WHO ELSE
writes like ?
A Readers' Guide to Fiction Authors

Compiled and edited by

Roy and Jeanne Huse

1996

Library & Information Statistics Unit
Department of Information and Library Studies

Loughborough
University

Who Else Writes Like ...?

Compiled and edited by Roy Huse, LISU, 1993

2nd edition, compiled and edited by Roy and Jeanne Huse, 1996

Published by
The Library and Information Statistics Unit (LISU)
Department of Information and Library Studies
Loughborough University, Loughborough, LE11 3TU
Tel: +44 (0)1509 223071 Fax: + 44 (0)1509 223072 E-mail: lisu@lboro.ac.uk

British Library Cataloguing in Publication Data may be obtained from the British Library

ISBN 0 948848 84 7

Cover design by Susan England

Printed and bound in Great Britain by St. Edmundsbury Press
Bury St. Edmunds, Suffolk

CONTENTS

INTRODUCTION

The Readers' Guide to Fiction Authors, was first compiled by Peter Mann and published in 1985. It was based on a list of 61 'Core' authors to which were added alternatives submitted by over 600 librarians.

A new edition under the current title was published in 1993. The entries were based mainly on the most popular authors according to the Public Lending Right lists with additional suggestions made by professional librarians and fiction specialists. Cross referenced through the use of Hypertext it proved to be a useful and popular reference book for library staff and their reading public. A user survey in the Autumn of 1994 confirmed the need for a revised edition.

This edition continues the principal features of its predecessor but it has been considerably enlarged. The number of authors has been increased by 20% to over 1200. Entries in the main sequence include the nationality or place of birth of those authors who are not English together with the date of birth (and death as appropriate) where known. The number of alternative authors has generally been limited to between 4 and 12.

Of course no author writes exactly like another; indeed everyone's creative work is unique. However there is often sufficient similarity within a style or content to link the novels of one author with those of another. Inevitably there will be disagreement with some suggestions but the Guide has been published to help readers and library staff explore the ever expanding, exciting world of contemporary fiction.

Many authors write exclusively within a category or genre. Where they do so this is indicated under their name in the main sequence and in the section *Authors Listed by Genre*. To give more information to readers parts of this section have been expanded in this latest edition, particularly in the fields of Adventure; Crime; Fantasy and Science Fiction.

An entirely new section compiled by two specialist librarians lists some 50 authors and titles of books for Teenagers. It is hoped that this feature will be useful to parents, teachers, librarians and of course to teenagers themselves.

Finally the Guide has an up-dated list of *Literary Prizes and Awards* and a revised *Bibliography* covering current guides to fiction reading.

Most of the authors listed in the Guide are those currently in print and popular in public libraries in the UK, the US and in many Commonwealth countries. Older favourites which are not usually so readily available and classic writers who need no introduction are not included: the Bibliographies listed at the back of the book should help readers find such authors.

While Copyright lies with the British Library there is no restriction on using appropriate parts of the Guide to promote a greater awareness of the wide range of fiction available to Library users.

It is hoped to produce a further edition in three years. If readers have constructive comments, they are invited to send them to the publisher, the Director of LISU, Loughborough University, Loughborough, Leicestershire, LE11 3TU.

ACKNOWLEDGEMENTS

This Guide could not have been produced without the active support of many Library Authorities and their staff who have willingly given a great deal of their time and professional expertise to the compilation of the lists of authors.

It is particularly encouraging that so many authorities and individuals who worked on the last edition wished to be involved again and we are especially grateful to the following Library Authorities, to the individual members of staff and to their colleagues who helped in the task. We hope they will be pleased with the result.

Initial compilation
BROMLEY LIBRARIES: John Levett, Anne Woods and colleagues
BUCKINGHAMSHIRE COUNTY LIBRARY: Jenny Varney, Gill Green
    and Mair Truelove
DORSET COUNTY LIBRARY: Lynne Cousins and colleagues
EAST SUSSEX COUNTY LIBRARY: Barry Foster and colleagues
HAMPSHIRE COUNTY LIBRARY: Barrie Kempthorne and colleagues
LEEDS CITY LIBRARIES: Vivien Cartwright and colleagues
TORFAEN LIBRARIES: Sue Johnson and colleagues
UNIVERSITY OF LIVERPOOL: Andy Sawyer, Librarian Science Fiction
    Foundation

Initial compilation and subsequent editing stages

ANGUS COUNCIL CULTURAL SERVICES: John MacRitchie

BERKSHIRE COUNTY LIBRARY: Yvonne Cope

BIRMINGHAM CITY LIBRARIES: Linda Saunders for her work on the Teenage Lists and Joan Billingham for work on the main lists

CHESHIRE COUNTY LIBRARY: Lesley Morgan and Liz Stafford

EALING LIBRARIES: Brian Cope

ESSEX COUNTY LIBRARY: Fredo Donnelly, Liz Boyle, Anthony Butlin, Anna Prince and Michael Wrenn together with Ann Christmas of Southend-on-Sea

HERTFORDSHIRE LIBRARIES: Bob Sharpe and Catherine Davies

WEST DUMBARTON LIBRARIES: Ian Baillie

WEST SUSSEX LIBRARY SERVICE: Trish Botten for her work on the Teenage Supplement and Keith Laker and colleagues

We are grateful to the Registrar of Public Lending Right for supplying statistics as the basis for the core list of authors and to Berkshire Libraries who supplied details of their genre authors.

We have, as always, received consistent support and encouragement from our publisher, John Sumsion, Director of LISU, and from the LISU Advisory Committee and The British Library Research and Innovation Centre.

Typesetting, co-ordination and work on Hypertext has been in the capable hands of Mary Ashworth and Sharon Fletcher who have, as for the previous edition, ensured that all has been produced to the highest possible standard. Their work has been absolutely invaluable.

Roy and Jeanne Huse

Aldwick   September 1996

NATIONALITY OR PLACE OF BIRTH

The nationality or place of birth (where known) of those authors who are not English is indicated in the main list by an abbreviation or, in a few places, by the name of the country in full. The following is a full list of these countries.

Aus	Australia	It	Italy
Austria	Austria	Ja	Japan
Can	Canada	Lebanon	Lebanon
Carib	Caribbean	Neth	Netherlands
Chi	Chile	NZ	New Zealand
Colombia	Colombia	Nigeria	Nigeria
Cz	Czechoslovakia	Pol	Poland
Den	Denmark	Rus	Russia
Fr	France	SA	South Africa
Ger	Germany	Sco	Scotland
Hu	Hungary	Swe	Sweden
Ind	India	US	United States of America
Ire	Ireland		
Isr	Israel	Wales	Wales

HOW TO USE THIS GUIDE

The arrangement is very simple. Look up the author you want in the Alphabetical List. The names which follow are suggested alternatives. For example: if you like Margaret FORSTER you might also enjoy books by Margaret DRABBLE or Deborah MOGGACH. There is no guarantee that you will, but they are authors who usually write in a similar style.

Where an author writes in a category or genre this is indicated. The alternative authors which then follow usually write in a similar genre. For example Ted ALLBEURY usually writes *Adventure* or *Spy Stories* and this is shown by the word *Adventure* under his name.

A few authors write under the same name but in two quite different genres. We have shown the alternatives under the two headings: for example Evelyn ANTHONY *(Adventure)* and Evelyn ANTHONY *(Historical)*.

Do remember that some authors who write frequently in one category will occasionally produce a book in a quite different genre. It is important to read the jacket details or summary of the book before you borrow.

If you only want a list of authors who write in a particular category or genre then turn straight to page 217. If you are a reader of Crime Fiction, Fantasy or Science Fiction, to make selection easier for you, we have sub-divided these popular genres.

Should you need to know the names of authors writing for Teenagers turn to page 207 for some fifty authors and suggested titles.

Novels which have been awarded a **Literary Prize** are sometimes overlooked when the initial publicity has subsided. The lists beginning on page 255 will help you trace the winners in recent years.

There are many other guides and lists which will also help you explore the world of fiction or assist you in finding the book or series you want. A selection is listed in the **Bibliography** on page 289. In this work we list only authors' writing names: there are separate dictionaries of **pseudonymns**.

This Guide is not infallible but it is easy to use. If you need more information library staff are there to help.

THE READERS' GUIDE: AN ALPHABETICAL LIST

Peter ABRAHAMS   Can   1919-
War

  Peter CAVE

  Shaun CLARKE

  W.E.B. GRIFFIN

  John HARRIS

  David MONNERY

  Derek ROBINSON

  Terence STRONG

Chinua ACHEBE   Nigeria   1930-
General

  James BALDWIN

  Saul BELLOW

  J.M. COETZEE

  V.S. NAIPAUL

  Ben OKRI

  Caryl PHILLIPS

  Wole SOYINKA

Peter ACKROYD   1949-
General

  John BANVILLE

  Julian BARNES

  Peter BENSON

  Anthony BURGESS

  Peter CAREY

  J.G. FARRELL

  John FOWLES

James HAMILTON-PATERSON

Robert NYE

Graham SWIFT

Barry UNSWORTH

Douglas ADAMS   1952-
Science Fiction

  Robert ASPRIN

  Ben ELTON

  Harry HARRISON

  Tom HOLT

  Grant NAYLOR

  Terry PRATCHETT

  Robert RANKIN

  Bob SHAW

  Robert SHECKLEY

Richard ADAMS   1920-
General

  Aeron CLEMENT

  Paul GALLICO

  William HORWOOD

  Garry D. KILWORTH

  A.R. LLOYD

  Henry WILLIAMSON

Elizabeth ADLER
Family Stories
  Aileen ARMITAGE
  Charlotte BINGHAM
  Brenda JAGGER
  Denise ROBERTSON
  Sidney SHELDON
  Janet TANNER
  Elizabeth VILLARS

Joan AIKEN   1924-
General
  Jane AUSTEN
  Elizabeth HARRIS
  Susan HILL
  Iris MURDOCH
  Emma TENNANT

Catherine AIRD   1930-
Crime
  Margery ALLINGHAM
  M.C. BEATON
  Simon BRETT
  W.J. BURLEY
  Ann CLEEVES
  Elizabeth FERRARS
  Ann GRANGER
  Elizabeth LEMARCHAND
  John PENN
  Betty ROWLANDS

Patricia WENTWORTH
Margaret YORKE

Brian W. ALDISS   1925-
Science Fiction
  Isaac ASIMOV
  Ray BRADBURY
  David BRIN
  Richard COWPER
  Joe HALDEMAN
  Harry HARRISON
  Robert A. HEINLEIN
  Frank HERBERT
  Paul J. MCAULEY
  Brian STABLEFORD
  Kurt VONNEGUT
  John WYNDHAM

Ted ALLBEURY   1917-
Adventure
  Evelyn ANTHONY
  Desmond BAGLEY
  Clive EGLETON
  Colin FORBES
  Frederick FORSYTH
  Brian FREEMANTLE
  Adam HALL
  Palma HARCOURT
  Robert LUDLUM

Charlotte Vale ALLEN Can
Family Stories   1941-

  Betty BURTON

  Janet DAILEY

  Cynthia FREEMAN

  Claire LORRIMER

  Maisie MOSCO

  Pamela OLDFIELD

  LaVyrle SPENCER

  Nicola THORNE

  Helen VAN SLYKE

  Elizabeth WALKER

Isabel ALLENDE Chi   1942-
General

  Margaret ATWOOD

  Gabriel GARCIA MARQUEZ

  Günter GRASS

  Milan KUNDERA

Margery ALLINGHAM   1904-66
Crime

  Catherine AIRD

  Nicholas BLAKE

  Agatha CHRISTIE

  Edmund CRISPIN

  Elizabeth FERRARS

  Michael INNES

  Ngaio MARSH

  Gladys MITCHELL

  Patricia MOYES

  Dorothy L. SAYERS

  Josephine TEY

  Patricia WENTWORTH

Catherine ALLIOTT
Glitz & Glamour

  Jilly COOPER

  Maeve HARAN

  Jill MANSELL

  Penny VINCENZI

Lisa ALTHER US   1944-
General

  Ethan CANIN

  Marilyn FRENCH

  Alice HOFFMAN

  Rona JAFFE

  Toni MORRISON

  Ann OAKLEY

  Marge PIERCY

  Judith ROSSNER

Eric AMBLER   1909-
Adventure

  John BUCHAN

  Victor CANNING

  Peter DRISCOLL

  Ian FLEMING

  John GARDNER

  Adam HALL

Palma HARCOURT

Geoffrey HOUSEHOLD

Robert LITTELL

J.K. MAYO

David LODGE

Ian McEWAN

Brian MOORE

Marianne WIGGINS

Stephen AMIDON   US   1959-
General

Evelyn ANTHONY

Ben ELTON

Dashiell HAMMETT

Jonathan KELLERMAN

Kingsley AMIS   1922-95
General

William BOYD

Malcolm BRADBURY

John BRAINE

William COOPER

Michael FRAYN

Nick HORNBY

David LODGE

David NOBBS

Keith WATERHOUSE

A.N. WILSON

Martin AMIS   1949-
General

Iain BANKS

Julian BARNES

Roddy DOYLE

Valerie ANAND   1937-
Historical

Philippa CARR

Dorothy DUNNETT

Cynthia HARROD-EAGLES

Morgan LLYWELYN

Edith PARGETER

Sharon PENMAN

Jean PLAIDY

Judith M. RILEY

Poul ANDERSON   US   1926-
Science Fiction

Isaac ASIMOV

Robert BLOCH

Ray BRADBURY

David BRIN

Jack L. CHALKER

Harlan ELLISON

Joe HALDEMAN

Fred SABERHAGEN

Robert SILVERBERG

Roger ZELAZNY

Lucilla ANDREWS   Sco   1919-
Romance
  Iris BROMIGE
  Marion CHESNEY
  Anne MATHER
  Miss READ
  Patricia ROBINS
  Elizabeth SEIFERT
  Jessica STEELE
  D.E. STEVENSON

Lyn ANDREWS
Family Stories
  Donna BAKER
  Louise BRINDLEY
  Josephine COX
  Kate FLYNN
  Helen FORRESTER
  Sara FRASER
  Ruth HAMILTON
  Maisie MOSCO
  Elvi RHODES
  Mary Jane STAPLES
  Margaret THORNTON

Virginia ANDREWS   US 1933-86
General
  Jane BRINDLE
  Virginia COFFMAN
  Suzanne GOODWIN

  Barbara MICHAELS
  Daoma WINSTON

Patricia ANGADI   1914-
General
  Lynne Reid BANKS
  Mary HOCKING
  Deborah MOGGACH
  Bernice RUBENS
  Titia SUTHERLAND
  Mary WESLEY
  Gillian WHITE

Evelyn ANTHONY   1928-
Adventure
  Ted ALLBEURY
  Colin FORBES
  Clare FRANCIS
  Adam HALL
  Helen MACINNES

Evelyn ANTHONY   1928-
Historical
  Barbara ERSKINE
  Catherine GAVIN
  Cynthia HARROD-EAGLES
  Genevieve LYONS
  Diana NORMAN
  Jean PLAIDY
  Philippa WIAT

Piers ANTHONY US   1934-
Science Fiction
- Isaac ASIMOV
- Greg BEAR
- Jack L. CHALKER
- Philip José FARMER
- Alan Dean FOSTER
- Harry HARRISON
- Frank HERBERT
- Michael MOORCOCK
- Terry PRATCHETT
- Brian STABLEFORD

Geoffrey ARCHER
Adventure
- Stephen COONTS
- Lionel DAVIDSON
- Robert LUDLUM
- Julian Jay SAVARIN
- Tim SEBASTIAN
- Craig THOMAS

Jeffrey ARCHER   1940-
General
- Susan CROSLAND
- Michael DOBBS
- Robert GODDARD
- William HAGGARD
- Arthur HAILEY
- David MASON

Sidney SHELDON
John TRENHAILE

Aileen ARMITAGE
Family Stories
- Elizabeth ADLER
- Brenda JAGGER
- Elvi RHODES
- Ann Victoria ROBERTS
- Kay STEPHENS
- Janet TANNER
- Nicola THORNE
- Elizabeth WALKER

Campbell ARMSTRONG   Sco
Adventure   1944-
- Colin FORBES
- Jack GERSON
- William HAGGARD
- Julian Jay SAVARIN
- John TRENHAILE

Doug ARMSTRONG
War
- Peter CAVE
- Shaun CLARKE
- Robin JAMES
- David MONNERY

Lindsay ARMSTRONG SA
Romance
  Penny JORDAN
  Carole MORTIMER
  Anne WEALE

Thomas ARMSTRONG 1899-1978
General
  Phyllis BENTLEY
  Taylor CALDWELL
  A.J. CRONIN
  R.F. DELDERFIELD
  J.B. PRIESTLEY
  Howard SPRING
  Marguerite STEEN

Isaac ASIMOV US   1920-92
Science Fiction
  Brian W. ALDISS
  Poul ANDERSON
  Piers ANTHONY
  James BLISH
  John BRUNNER
  Arthur C. CLARKE
  Philip K. DICK
  Robert A. HEINLEIN
  Frank HERBERT
  Larry NIVEN
  Frederik POHL
  Fred SABERHAGEN
  Clifford D. SIMAK

Robert ASPRIN US   1946-
Fantasy
  Douglas ADAMS
  Craig Shaw GARDNER
  Tom HOLT
  Dan McGIRT
  Grant NAYLOR
  Terry PRATCHETT
  Robert RANKIN
  Christopher STASHEFF
  Harry TURTLEDOVE

Judy ASTLEY
General
  Marika COBBOLD
  E.M. DELAFIELD
  Kathleen ROWNTREE
  Mary WESLEY

Margaret ATWOOD Can 1939-
General
  Isabel ALLENDE
  Pat BARKER
  Barbara COMYNS
  Anita DESAI
  Janice ELLIOTT
  Nadine GORDIMER
  Ruth Prawer JHABVALA
  E. Annie PROULX
  Carol SHIELDS
  Fay WELDON
  Marianne WIGGINS

Jean M. AUEL US   1936-
Fantasy
  Louise COOPER
  Stephen DONALDSON
  Garry D. KILWORTH
  Nicholas LUARD
  Linda Lay SHULER

Jane AUSTEN   1775-1817
General
  Joan AIKEN
  Ivy COMPTON-BURNETT
  Penelope FITZGERALD
  Georgette HEYER
  Barbara PYM
  Emma TENNANT
  Edith WHARTON

Jonathan AYCLIFFE   1949-
also writes as Daniel EASTERMAN
Supernatural
  Joe DONNELLY
  Dean R. KOONTZ
  Stephen LAWS
  Robert McCAMMON
  Kim NEWMAN
  Philip RICKMAN
  Peter STRAUB
  Dennis WHEATLEY

Marian BABSON US
Crime
  Simon BRETT
  Pat BURDEN
  Elizabeth FERRARS
  Anthea FRASER
  Elizabeth LEMARCHAND
  Patricia MOYES
  Magdalen NABB
  Frank PARRISH
  Simon SHAW
  Neville STEED
  Barbara WHITEHEAD

Margaret BACON
General
  Caroline BRIDGWOOD
  Marika COBBOLD
  Sybil MARSHALL
  Titia SUTHERLAND
  Joanna TROLLOPE

Desmond BAGLEY   1923-83
Adventure
  Ted ALLBEURY
  Jon CLEARY
  James FOLLETT
  Ken FOLLETT
  John GARDNER
  Jack HIGGINS
  Hammond INNES

Desmond BAGLEY (cont.)

  Geoffrey JENKINS

  Duncan KYLE

  Andrew MACALLAN

  Alistair MACLEAN

  Gerald SEYMOUR

Hilary BAILEY   1936-
General

  Nina BAWDEN

  Charlotte BINGHAM

  Elizabeth DAISH

  Alice Thomas ELLIS

  Jane GARDAM

  Angela LAMBERT

  Hilary MANTEL

  James MITCHELL

Paul BAILEY   1937-
General

  David COOK

  Ian McEWAN

  Brian MOORE

  Piers Paul READ

  Paul SAYER

  Graham SWIFT

Beryl BAINBRIDGE   1934-
General

  Pat BARKER

  Alice Thomas ELLIS

  Penelope FITZGERALD

  Margaret FORSTER

  George GROSSMITH

  Susan HILL

  Penelope MORTIMER

  Bernice RUBENS

  Fay WELDON

Anne BAKER
Family Stories

  Kate FLYNN

  Helen FORRESTER

  Sheila JANSEN

  Joan JONKER

  Lena KENNEDY

  Elizabeth MURPHY

Donna BAKER   1939-
Family Stories

  Lyn ANDREWS

  Rosemary ENRIGHT

  Iris GOWER

  Lena KENNEDY

  Maisie MOSCO

  Malcolm ROSS

  Susan SALLIS

  Jean STUBBS

  Sue SULLY

  Margaret SUNLEY

  E.V. THOMPSON

James BALDWIN US 1924-87
General
- Chinua ACHEBE
- Rosa GUY
- Toni MORRISON
- Alan PATON
- Alice WALKER
- Edmund WHITE

J.G. BALLARD 1930-
Science Fiction
- Anthony BURGESS
- Philip K. DICK
- Thomas M. DISCH
- Joe HALDEMAN
- Frank HERBERT
- Kim NEWMAN
- Christopher PRIEST
- Kurt VONNEGUT
- Ian WATSON

Iain BANKS Sco 1954-
also writes as Iain M. BANKS
General
- Martin AMIS
- Peter BENSON
- Guy BURT
- Ian McEWAN

Iain M. BANKS Sco 1954-
also writes as Iain BANKS
Science Fiction
- Ray BRADBURY
- Orson Scott CARD
- Christopher PRIEST
- Ian WATSON

Lynne Reid BANKS 1929-
General
- Patricia ANGADI
- Monica DICKENS
- Margaret DRABBLE
- Nell DUNN
- Nadine GORDIMER
- Olivia MANNING
- Edna O'BRIEN
- Muriel SPARK

Russell BANKS US 1940-
General
- Pete DEXTER
- Shusaku ENDO
- Kazuo ISHIGURO
- Yukio MISHIMA
- Haruki MURAKAMI
- J.D. SALINGER

John BANVILLE   Ire   1945-
General

  Peter ACKROYD

  Peter CAREY

  James HAMILTON-PATERSON

  John McGAHERN

  Barry UNSWORTH

Noel BARBER   1909-88
General

  Dirk BOGARDE

  Janice Young BROOKS

  Fiona BULLEN

  James CLAVELL

  Elizabeth DARRELL

  Robert ELEGANT

  Christopher HUDSON

  Peter LING

  Malcolm MACDONALD

  James A. MICHENER

  Owen SELA

  Janet TANNER

Tessa BARCLAY   Sco   1928-
Family Stories

  Louise BRINDLEY

  Betty BURTON

  Elizabeth DAISH

  Margaret Thomson DAVIS

  Rosemary ENRIGHT

  Pamela EVANS

  Margaret GRAHAM

  Audrey HOWARD

  Marie JOSEPH

  Pamela OLDFIELD

  Denise ROBERTSON

  T.R. WILSON

A.L. BARKER   1918-
General

  Anita BROOKNER

  Barbara COMYNS

  Barbara PYM

  Emma TENNANT

Pat BARKER   1943-
General

  Margaret ATWOOD

  Beryl BAINBRIDGE

  Stan BARSTOW

  Heinrich BÖLL

  Geoff DYER

  Janice ELLIOTT

  Zoe FAIRBAIRNS

  Sebastian FAULKS

  Erich Maria REMARQUE

  Rebecca WEST

Robert BARNARD   1936-
Crime

  Colin DEXTER

  Peter DICKINSON

  Jonathan GASH

  John HARVEY

  Mark HEBDEN

  Charlotte MACLEOD

  Simon SHAW

John BARNES   US
Science Fiction

  Orson Scott CARD

  Kim Stanley ROBINSON

  Neal STEPHENSON

  Bruce STERLING

Julian BARNES   1946-
also writes as Dan KAVANAGH
General

  Peter ACKROYD

  Martin AMIS

  Peter BENSON

  William BOYD

  Bruce CHATWIN

  Jonathan COE

  Sebastian FAULKS

  Kazuo ISHIGURO

  Ian McEWAN

  Timothy MO

  Graham SWIFT

  D.M. THOMAS

  A.N. WILSON

Linda BARNES   US   1949-
Crime

  Liza CODY

  Amanda CROSS

  Janet EVANOVICH

  Sue GRAFTON

  Karen KIJEWSKI

  Susan MOODY

  Marcia MULLER

  Sara PARETSKY

Stan BARSTOW   1928-
General

  Pat BARKER

  H.E. BATES

  Melvyn BRAGG

  John BRAINE

  D.H. LAWRENCE

  Stanley MIDDLETON

  Alan SILLITOE

  David STOREY

  Tony WARREN

H.E. BATES   1905-74
General

  Stan BARSTOW

  Melvyn BRAGG

H.E. BATES (cont.)

R.F. DELDERFIELD

Monica DICKENS

Paul GALLICO

Annie LEITH

Howard SPRING

H.E. BATES 1905-74

Humour

E.F. BENSON

George Macdonald FRASER

Tom HOLT

Garrison KEILLOR

David NOBBS

Peter TINNISWOOD

Keith WATERHOUSE

Nina BAWDEN 1925-

General

Hilary BAILEY

Jenny DISKI

Margaret DRABBLE

Margaret FORSTER

Caro FRASER

Jane GARDAM

Nadine GORDIMER

Penelope LIVELY

Alison LURIE

Muriel SPARK

Stephen BAXTER 1957-

Science Fiction

Greg BEAR

Gregory BENFORD

Arthur C. CLARKE

Jules VERNE

H.G. WELLS

William BAYER US 1939-

Crime

Lawrence BLOCK

James Lee BURKE

Loren D. ESTLEMAN

Thomas HARRIS

David L. LINDSEY

Phillip M. MARGOLIN

John SANDFORD

Greg BEAR US 1951-

Science Fiction

Piers ANTHONY

Stephen BAXTER

Gregory BENFORD

C.J. CHERRYH

Arthur C. CLARKE

Greg EGAN

Philip José FARMER

Alan Dean FOSTER

Paul J. MCAULEY

Frederik POHL

Kim Stanley ROBINSON

Bob SHAW

David WINGROVE

M.C. BEATON   Sco   1936-
also writes as Marion CHESNEY
Crime

Catherine AIRD

Ann GRANGER

Bill KNOX

T. Jefferson PARKER

Ann QUINTON

C.F. ROE

R.D. WINGFIELD

Sally BEAUMAN   1944-
Glitz & Glamour

Julie BURCHILL

Jackie COLLINS

Jilly COOPER

Julie ELLIS

Shirley ESKAPA

Elizabeth GAGE

Rupert LEGGE

Susan LEWIS

Una-Mary PARKER

Guy BELLAMY
Humour

Dan BINCHY

Michael CARSON

Jonathan COE

Michael FRAYN

Patrick GALE

Nick HORNBY

David NOBBS

Ann OAKLEY

Tom SHARPE

Peter TINNISWOOD

Nigel WILLIAMS

Pamela BELLE   1952-
Historical

Philippa CARR

Elizabeth CHADWICK

Catherine COULTER

Elizabeth DAISH

Emma DRUMMOND

Cynthia HARROD-EAGLES

Rosalind LAKER

Diana NORMAN

Sharon PENMAN

Judith M. RILEY

Anya SETON

E.V. THOMPSON

Saul BELLOW   US   1915-
General

Chinua ACHEBE

Anthony BURGESS

Don DELILLO

William FAULKNER

Saul BELLOW (cont.)

Joseph HELLER

Cormac McCARTHY

V.S. NAIPAUL

Chaim POTOK

Philip ROTH

Isaac Bashevis SINGER

William STYRON

Paul THEROUX

John UPDIKE

Peter BENCHLEY　US　　1940-
General

Richard CONDON

Michael CRICHTON

Arthur HAILEY

Gregory BENFORD　US　　1941-
Science Fiction

Stephen BAXTER

Greg BEAR

Greg EGAN

Bob SHAW

E.F. BENSON　　1867-1940
Humour

H.E. BATES

Vernon COLEMAN

E.M. DELAFIELD

Tom HOLT

Annie LEITH

Angela THIRKELL

Evelyn WAUGH

P.G. WODEHOUSE

Peter BENSON　　1956-
General

Peter ACKROYD

Iain BANKS

Julian BARNES

William BOYD

Graham SWIFT

Phyllis BENTLEY　　1894-1977
General

Thomas ARMSTRONG

Elizabeth BOWEN

Taylor CALDWELL

Lettice COOPER

Dorothy EDEN

John GALSWORTHY

Elizabeth GOUDGE

Winifred HOLTBY

Richard LLEWELLYN

J.B. PRIESTLEY

Rachel BILLINGTON　　1942-
General

Anne FINE

Penelope FITZGERALD

Elizabeth Jane HOWARD
Penelope LIVELY
Alison LURIE
Deborah MOGGACH
Gillian TINDALL

Dan BINCHY   Ire   1940-
Humour
  Guy BELLAMY
  Roy CLARKE
  Roddy DOYLE
  Garrison KEILLOR
  Tom SHARPE

Maeve BINCHY   Ire   1940-
Family Stories
  Elaine CROWLEY
  Frank DELANEY
  Molly KEANE
  Genevieve LYONS
  Mary MINTON
  M.R. O'DONNELL
  Rosamunde PILCHER
  Erin PIZZEY
  Deirdre PURCELL
  Malcolm ROSS
  Mary RYAN

Charlotte BINGHAM   1942-
General
  Elizabeth ADLER
  Hilary BAILEY
  Elizabeth BUCHAN
  Jilly COOPER
  Lucinda EDMONDS
  Maeve HARAN
  Sarah HARRISON
  Audrey SLAUGHTER

Emma BLAIR   Sco   1942-
Family Stories
  Margaret Thomson DAVIS
  Pamela EVANS
  Christine Marion FRASER
  Audrey HOWARD
  Sheelagh KELLY
  Beryl KINGSTON
  Elisabeth McNEILL
  Agnes SHORT
  Eileen STAFFORD
  Emma STIRLING
  Jessica STIRLING

Nicholas BLAKE   Ire   1904-72
Crime
  Margery ALLINGHAM
  John Dickson CARR
  Agatha CHRISTIE
  Edmund CRISPIN

John BLAZE
Western
  Max BRAND
  Al CODY
  J.T. EDSON
  Lee F. GREGSON
  Jack SCHAEFER

James BLISH   US   1921-75
Science Fiction
  Isaac ASIMOV
  Ray BRADBURY
  Arthur C. CLARKE
  John WYNDHAM

Robert BLOCH   US   1917-
Fantasy
  Poul ANDERSON
  Ray BRADBURY
  August DERLETH
  H.P. LOVECRAFT
  Brian LUMLEY

Lawrence BLOCK   US   1938-
Crime
  William BAYER
  James ELLROY
  Loren D. ESTLEMAN
  George V. HIGGINS
  Eugene IZZI

  Elmore LEONARD
  John D. MACDONALD
  Ross MACDONALD
  Robert B. PARKER
  Ross THOMAS
  Charles WILLEFORD

Philip BOAST   1952-
Family Stories
  Roy HATTERSLEY
  Lena KENNEDY
  Beryl KINGSTON
  Peter LING
  Connie MONK
  Gilda O'NEILL
  Mary Jane STAPLES

Dirk BOGARDE   1921-
General
  Noel BARBER
  Elizabeth BOWEN
  Robert GODDARD
  Rumer GODDEN
  Christopher HUDSON
  Tony WARREN

Heinrich BÖLL   Ger   1917-85
General
  Pat BARKER
  Günter GRASS

Franz KAFKA
Francis KING
Alexander SOLZHENITSYN
Henry WILLIAMSON

Eric LUSTBADER
Christopher NICOLE
Marc OLDEN

Larry BOND   US
Adventure
Dale BROWN
George BROWN
Tom CLANCY
Stephen COONTS
Michael HARTLAND
Richard HERMAN
Stephen LEATHER
David MACE

Pat BOOTH   1942-
Glitz & Glamour
Sandra BROWN
Julie BURCHILL
Jackie COLLINS
Lucinda EDMONDS
Shirley ESKAPA
Olivia GOLDSMITH
Judith KRANTZ
Lynda LA PLANTE
Harold ROBBINS
Sidney SHELDON
Penny VINCENZI

Michael BOND   1926-
Crime
Lilian Jackson BRAUN
Ruth Dudley EDWARDS
Roderic JEFFRIES
Simon SHAW
Colin WATSON

Rose BOUCHERON
Family Stories
Harry BOWLING
Patricia BURNS
Josephine COX
Beryl KINGSTON

Martin BOOTH   1944-
Adventure
George BROWN
James CLAVELL
Bryce COURTENAY
Anthony GREY

Elizabeth BOWEN Ire 1899-1973
General
Phyllis BENTLEY
Dirk BOGARDE
Anita BROOKNER

Elizabeth BOWEN (cont.)

Ivy COMPTON-BURNETT

Graham GREENE

Molly KEANE

Rosamond LEHMANN

Olivia MANNING

Iris MURDOCH

May SARTON

Virginia WOOLF

Harry BOWLING   1931-
Family Stories

Rose BOUCHERON

Patricia BURNS

Pamela EVANS

Helen FORRESTER

Ruth HAMILTON

Beryl KINGSTON

Peter LING

Brenda McBRYDE

Gilda O'NEILL

Judith SAXTON

Mary Jane STAPLES

Elizabeth WAITE

William BOYD   1952-
General

Kingsley AMIS

Julian BARNES

Peter BENSON

Nick HORNBY

Kazuo ISHIGURO

Howard JACOBSON

Thomas KENEALLY

David LODGE

Paul MICOU

Brian MOORE

V.S. PRITCHETT

Paul THEROUX

Clare BOYLAN   Ire   1948-
Family Stories

Kathleen CONLON

Edna O'BRIEN

Wendy PERRIAM

Mary RYAN

Sue TOWNSEND

Malcolm BRADBURY   1932-
General

Kingsley AMIS

Melvyn BRAGG

William COOPER

Robertson DAVIES

Louis DE BERNIÈRES

Michael FRAYN

Howard JACOBSON

Thomas KENEALLY

David LODGE

John MORTIMER

Keith WATERHOUSE

A.N. WILSON

20

Ray **BRADBURY** US 1920-
Fantasy

- Brian W. ALDISS
- Poul ANDERSON
- Iain M. BANKS
- James BLISH
- Robert BLOCH
- Harlan ELLISON
- Robert A. HEINLEIN
- H.P. LOVECRAFT
- Michael MOORCOCK
- Kim Stanley ROBINSON
- Clifford D. SIMAK
- Jules VERNE
- Roger ZELAZNY

Barbara Taylor **BRADFORD**
Family Stories 1933-

- Jacqueline BRISKIN
- Brenda CLARKE
- Rosemary ENRIGHT
- Cynthia FREEMAN
- Sheelagh KELLY
- Adam KENNEDY
- Danielle STEEL
- Nicola THORNE
- Elizabeth VILLARS
- Elizabeth WAITE
- Elizabeth WALKER

Marion Zimmer **BRADLEY** US
Fantasy 1930-

- Raymond E. FEIST
- David A. GEMMELL
- Patricia KENNEALY
- Garry D. KILWORTH
- Mercedes LACKEY
- Anne McCAFFREY
- Melanie RAWN
- Sheri S. TEPPER
- Tad WILLIAMS

Gillian **BRADSHAW** US 1956-
Historical

- Dorothy DUNNETT
- Robert GRAVES
- Mary RENAULT
- Rosemary SUTCLIFF
- Gore VIDAL

Melvyn **BRAGG** 1939-
General

- Stan BARSTOW
- H.E. BATES
- Malcolm BRADBURY
- Lettice COOPER
- Margaret DRABBLE
- John FOWLES
- Roy HATTERSLEY
- D.H. LAWRENCE

Melvyn BRAGG (cont.)

William McILVANNEY

Stanley MIDDLETON

Hugh WALPOLE

John BRAINE   1922-86
General

Kingsley AMIS

Stan BARSTOW

William COOPER

Alan SILLITOE

Leslie THOMAS

Tony WARREN

Sally BRAMPTON   1955-
General

Maeve HARAN

Kathy LETTE

Nancy MITFORD

Rosie THOMAS

Max BRAND US   1892-1944
Western

Al CODY

John BLAZE

J.T. EDSON

Zane GREY

Louis L'AMOUR

Nelson NYE

Lilian Jackson BRAUN US
Crime

Michael BOND

Amanda CROSS

Colin DEXTER

Elizabeth PETERS

Celia BRAYFIELD   1945-
Glitz & Glamour

Jacqueline BRISKIN

Jackie COLLINS

Shirley CONRAN

Jilly COOPER

Lucinda EDMONDS

Elizabeth GAGE

Lynda LA PLANTE

Harold ROBBINS

Penny VINCENZI

Chaz BRENCHLEY
Supernatural

Nancy COLLINS

Stephen GALLAGHER

Madeleine BRENT   1920-
Historical

Catherine COULTER

Dorothy EDEN

Victoria HOLT

Sara HYLTON

Carola SALISBURY

Anya SETON

Mary STEWART

Phyllis A. WHITNEY

Dick FRANCIS

Adam HALL

Robert HARRIS

John LE CARRÉ

Helen MACINNES

Simon BRETT　　　　1945-
Crime

Catherine AIRD

Marian BABSON

Jane DENTINGER

Jonathan GASH

Martha GRIMES

Tim HEALD

Iain PEARS

Mike RIPLEY

Simon SHAW

Mark TIMLIN

Colin WATSON

Freda BRIGHT　US　　1929-
Glitz & Glamour

Jacqueline BRISKIN

Julie ELLIS

Judith KRANTZ

June Flaum SINGER

David BRIN　US　　1950-
Science Fiction

Brian W. ALDISS

Poul ANDERSON

John BRUNNER

Philip K. DICK

Greg EGAN

Kim Stanley ROBINSON

Bruce STERLING

Caroline BRIDGWOOD　1960-
General

Margaret BACON

Marika COBBOLD

Sybil MARSHALL

Audrey SLAUGHTER

Jane BRINDLE　　　　1938-
also writes as Josephine COX
General

Virginia ANDREWS

Mary Higgins CLARK

Susan HILL

Barbara MICHAELS

David BRIERLEY　　　1936-
Adventure

Evelyn ANTHONY

Len DEIGHTON

Louise BRINDLEY
Family Stories
   Lyn ANDREWS
   Tessa BARCLAY
   Rosemary ENRIGHT
   Sara HYLTON
   Maisie MOSCO
   Denise ROBERTSON
   Susan SALLIS
   Dee WILLIAMS

Iris BROMIGE   1910-
Romance
   Lucilla ANDREWS
   Elizabeth CADELL
   Dorothy EDEN
   Charlotte LAMB
   Mary PEARCE
   Rosamunde PILCHER
   D.E. STEVENSON
   Essie SUMMERS
   Elswyth THANE

Andre BRINK   SA   1935-
General
   J.M. COETZEE
   Buchi EMECHETA
   Nadine GORDIMER
   Christopher HOPE
   Thomas KENEALLY
   Arthur KOESTLER
   Alan PATON

Anita BROOKNER   1928-
General
   A.L. BARKER
   Elizabeth BOWEN
   A.S. BYATT
   Isabel COLEGATE
   Julian FANE
   Penelope FITZGERALD
   Penelope LIVELY
   Alison LURIE
   Barbara PYM
   Bernice RUBENS
   Carol SHIELDS
   Titia SUTHERLAND

Jacqueline BRISKIN   US   1927-
Glitz & Glamour
   Barbara Taylor BRADFORD
   Celia BRAYFIELD
   Freda BRIGHT
   Lucinda EDMONDS
   Judith KRANTZ
   June Flaum SINGER

Janice Young BROOKS   US
General
   Noel BARBER
   Fiona BULLEN

Belva PLAIN

Janet TANNER

Diana NORMAN

Nigel TRANTER

Terry BROOKS   US   1944-
Fantasy

Jack L. CHALKER

Stephen DONALDSON

Dave DUNCAN

David EDDINGS

Raymond E. FEIST

David A. GEMMELL

Robert JORDAN

Melanie RAWN

Margaret WEIS

Jonathan WYLIE

Dale BROWN   US   1956-
Adventure

Larry BOND

Tom CLANCY

Stephen COONTS

Clive CUSSLER

Richard HERMAN

Graham HURLEY

Julian Jay SAVARIN

Douglas TERMAN

Craig THOMAS

Brigid BROPHY   1929-95
General

Nadine GORDIMER

Iris MURDOCH

Edna O'BRIEN

Muriel SPARK

George BROWN
Adventure

Larry BOND

Martin BOOTH

Tom CLANCY

Len DEIGHTON

Gavin ESLER

Ian FLEMING

James FOLLETT

Colin FORBES

Michael HARTLAND

Robert LUDLUM

Eric LUSTBADER

D.K. BROSTER   1877-1950
Historical

Elizabeth BYRD

Elizabeth CHADWICK

Georgette HEYER

Neil MUNRO

Sandra BROWN US   1948-
Glitz & Glamour
- Pat BOOTH
- Julie BURCHILL
- Elizabeth GAGE
- Olivia GOLDSMITH
- Jayne Ann KRENTZ
- Harold ROBBINS
- June Flaum SINGER
- Penny VINCENZI

John BRUNNER   1934-
Science Fiction
- Isaac ASIMOV
- David BRIN
- Thomas M. DISCH
- William GIBSON
- Kim Stanley ROBINSON
- Bruce STERLING
- Jack VANCE

Elizabeth BUCHAN   1948-
Romance
- Charlotte BINGHAM
- Angela HUTH
- Reay TANNAHILL
- Joanna TROLLOPE
- Fay WELDON

John BUCHAN   Sco   1875-1940
Adventure
- Eric AMBLER
- Lionel DAVIDSON
- Peter DRISCOLL
- Robert GODDARD
- Geoffrey HOUSEHOLD
- Duncan KYLE
- Helen MACINNES

Edna BUCHANAN   US   1939-
Crime
- James Lee BURKE
- Robert CAMPBELL
- Raymond CHANDLER
- Carl HIAASEN

Fiona BULLEN
General
- Noel BARBER
- Janice Young BROOKS
- Una-Mary PARKER

Julie BURCHILL   1959-
Glitz & Glamour
- Sally BEAUMAN
- Pat BOOTH
- Sandra BROWN
- Jackie COLLINS
- Joan COLLINS

Elizabeth GAGE

Rupert LEGGE

Harold ROBBINS

Pat BURDEN

Crime

Marian BABSON

Caroline GRAHAM

Ann GRANGER

Hazel HOLT

Elizabeth LEMARCHAND

Anne MORICE

Emma PAGE

Betty ROWLANDS

June THOMSON

Anthony BURGESS   1917-93

General

Peter ACKROYD

J.G. BALLARD

Saul BELLOW

Robertson DAVIES

Gabriel GARCIA MARQUEZ

William GOLDING

Robert GRAVES

George ORWELL

Salman RUSHDIE

Paul THEROUX

Angus WILSON

Anita BURGH   1937-

also writes as Annie LEITH

General

Teresa CRANE

Daphne DU MAURIER

Winston GRAHAM

James Lee BURKE   US   1936-

Crime

William BAYER

Edna BUCHANAN

James HALL

Tony HILLERMAN

Tom KAKONIS

Joseph KOENIG

Elmore LEONARD

David L. LINDSEY

Sara PARETSKY

John SANDFORD

W.J. BURLEY   1914-

Crime

Catherine AIRD

Ann CLEEVES

Jonathan GASH

B.M. GILL

Roy HART

John Buxton HILTON

Roger ORMEROD

John PENN

Ann QUINTON

W.J. BURLEY (cont.)

Jonathan ROSS

June THOMSON

M.J. TROW

Ted WOOD

Patricia BURNS
Family Stories

Rose BOUCHERON

Harry BOWLING

Lena KENNEDY

Beryl KINGSTON

Guy BURT
General

Iain BANKS

Patrick GALE

William GOLDING

Patrick McCABE

Betty BURTON
Family Stories

Charlotte Vale ALLEN

Tessa BARCLAY

Virginia COFFMAN

Elizabeth DAISH

Elizabeth DARRELL

Gwendoline BUTLER
also writes as Jennie MELVILLE
Crime

Ann CLEEVES

Alanna KNIGHT

Jennie MELVILLE

Iain PEARS

Anne PERRY

Michael UNDERWOOD

A.S. BYATT   1936-
General

Anita BROOKNER

Angela CARTER

Margaret DRABBLE

Elizabeth Jane HOWARD

Angela HUTH

Penelope LIVELY

Candia McWILLIAM

Marina WARNER

Marianne WIGGINS

Elizabeth BYRD
Historical

D.K. BROSTER

Elizabeth CADELL

Elizabeth CHADWICK

Neil MUNRO

Anya SETON

Jean STUBBS

Elizabeth CADELL   1910-89
Romance
  Iris BROMIGE
  Elizabeth BYRD
  D.E. STEVENSON
  Essie SUMMERS
  Elswyth THANE

James M. CAIN   US   1892-1977
Crime
  Robert CAMPBELL
  James Hadley CHASE
  James ELLROY
  John D. MACDONALD
  Ross THOMAS
  Jim THOMPSON
  Andrew VACHSS

Erskine CALDWELL US 1903-87
General
  Truman CAPOTE
  William FAULKNER
  Ernest HEMINGWAY
  Carson McCULLERS

Taylor CALDWELL Sco 1900-85
General
  Thomas ARMSTRONG
  Phyllis BENTLEY
  A.J. CRONIN

  Daphne DU MAURIER
  Marguerite STEEN

Brian CALLISON   Sco   1934-
Sea
  Alan EVANS
  Alexander FULLERTON
  Geoffrey JENKINS
  Philip McCUTCHAN
  Douglas REEMAN
  Douglas SCOTT
  Antony TREW
  Charles WHITING
  John WINGATE
  Richard WOODMAN

Ramsey CAMPBELL   1946-
Supernatural
  August DERLETH
  Joe DONNELLY
  Christopher FOWLER
  Steve HARRIS
  James HERBERT
  Stephen KING
  Dean R. KOONTZ
  H.P. LOVECRAFT
  Graham MASTERTON
  Whitley STRIEBER
  T.M. WRIGHT

Robert CAMPBELL US 1927-
Crime

  Edna BUCHANAN

  James M. CAIN

  Andrew COBURN

  K.C. CONSTANTINE

  Tom KAKONIS

Albert CAMUS Fr 1913-60
General

  William GOLDING

  Günter GRASS

  Franz KAFKA

  Jack KEROUAC

Ethan CANIN US 1960-
General

  Lisa ALTHER

  Jon COHEN

  Garrison KEILLOR

  Sue MILLER

  Mary McGarry MORRIS

  John UPDIKE

Victor CANNING 1911-86
Adventure

  Eric AMBLER

  Jon CLEARY

  Robert LUDLUM

  Alistair MACLEAN

  Nevil SHUTE

Truman CAPOTE US 1924-84
General

  Erskine CALDWELL

  Ernest HEMINGWAY

  Armistead MAUPIN

  Carson McCULLERS

  J.D. SALINGER

  Gore VIDAL

Orson Scott CARD US 1951-
Science Fiction

  Iain M. BANKS

  John BARNES

  Arthur C. CLARKE

  Alan Dean FOSTER

  Stephen KING

  Kim Stanley ROBINSON

  Gene WOLFE

Peter CAREY Aus 1943-
General

  Peter ACKROYD

  John BANVILLE

  Rodney HALL

  Thomas KENEALLY

  David MALOUF

  Patrick WHITE

  Tim WINTON

J.L. CARR 1912-94
Humour

Roy CLARKE

Michael FRAYN

David NOBBS

Tom SHARPE

John Dickson CARR US 1906-77
Crime

Nicholas BLAKE

John Newton CHANCE

John CREASEY

Edmund CRISPIN

Michael INNES

H.R.F. KEATING

Ngaio MARSH

Gladys MITCHELL

Dorothy L. SAYERS

Rex STOUT

Josephine TEY

Sara WOODS

Philippa CARR 1906-93
also writes as Victoria HOLT & Jean PLAIDY
Historical

Valerie ANAND

Pamela BELLE

Emma DRUMMOND

Barbara ERSKINE

Diana GABALDON

Valerie GEORGESON

Philippa GREGORY

Pamela HILL

Isabelle HOLLAND

Dinah LAMPITT

Diana NORMAN

Nigel TRANTER

Michael CARSON 1946-
General

Guy BELLAMY

Patrick GALE

Alan HOLLINGHURST

David LEAVITT

Adam MARS-JONES

Armistead MAUPIN

Tony WARREN

Edmund WHITE

Angela CARTER 1940-92
General

A.S. BYATT

Alice Thomas ELLIS

John FOWLES

Gabriel GARCIA MARQUEZ

Elizabeth JOLLEY

Michèle ROBERTS

Salman RUSHDIE

Isaac Bashevis SINGER

Marina WARNER

Fay WELDON

Jeanette WINTERSON

Brian CARTER
General
  Aeron CLEMENT
  William HORWOOD
  A.R. LLOYD
  Brian PARVIN

Sarah CAUDWELL
Crime
  Frances FYFIELD
  Donna LEON
  Joyce PORTER
  Annette ROOME

Barbara CARTLAND   1901-
Romance
  Marion CHESNEY
  Caroline COURTNEY
  Clare DARCY
  Penny JORDAN
  Sheila WALSH

Harry CAULEY US
General
  Garrison KEILLOR
  Jane SMILEY
  Anne TYLER
  Robert James WALLER

Raymond CARVER US 1939-88
General
  John CHEEVER
  Richard FORD
  David GATES
  Jim HARRISON
  Bobbie Ann MASON

Peter CAVE
War
  Peter ABRAHAMS
  Doug ARMSTRONG
  Shaun CLARKE
  Robin JAMES
  David MONNERY

Joyce CARY   1888-1957
General
  Ivy COMPTON-BURNETT
  Nadine GORDIMER
  Doris LESSING
  Marguerite STEEN

Elizabeth CHADWICK
Historical
  Pamela BELLE
  D.K. BROSTER
  Elizabeth BYRD
  Georgette HEYER
  Norah LOFTS

Jack L. CHALKER US   1944-
Science Fiction
  Poul ANDERSON
  Piers ANTHONY
  Terry BROOKS
  Gordon R. DICKSON
  Philip José FARMER
  Fred SABERHAGEN
  Robert SILVERBERG
  Roger ZELAZNY

John Newton CHANCE 1911-83
Crime
  John Dickson CARR
  Raymond CHANDLER
  Ed McBAIN
  James PATTINSON

Raymond CHANDLER   US
Crime   1888-1959
  Edna BUCHANAN
  John Newton CHANCE
  James Hadley CHASE
  Andrew COBURN
  Loren D. ESTLEMAN
  Erle Stanley GARDNER
  Dashiell HAMMETT
  John D. MACDONALD
  Gregory MCDONALD
  Walter MOSLEY
  Robert B. PARKER

Walter SATTERTHWAIT
Rex STOUT

Kate CHARLES US   1950-
Crime
  D.M. GREENWOOD
  Paul HARDING
  Ellis PETERS
  Dorothy L. SAYERS
  Kate SEDLEY
  Barbara WHITEHEAD
  Derek WILSON

James Hadley CHASE 1906-85
Crime
  James M. CAIN
  Raymond CHANDLER
  K.C. CONSTANTINE
  Dashiell HAMMETT
  John D. MACDONALD
  Ross MACDONALD
  Ed McBAIN
  Robert B. PARKER
  Rex STOUT

Bruce CHATWIN   1940-1989
General
  Julian BARNES
  David COOK
  John FOWLES

Bruce CHATWIN (cont.)

   Patrick McCABE

   Robert NYE

   Barry UNSWORTH

Amit CHAUDHURI   Ind   1962-
General

   Farrukh DHONDY

   Russell LUCAS

   John MASTERS

   Gita MEHTA

   R.K. NARAYAN

   Vikram SETH

Mavis CHEEK
Humour

   Caro FRASER

   Helen MUIR

   Elizabeth PETERS

   Nigel WILLIAMS

John CHEEVER   US   1912-82
General

   Raymond CARVER

   William KENNEDY

   John O'HARA

   Anne TYLER

   John UPDIKE

   Gore VIDAL

C.J. CHERRYH   US   1942-
Science Fiction

   Greg BEAR

   Thomas M. DISCH

   Colin GREENLAND

   Mercedes LACKEY

   Anne McCAFFREY

   Frederik POHL

   Bob SHAW

Marion CHESNEY   Sco   1936-
also writes as M.C. BEATON
Romance

   Lucilla ANDREWS

   Barbara CARTLAND

   Catherine COULTER

   Caroline COURTNEY

   Clare DARCY

   Georgette HEYER

   Patricia ROBINS

   Sheila WALSH

Matt CHISHOLM   1919-83
Western

   J.T. EDSON

   Louis L'AMOUR

   Bill WADE

Agatha CHRISTIE   1890-1976
Crime

   Margery ALLINGHAM

   Nicholas BLAKE

John CREASEY
Elizabeth LEMARCHAND
Ngaio MARSH
Gladys MITCHELL
Dorothy L. SAYERS
Julian SYMONS
June THOMSON
Patricia WENTWORTH

Tom CLANCY   US   1947-
Adventure
Larry BOND
Dale BROWN
George BROWN
Stephen COONTS
Harold COYLE
Clive CUSSLER
Nelson DE MILLE
Daniel EASTERMAN
Colin FORBES
Jack HIGGINS
Stephen LEATHER
Douglas TERMAN

Douglas CLARK   1919-93
Crime
Arthur DOUGLAS
Dick FRANCIS
Gerald HAMMOND
Roy HART
June THOMSON

Mary Higgins CLARK   US 1929-
General
Jane BRINDLE
Ursula CURTISS
Joy FIELDING
Frances HEGARTY
Jonathan KELLERMAN
Judith KELMAN
Mary McMULLEN
Barbara MICHAELS
Anita SHREVE
Bernard TAYLOR
David WILTSE

Arthur C. CLARKE   1917-
Science Fiction
Isaac ASIMOV
Stephen BAXTER
Greg BEAR
James BLISH
Orson Scott CARD
Richard COWPER
Robert A. HEINLEIN
Stanislaw LEM
Larry NIVEN
Frederik POHL
Kim Stanley ROBINSON
Bob SHAW

Brenda CLARKE　　　1926-
also writes as Kate SEDLEY
Family Stories

Barbara Taylor BRADFORD

Vera COWIE

Suzanne GOODWIN

Elizabeth Jane HOWARD

Brenda JAGGER

Mary MINTON

Kay STEPHENS

Roy CLARKE
Humour

Dan BINCHY

J.L. CARR

David NOBBS

Peter TINNISWOOD

Sue TOWNSEND

Shaun CLARKE
War

Peter ABRAHAMS

Doug ARMSTRONG

Peter CAVE

Robin JAMES

David MONNERY

James CLAVELL　US　　1924-94
Adventure

Noel BARBER

Martin BOOTH

Robert ELEGANT

Colin FALCONER

Anthony GREY

Nicholas GUILD

Michael HARTLAND

Gary JENNINGS

Eric LUSTBADER

Amin MAALOUF

John MASTERS

Christopher NICOLE

Alan SAVAGE

Owen SELA

Jon CLEARY　Aus　　　1917-
Adventure

Desmond BAGLEY

Victor CANNING

Colin FORBES

John HARRIS

Hammond INNES

Geoffrey JENKINS

Duncan KYLE

Derek LAMBERT

Gavin LYALL

Nevil SHUTE

Wilbur SMITH

Eric WRIGHT

Ann CLEEVES　　　1954-
Crime

Catherine AIRD

W.J. BURLEY

Gwendoline BUTLER

Alan HUNTER

Candace ROBB

Peter TREMAYNE

Aeron CLEMENT
General

Richard ADAMS

Brian CARTER

William HORWOOD

Brian PARVIN

Carol CLEWLOW
General

Wendy PERRIAM

Michèle ROBERTS

Anita SHREVE

Fay WELDON

Daoma WINSTON

Jeanette WINTERSON

Michael CLYNES
Crime

Lindsey DAVIS

P.C. DOHERTY

Elizabeth EYRE

D.M. GREENWOOD

Martha GRIMES

Paul HARDING

Domini HIGHSMITH

William KIENZLE

Ellis PETERS

Marika COBBOLD　　Swe
General

Judy ASTLEY

Margaret BACON

Caroline BRIDGWOOD

Katie FFORDE

Nora NAISH

Ann PURSER

Kathleen ROWNTREE

Titia SUTHERLAND

Joanna TROLLOPE

Mary WESLEY

Andrew COBURN　　US　　1932-
Crime

Robert CAMPBELL

Raymond CHANDLER

K.C. CONSTANTINE

Stuart M. KAMINSKY

Robert B. PARKER

Ian COCHRANE　　Ire
General

Roddy DOYLE

James HAMILTON-PATERSON

Ian McEWAN

Al CODY 1928-
Western
  John BLAZE
  Max BRAND
  J.T. EDSON
  Zane GREY
  Louis L'AMOUR

Jess CODY 1899-
Western
  J.T. EDSON
  Louis L'AMOUR
  Chuck MARTIN
  T.C. OLSEN

Liza CODY 1944-
Crime
  Linda BARNES
  Sarah DUNANT
  Sue GRAFTON
  Christine GREEN
  Karen KIJEWSKI
  Sara LACEY
  Val MCDERMID
  Susan MOODY
  Marcia MULLER
  Sara PARETSKY
  Robert B. PARKER

Jonathan COE 1961-
Humour
  Julian BARNES
  Guy BELLAMY
  John IRVING
  David LODGE
  Nigel WILLIAMS

J.M. COETZEE SA 1940-
General
  Chinua ACHEBE
  Andre BRINK
  Nadine GORDIMER
  Alan PATON
  Amanda PRANTERA
  Barry UNSWORTH

Virginia COFFMAN US 1914-
Family Stories
  Virginia ANDREWS
  Betty BURTON
  Barbara MICHAELS
  LaVyrle SPENCER
  Helen VAN SLYKE
  Phyllis A. WHITNEY
  Mary WILLIAMS
  Daoma WINSTON

Anthea COHEN 1913-
Crime
  B.M. GILL
  Lesley GRANT-ADAMSON
  Christine GREEN
  Patricia HIGHSMITH
  Simon SHAW

Jon COHEN US
General
  Ethan CANIN
  Joseph HELLER
  Sue MILLER
  Mary McGarry MORRIS

Martina COLE
General
  Lynda LA PLANTE
  Michael MOLLOY
  Gilda O'NEILL
  James PATTINSON

Isabel COLEGATE 1931-
General
  Anita BROOKNER
  Margaret DRABBLE
  Penelope FITZGERALD
  Anthony POWELL
  Muriel SPARK
  Elizabeth TAYLOR

Vernon COLEMAN
General
  E.F. BENSON
  E.M. DELAFIELD
  Colin DOUGLAS
  Annie LEITH
  Angela THIRKELL

Catrin COLLIER Wales 1948-
Family Stories
  Alexander CORDELL
  Hilda McKENZIE
  Catrin MORGAN
  Sarah SHEARS
  Grace THOMPSON

Jackie COLLINS
Glitz & Glamour
  Sally BEAUMAN
  Pat BOOTH
  Celia BRAYFIELD
  Julie BURCHILL
  Joan COLLINS
  Shirley CONRAN
  Judith GOULD
  Erica JONG
  Judith KRANTZ
  Harold ROBBINS
  June Flaum SINGER
  Penny VINCENZI

Joan COLLINS   1933-
Glitz & Glamour

  Julie BURCHILL

  Jackie COLLINS

  Elizabeth GAGE

  Harold ROBBINS

Nancy COLLINS   US
Supernatural

  Chaz BRENCHLEY

  Christopher FOWLER

  George R. MARTIN

  Anne RICE

  Dan SIMMONS

Ivy COMPTON-BURNETT
General   1884-1969

  Jane AUSTEN

  Elizabeth BOWEN

  Joyce CARY

  Pamela Hansford JOHNSON

  Marguerite STEEN

  Evelyn WAUGH

Barbara COMYNS   1909-
General

  Margaret ATWOOD

  A.L. BARKER

  Janice ELLIOTT

  Joanna TROLLOPE

Richard CONDON   US   1915-96
Adventure

  Peter BENCHLEY

  Richard COX

  Michael CRICHTON

  Arthur HAILEY

  John LE CARRÉ

  Sidney SHELDON

  Leslie WALLER

Kathleen CONLON   1943-
Family Stories

  Clare BOYLAN

  Frank DELANEY

  Elizabeth Jane HOWARD

  Molly KEANE

Joseph CONRAD   1857-1924
General

  Louis DE BERNIÈRES

  Ford Madox FORD

  James HAMILTON-PATERSON

  Ernest HEMINGWAY

  Henry JAMES

  W. Somerset MAUGHAM

  Patrick O'BRIAN

  Paul THEROUX

Shirley CONRAN 1932-
Glitz & Glamour
  Celia BRAYFIELD
  Jackie COLLINS
  Jilly COOPER
  Lucinda EDMONDS
  Shirley ESKAPA
  Olivia GOLDSMITH
  Susan LEWIS
  Erin PIZZEY
  Harold ROBBINS
  Penny VINCENZI

K.C. CONSTANTINE US
Crime
  Robert CAMPBELL
  James Hadley CHASE
  Andrew COBURN
  Ed McBAIN
  Hilary WAUGH

Storm CONSTANTINE
Fantasy
  Mary GENTLE
  Guy Gavriel KAY
  Patricia KENNEALY
  Anne RICE
  Michael Scott ROHAN

David COOK 1940-
General
  Paul BAILEY
  Bruce CHATWIN
  Janet FRAME
  Ken KESEY
  David L. LINDSEY
  Ian McEWAN
  Brian MOORE
  Paul SAYER

Thomas H. COOK US 1947-
Crime
  Celia FREMLIN
  Thomas HARRIS
  Patricia HIGHSMITH
  David L. LINDSEY
  David WILTSE

Catherine COOKSON 1906-
Family Stories
  Kate FLYNN
  Iris GOWER
  Audrey HOWARD
  Sheila JANSEN
  Marie JOSEPH
  Mary E. PEARCE
  Elvi RHODES
  Janet TANNER
  Grace THOMPSON
  Dee WILLIAMS

Stephen COONTS   US   1946-
Adventure

  Geoffrey ARCHER

  Larry BOND

  Dale BROWN

  Tom CLANCY

  Clive CUSSLER

  Richard HERMAN

  Graham HURLEY

  David MACE

  Julian Jay SAVARIN

  Douglas TERMAN

Jilly COOPER   1937-
Glitz & Glamour

  Catherine ALLIOTT

  Sally BEAUMAN

  Charlotte BINGHAM

  Celia BRAYFIELD

  Shirley CONRAN

  Lucinda EDMONDS

  Judith GOULD

  Judith KRANTZ

  Rupert LEGGE

  Jill MANSELL

  Fiona WALKER

Lettice COOPER   1897-1994
General

  Phyllis BENTLEY

  Melvyn BRAGG

  Winifred HOLTBY

  Angela THIRKELL

Louise COOPER   1952-
Fantasy

  Jean M. AUEL

  David A. GEMMELL

  Robert JORDAN

  Katherine KERR

  Melanie RAWN

Natasha COOPER
Crime

  Frances FYFIELD

  Susan KELLY

  Jennie MELVILLE

  Janet NEEL

  Betty ROWLANDS

  Veronica STALLWOOD

William COOPER   1910-
General

  Kingsley AMIS

  Malcolm BRADBURY

  John BRAINE

  Stanley MIDDLETON

  C.P. SNOW

Alexander CORDELL 1914-
General
  Catrin COLLIER
  A.J. CRONIN
  R.F. DELDERFIELD
  Winston GRAHAM
  Richard LLEWELLYN
  Malcolm MACDONALD
  E.V. THOMPSON

Barry CORK
Crime
  Mark DANIEL
  Dick FRANCIS
  John FRANCOME
  Richard PITMAN
  Richard RUSSELL

Bernard CORNWELL 1944-
Adventure
  Alan EVANS
  C.S. FORESTER
  Alexander FULLERTON
  Max HENNESSY
  Alexander KENT
  Sam LLEWELLYN
  Patrick O'BRIAN
  Douglas REEMAN
  Nigel TRANTER

Patricia D. CORNWELL US
Crime 1956-
  Joy FIELDING
  Frances FYFIELD
  Elizabeth GEORGE
  Sue GRAFTON
  John GRISHAM
  Faye KELLERMAN
  Jonathan KELLERMAN
  Ridley PEARSON
  Ruth RENDELL
  Minette WALTERS

William J. COUGHLIN US
Crime
  Dexter DIAS
  Philip FRIEDMAN
  John GRISHAM
  Steve MARTINI

Catherine COULTER US
Historical
  Pamela BELLE
  Madeleine BRENT
  Marion CHESNEY
  Teresa CRANE
  Judith McNAUGHT
  Sheila WALSH

Bryce COURTENAY SA
Adventure
   Martin BOOTH
   Eric LUSTBADER
   Amin MAALOUF
   Wilbur SMITH

Caroline COURTNEY 1920-
Romance
   Barbara CARTLAND
   Marion CHESNEY
   Clare DARCY
   Joyce DINGWELL
   Jane DONNELLY

Vera COWIE
Glitz & Glamour
   Brenda CLARKE
   Vanessa FOX
   Susan LEWIS
   Penny VINCENZI

Richard COWPER 1926-
Science Fiction
   Brian W. ALDISS
   Arthur C. CLARKE
   Clifford D. SIMAK
   Brian STABLEFORD

Josephine COX 1938-
also writes as Jane BRINDLE
General
   Lyn ANDREWS
   Rose BOUCHERON
   Kate FLYNN
   Sara FRASER
   Suzanne GOODWIN
   Iris GOWER
   Marie JOSEPH
   Lena KENNEDY
   Maisie MOSCO
   Wendy ROBERTSON

Richard COX 1931-
Adventure
   Richard CONDON
   Clare FRANCIS
   Arthur HAILEY
   Leslie WALLER

Harold COYLE US 1952-
Adventure
   Tom CLANCY
   Clive CUSSLER
   W.E.B. GRIFFIN
   Sven HASSEL
   Jack HIGGINS
   Graham HURLEY
   Leo KESSLER
   Craig THOMAS

Amanda CRAIG   1959-
General
  Janice GALLOWAY
  Jane GARDAM
  A.L. KENNEDY
  Amanda PRANTERA
  Barbara TRAPIDO

Teresa CRANE
Historical
  Anita BURGH
  Catherine COULTER
  Catherine GASKIN
  Genevieve LYONS
  Elisabeth McNEILL
  Belva PLAIN
  Judith SAXTON
  Eileen TOWNSEND

John CREASEY   1908-73
Crime
  John Dickson CARR
  Agatha CHRISTIE
  John Buxton HILTON
  Jonathan ROSS
  Georges SIMENON

Michael CRICHTON US 1942-
General
  Peter BENCHLEY
  Richard CONDON

Dean R. KOONTZ
Sidney SHELDON

Edmund CRISPIN   1921-78
Crime
  Margery ALLINGHAM
  Nicholas BLAKE
  John Dickson CARR
  Georgette HEYER
  Michael INNES
  Gladys MITCHELL
  Josephine TEY
  Colin WATSON

A.J. CRONIN Sco 1896-1981
General
  Thomas ARMSTRONG
  Taylor CALDWELL
  Alexander CORDELL
  R.F. DELDERFIELD
  Winston GRAHAM
  Richard LLEWELLYN
  J.B. PRIESTLEY
  Howard SPRING

Susan CROSLAND US
General
  Jeffrey ARCHER
  Bertie DENHAM
  Michael DOBBS

Susan CROSLAND (cont.)

Dominic DUNNE

Robert GODDARD

Amanda CROSS   US   1926-
Crime

Linda BARNES

Lilian Jackson BRAUN

Ruth Dudley EDWARDS

Antonia FRASER

Elizabeth GEORGE

Sue GRAFTON

P.D. JAMES

Emma LATHEN

Dorothy L. SAYERS

Elaine CROWLEY   Ire
Family Stories

Maeve BINCHY

Frank DELANEY

Beryl KINGSTON

Elvi RHODES

Ursula CURTISS
Romance

Mary Higgins CLARK

Isabelle HOLLAND

Mary McMULLEN

Phyllis A. WHITNEY

Margaret YORKE

Clive CUSSLER   US   1931-
Adventure

Dale BROWN

Tom CLANCY

Stephen COONTS

Harold COYLE

Alan EVANS

Graham HURLEY

Hammond INNES

Alistair MACLEAN

Julian Jay SAVARIN

Gerald SEYMOUR

Craig THOMAS

David DABYDEEN   1956-
General

Buchi EMECHETA

V.S. NAIPAUL

Ben OKRI

Caryl PHILLIPS

Janet DAILEY   US   1944-
Family Stories

Charlotte Vale ALLEN

Judith SAXTON

LaVyrle SPENCER

Diana STAINFORTH

Danielle STEEL

Margaret SUNLEY

Helen VAN SLYKE

Elizabeth WAITE

Elizabeth WARNE

Daoma WINSTON

Elizabeth DAISH
Family Stories

Hilary BAILEY

Tessa BARCLAY

Pamela BELLE

Betty BURTON

Elizabeth DARRELL

Margaret Thomson DAVIS

Iris GOWER

Reay TANNAHILL

Barbara WHITNELL

Mark DANIEL   1954-
Crime

Barry CORK

Arthur DOUGLAS

Dick FRANCIS

John FRANCOME

Richard PITMAN

Richard RUSSELL

Clare DARCY   US
Romance

Barbara CARTLAND

Marion CHESNEY

Caroline COURTNEY

Georgette HEYER

Elizabeth DARRELL
also writes as Emma DRUMMOND
Family Stories

Noel BARBER

Betty BURTON

Elizabeth DAISH

Peter LING

Doris DAVIDSON   Sco
Family Stories

Margaret Thomson DAVIS

Evelyn HOOD

Gwen KIRKWOOD

Agnes SHORT

Emma STIRLING

Jessica STIRLING

Anne VIVIS

Lionel DAVIDSON   1922-
Adventure

Geoffrey ARCHER

John BUCHAN

Len DEIGHTON

Ken FOLLETT

Alan FURST

Hammond INNES

John LE CARRÉ

Duncan KYLE

Anthony PRICE

Julian RATHBONE

Tim SEBASTIAN

Robertson DAVIES   Can
General   1913-95
  Malcolm BRADBURY
  Anthony BURGESS
  John IRVING
  Angus WILSON

John Gordon DAVIS   SA
General
  Nelson DE MILLE
  Colleen McCULLOUGH
  Patricia SHAW
  Wilbur SMITH

Lindsey DAVIS
Crime
  Michael CLYNES
  P.C. DOHERTY
  Elizabeth EYRE
  Paul HARDING
  John Buxton HILTON
  Michael PEARCE
  Ellis PETERS
  Candace ROBB
  Peter TREMAYNE

Margaret Thomson DAVIS   Sco
Family Stories
  Tessa BARCLAY
  Emma BLAIR

Elizabeth DAISH
Doris DAVIDSON
Christine Marion FRASER
Iris GOWER
Evelyn HOOD
Marie JOSEPH
Alison Scott SKELTON
Jessica STIRLING
Nicola THORNE

Louis DE BERNIÈRES   1954-
General
  Malcolm BRADBURY
  Joseph CONRAD
  James HAMILTON-PATERSON
  Christopher HUDSON
  Jay McINERNEY

Nelson DE MILLE   US   1943-
Adventure
  Tom CLANCY
  John Gordon DAVIS
  Pete DEXTER
  Daniel EASTERMAN
  Ken FOLLETT
  Gary JENNINGS
  Sidney SHELDON
  John TRENHAILE

Colin DE SILVA Sri Lan
Historical

  Peter DRISCOLL

  M.M. KAYE

  John MASTERS

Len DEIGHTON 1929-
Adventure

  David BRIERLEY

  George BROWN

  Lionel DAVIDSON

  Clive EGLETON

  Bryan FORBES

  Robert HARRIS

  Philip KERR

  John LE CARRÉ

  Robert LITTELL

  Gavin LYALL

  Anthony PRICE

  Nigel WEST

E.M. DELAFIELD 1890-1943
General

  Judy ASTLEY

  E.F. BENSON

  Vernon COLEMAN

  Annie LEITH

  Miss READ

  Kathleen ROWNTREE

  Angela THIRKELL

  Joanna TROLLOPE

Frank DELANEY Ire 1942-
Family Stories

  Maeve BINCHY

  Kathleen CONLON

  Elaine CROWLEY

  Audrey HOWARD

  Genevieve LYONS

  Deirdre PURCELL

  Mary RYAN

Samuel R. DELANY US 1942-
Science Fiction

  Harlan ELLISON

  Michael MOORCOCK

  Joanna RUSS

  Roger ZELAZNY

R.F. DELDERFIELD 1912-72
Family Stories

  Thomas ARMSTRONG

  H.E. BATES

  Alexander CORDELL

  A.J. CRONIN

  John GALSWORTHY

  Winston GRAHAM

  Malcolm MACDONALD

  J.B. PRIESTLEY

  Howard SPRING

  E.V. THOMPSON

  Hugh WALPOLE

Don DELILLO US   1936-
General

  Saul BELLOW

  William STYRON

  John UPDIKE

  Gore VIDAL

Barbara DELINSKY US   1945-
Family Stories

  Doris MORTMAN

  Belva PLAIN

  LaVyrle SPENCER

  Danielle STEEL

Jane DENTINGER US
Crime

  Simon BRETT

  Emma LATHEN

  Janet LAURENCE

  Anne MORICE

  Emma PAGE

  Simon SHAW

August DERLETH US   1909-71
Fantasy

  Robert BLOCH

  Ramsey CAMPBELL

  H.P. LOVECRAFT

  Brian LUMLEY

Alan M. DERSHOWITZ US
Crime

  Philip FRIEDMAN

  John GRISHAM

  Scott TUROW

Anita DESAI Ind   1937-
General

  Margaret ATWOOD

  Marita GOLDEN

  Ruth Prawer JHABVALA

  Russell LUCAS

  R.K. NARAYAN

  Salman RUSHDIE

Eileen DEWHURST   1929-
Crime

  Alan HUNTER

  Ann QUINTON

  Sheila RADLEY

  Jonathan ROSS

Colin DEXTER   1930-
Crime

  Robert BARNARD

  Lilian Jackson BRAUN

  Nicolas FREELING

  Ann GRANGER

  John HARVEY

  Bill JAMES

P.D. JAMES

Roger ORMEROD

John PENN

Ian RANKIN

Ruth RENDELL

Peter ROBINSON

R.D. WINGFIELD

Richard North PATTERSON

Scott TUROW

Michael DIBDIN   1947-
Crime

Peter DICKINSON

Juliet HEBDEN

P.D. JAMES

Donna LEON

James McCLURE

Magdalen NABB

Ruth RENDELL

Pete DEXTER US   1943-
General

Russell BANKS

Nelson DE MILLE

William FAULKNER

Richard FORD

David GATES

Jim HARRISON

William KENNEDY

Thomas McGUANE

Larry WATSON

Philip K. DICK US   1928-82
Science Fiction

Isaac ASIMOV

J.G. BALLARD

David BRIN

William GIBSON

Robert A. HEINLEIN

Stanislaw LEM

Christopher PRIEST

Kim Stanley ROBINSON

Ian WATSON

Farrukh DHONDY Ind   1944-
General

Amit CHAUDHURI

Hanif KUREISHI

Salman RUSHDIE

Monica DICKENS   1915-92
Family Stories

Lynne Reid BANKS

H.E. BATES

Margaret FORSTER

Dexter DIAS
Crime

William J. COUGHLIN

Philip FRIEDMAN

Monica DICKENS (cont.)

Rumer GODDEN

Elizabeth Jane HOWARD

Mary E. PEARCE

D.E. STEVENSON

Elizabeth TAYLOR

Peter DICKINSON   1927-
Crime

Robert BARNARD

Michael DIBDIN

Patricia HIGHSMITH

P.D. JAMES

Gordon R. DICKSON   US 1923-
Science Fiction

Jack L. CHALKER

Robert JORDAN

Robert SILVERBERG

Clifford D. SIMAK

Roger ZELAZNY

William DIEHL   US
Crime

Ed McBAIN

Richard North PATTERSON

Ross THOMAS

Scott TUROW

Joyce DINGWELL   Aus   1912-
Romance

Caroline COURTNEY

Charlotte LAMB

Anne MATHER

Carole MORTIMER

Jessica STEELE

Thomas M. DISCH   US   1940-
Science Fiction

J.G. BALLARD

John BRUNNER

C.J. CHERRYH

Jenny DISKI   1947-
General

Nina BAWDEN

Lesley GLAISTER

Frances HEGARTY

Joyce Carol OATES

Michael DOBBS
General

Jeffrey ARCHER

Susan CROSLAND

E.L. DOCTOROW US 1931-
General
F. Scott FITZGERALD
Thomas KENEALLY
William KENNEDY
Toni MORRISON
Jane SMILEY
John UPDIKE

P.C. DOHERTY
Crime
Michael CLYNES
Lindsey DAVIS
Elizabeth EYRE
D.M. GREENWOOD
Martha GRIMES
Paul HARDING
William KIENZLE
Anne PERRY
Ellis PETERS
Candace ROBB
Peter TREMAYNE

David DONACHIE Sco 1944-
Sea
C.S. FORESTER
Alexander KENT
Patrick O'BRIAN
Dudley POPE
Vivian STUART
Richard WOODMAN

Anabel DONALD
Crime
Sarah DUNANT
Anne FINE
Susan ISAACS
Sara LACEY
Joan SMITH
Veronica STALLWOOD
Minette WALTERS

Stephen DONALDSON US
Fantasy 1947-
Jean M. AUEL
Terry BROOKS
David EDDINGS
Stephen KING
Julian MAY
J.R.R. TOLKIEN

J.P. DONLEAVY Ire 1926-
General
John IRVING
Flann O'BRIEN
Tom SHARPE

Jane DONNELLY
Romance
Caroline COURTNEY
Charlotte LAMB
Anne MATHER
Carole MORTIMER
Jessica STEELE

Joe DONNELLY Sco 1950-
Supernatural
  Jonathan AYCLIFFE
  Ramsey CAMPBELL
  Stephen GALLAGHER
  Steve HARRIS
  Peter JAMES
  Stephen LAWS
  Graham MASTERTON
  Mark MORRIS
  Kim NEWMAN
  Philip RICKMAN
  Dennis WHEATLEY

Arthur DOUGLAS 1926-
also writes as Gerald HAMMOND
Crime
  Douglas CLARK
  Mark DANIEL
  Dick FRANCIS

Colin DOUGLAS Sco 1945-
Humour
  Vernon COLEMAN
  Tom HOLT
  David LODGE
  David NOBBS
  Nigel WILLIAMS

Ellen DOUGLAS US 1921-
General
  Ellen GILCHRIST
  David GUTERSON
  Gloria NAYLOR
  Alice WALKER

Roddy DOYLE Ire 1958-
Humour
  Martin AMIS
  Dan BINCHY
  Ian COCHRANE
  Geoff DYER
  James KELMAN
  A.L. KENNEDY
  Patrick MCCABE
  David NOBBS
  Irvine WELSH

Margaret DRABBLE 1939-
General
  Lynne Reid BANKS
  Nina BAWDEN
  Melvyn BRAGG
  A.S. BYATT
  Isabel COLEGATE
  Penelope FITZGERALD
  Margaret FORSTER
  Penelope MORTIMER
  Edna O'BRIEN
  Bernice RUBENS

Gillian TINDALL

Fay WELDON

Anya SETON

Mary STEWART

Peter DRISCOLL   1942-
Adventure

Eric AMBLER

John BUCHAN

Colin DE SILVA

Nicholas GUILD

J.K. MAYO

Wilbur SMITH

Sarah DUNANT   1950-
Crime

Liza CODY

Anabel DONALD

Lesley GRANT-ADAMSON

Val McDERMID

Joan SMITH

Minette WALTERS

Emma DRUMMOND
also writes as Elizabeth DARRELL
Historical

Pamela BELLE

Philippa CARR

Cynthia HARROD-EAGLES

Georgette HEYER

Victoria HOLT

Patricia SHAW

Laramie DUNAWAY   US
Glitz & Glamour

Lucinda EDMONDS

Elizabeth GAGE

Erica JONG

Rupert LEGGE

Kathy LETTE

Dave DUNCAN   Can   1933-
Fantasy

Terry BROOKS

David EDDINGS

Raymond E. FEIST

David A. GEMMELL

Daphne DU MAURIER   1907-89
General

Anita BURGH

Taylor CALDWELL

Robert GODDARD

Winston GRAHAM

Susan HILL

Susan HOWATCH

Jane DUNCAN   Sco
Family Stories
  Miss READ
  Sarah SHEARS
  D.E. STEVENSON

Nell DUNN   1936-
General
  Lynne Reid BANKS
  Edna O'BRIEN

Dominick DUNNE   US   1925-
General
  Susan CROSLAND
  Adam KENNEDY
  Marge PIERCY
  Tom WOLFE

Dorothy DUNNETT   US/Sco
Historical   1923-
  Valerie ANAND
  Gillian BRADSHAW
  Diana GABALDON
  Naomi MITCHISON
  Sharon PENMAN
  Jean PLAIDY
  Mary RENAULT
  Judith M. RILEY
  Stewart ROSS

Reay TANNAHILL
Nigel TRANTER

Lawrence DURRELL   1912-90
General
  John FOWLES
  Robert GRAVES
  Olivia MANNING
  C.P. SNOW
  Evelyn WAUGH

Geoff DYER   1958-
General
  Pat BARKER
  Roddy DOYLE
  Sebastian FAULKS
  J.D. SALINGER

Daniel EASTERMAN   1949-
also writes as Jonathan AYCLIFFE
Adventure
  Tom CLANCY
  Nelson DE MILLE
  James FOLLETT
  Amin MAALOUF
  John TRENHAILE

David EDDINGS US   1931-
Fantasy

  Terry BROOKS

  Stephen DONALDSON

  Dave DUNCAN

  Raymond E. FEIST

  Maggie FUREY

  David A. GEMMELL

  Garry D. KILWORTH

  Julian MAY

  Anne McCAFFREY

  Melanie RAWN

  Margaret WEIS

  Tad WILLIAMS

  Jonathan WYLIE

Dorothy EDEN NZ   1912-82
General

  Phyllis BENTLEY

  Madeleine BRENT

  Iris BROMIGE

  Barbara MICHAELS

  Anya SETON

  Marguerite STEEN

  Anne STEVENSON

  Mary STEWART

  Essie SUMMERS

  Barbara WHITNELL

  Phyllis A. WHITNEY

Lucinda EDMONDS   1966-
Glitz & Glamour

  Charlotte BINGHAM

  Pat BOOTH

  Celia BRAYFIELD

  Jacqueline BRISKIN

  Shirley CONRAN

  Jilly COOPER

  Laramie DUNAWAY

  Fiona WALKER

J.T. EDSON   1928-
Western

  John BLAZE

  Max BRAND

  Matt CHISHOLM

  Al CODY

  Jess CODY

  Lee F. GREGSON

  Louis L'AMOUR

  Nelson NYE

Martin EDWARDS   1955-
Crime

  Frances FYFIELD

  Reginald HILL

  Bill JAMES

  Val McDERMID

Ruth Dudley EDWARDS Ire
Crime
  Michael BOND
  Amanda CROSS
  Tim HEALD
  Colin WATSON

Greg EGAN Aus
Science Fiction
  Greg BEAR
  Gregory BENFORD
  David BRIN
  Paul J. McAULEY

Lesley EGAN US   1921-88
also writes as Dell SHANNON
Crime
  Eugene IZZI
  Ed McBAIN
  Dell SHANNON
  Peter TURNBULL
  Janwillem VAN DE WETERING
  Hillary WAUGH

Clive EGLETON   1927-
Adventure
  Ted ALLBEURY
  Len DEIGHTON
  Bryan FORBES
  Colin FORBES
  Frederick FORSYTH

  Palma HARCOURT
  John LE CARRÉ
  Robert LUDLUM
  Alistair MACLEAN
  Anthony PRICE

Robert ELEGANT US   1928-
General
  Noel BARBER
  James CLAVELL
  Derek LAMBERT
  Eric LUSTBADER
  James A. MICHENER
  Alan SAVAGE

Elizabeth ELGIN
Family Stories
  Rosemary ENRIGHT
  Lilian HARRY
  Wendy ROBERTSON
  Susan SALLIS

Janice ELLIOTT   1931-
General
  Margaret ATWOOD
  Pat BARKER
  Barbara COMYNS
  Penelope LIVELY
  Barbara PYM

Alice Thomas ELLIS   1932-
General
  Hilary BAILEY
  Beryl BAINBRIDGE
  Angela CARTER
  Jennifer JOHNSTON
  Molly KEANE
  Penelope LIVELY
  Deborah MOGGACH
  Edna O'BRIEN
  Barbara PYM
  Bernice RUBENS
  Barbara TRAPIDO

Julie ELLIS US   1933-
Glitz & Glamour
  Sally BEAUMAN
  Freda BRIGHT
  Shirley ESKAPA
  Judith KRANTZ
  Lynda LA PLANTE
  Una-Mary PARKER
  June Flaum SINGER

Harlan ELLISON US   1934-
Science Fiction
  Poul ANDERSON
  Ray BRADBURY
  Samuel R. DELANY

James ELLROY US   1948-
Crime
  Lawrence BLOCK
  James M. CAIN
  Loren D. ESTLEMAN
  Dashiell HAMMETT
  George V. HIGGINS
  Eugene IZZI
  Elmore LEONARD
  Walter MOSLEY
  Jim THOMPSON

Ben ELTON   1959-
General
  Douglas ADAMS
  Stephen AMIDON
  Peter TINNISWOOD
  Keith WATERHOUSE

Buchi EMECHETA Nigeria 1944-
General
  Andre BRINK
  David DABYDEEN
  Toni MORRISON
  Wole SOYINKA

Sally EMERSON
General
  Janice GALLOWAY
  Candia McWILLIAM
  Jane ROGERS

Shusaku ENDO Ja   1923-
General
Russell BANKS
Kazuo ISHIGURO
Yukio MISHIMA
Haruki MURAKAMI

Rosemary ENRIGHT
Family Stories
Donna BAKER
Tessa BARCLAY
Barbara Taylor BRADFORD
Louise BRINDLEY
Elizabeth ELGIN
Ruth HAMILTON
Lilian HARRY
Maisie MOSCO
Pamela OLDFIELD
Sue SULLY

Louise ERDRICH US   1954-
General
William FAULKNER
Alice HOFFMAN
Alison LURIE
Lorrie MOORE
E. Annie PROULX
Jane SMILEY
Anne TYLER
Larry WATSON

Barbara ERSKINE   1944-
Historical
Evelyn ANTHONY
Philippa CARR
Diana GABALDON
Elizabeth HARRIS
Cynthia HARROD-EAGLES
Domini HIGHSMITH
Dinah LAMPITT
Reay TANNAHILL

Margaret ERSKINE
Family Stories
Catherine GASKIN
Judith GLOVER
Reay TANNAHILL

Shirley ESKAPA SA
Glitz & Glamour
Sally BEAUMAN
Pat BOOTH
Shirley CONRAN
Julie ELLIS
Una-Mary PARKER
Penny VINCENZI

Gavin ESLER Sco
Adventure
George BROWN
Stephen LEATHER

Kenneth ROYCE

Tim SEBASTIAN

Gerald SEYMOUR

Douglas SCOTT

Peter TONKIN

Loren D. ESTLEMAN US 1952-
Crime

William BAYER

Lawrence BLOCK

Raymond CHANDLER

James ELLROY

Dashiell HAMMETT

Eugene IZZI

Elmore LEONARD

Janet EVANOVICH US
Crime

Linda BARNES

Susan ISAACS

Sara LACEY

Joan SMITH

Alan EVANS 1930-
Adventure

Brian CALLISON

Bernard CORNWELL

Clive CUSSLER

Duncan HARDING

Max HENNESSY

Richard HOUGH

Pamela EVANS
Family Stories

Tessa BARCLAY

Emma BLAIR

Harry BOWLING

Mary MINTON

Gilda O'NEILL

Denise ROBERTSON

Eileen STAFFORD

Mary Jane STAPLES

Elizabeth WAITE

Elizabeth WARNE

Jeanne WHITMEE

Dee WILLIAMS

Elizabeth EYRE
also writes as STAYNES & STOREY
Crime

Michael CLYNES

Lindsey DAVIS

P.C. DOHERTY

Paul HARDING

Ellis PETERS

Candace ROBB

Kate ROSS

Zoe FAIRBAIRNS 1948-
Family Stories
  Pat BARKER
  Kate FLYNN
  Philippa GREGORY
  Susan HOWATCH
  Kate SAUNDERS
  T.R. WILSON

Colin FALCONER
Adventure
  James CLAVELL
  Nicholas GUILD
  Eric LUSTBADER
  Christopher NICOLE

Julian FANE 1927-
General
  Anita BROOKNER
  Barbara PYM

Philip José FARMER US 1918-
Science Fiction
  Piers ANTHONY
  Greg BEAR
  Jack L. CHALKER
  Michael MOORCOCK

J.G. FARRELL 1935-79
General
  Peter ACKROYD
  Christopher HUDSON
  Ruth Prawer JHABVALA
  John MASTERS
  M.R. O'DONNELL

John FARRIS
Supernatural
  Stephen GALLAGHER
  Stephen KING
  Robert McCAMMON
  Anne RICE
  Peter STRAUB
  Whitley STRIEBER

Howard FAST US 1914-92
General
  Winston GRAHAM
  Leon URIS
  Herman WOUK

William FAULKNER US
General 1897-1962
  Saul BELLOW
  Erskine CALDWELL
  Pete DEXTER
  Louise ERDRICH
  F. Scott FITZGERALD

Richard FORD
Ellen GILCHRIST
Ernest HEMINGWAY
Sinclair LEWIS
Cormac McCARTHY
John STEINBECK
William STYRON

Sebastian FAULKS   1953-
General
Pat BARKER
Julian BARNES
Geoff DYER
Ronald FRAME
Milan KUNDERA
Erich Maria REMARQUE
Paul WATKINS

Raymond E. FEIST   US   1945-
Fantasy
Marion Zimmer BRADLEY
Terry BROOKS
Dave DUNCAN
David EDDINGS
Mary GENTLE
Robert JORDAN
Anne McCAFFREY
Melanie RAWN
R.A. SALVATORE
Margaret WEIS
Janny WURTS

Elizabeth FERRARS   1907-95
Crime
Catherine AIRD
Margery ALLINGHAM
Marian BABSON
Anthea FRASER
Emma LATHEN
Ngaio MARSH
Roger ORMEROD
John PENN
Dorothy SIMPSON
June THOMSON
Barbara WHITEHEAD
Margaret YORKE

Katie FFORDE
General
Marika COBBOLD
Elizabeth PALMER
Rosamund PILCHER
Titia SUTHERLAND
Joanna TROLLOPE
Mary WESLEY

Joy FIELDING
Crime
Mary Higgins CLARK
Patricia D. CORNWELL
Thomas HARRIS
Faye KELLERMAN
Jonathan KELLERMAN

Joy FIELDING (cont.)

Judith KELMAN

Nancy Taylor ROSENBERG

Anne FINE   1947-
General

Rachel BILLINGTON

Anabel DONALD

Lesley GLAISTER

Alasdair GRAY

Joan LINGARD

Will SELF

F. Scott FITZGERALD   US
General   1896-1940

E.L. DOCTOROW

William FAULKNER

Ford Madox FORD

E.M. FORSTER

Ernest HEMINGWAY

Sinclair LEWIS

Carson McCULLERS

John O'HARA

John STEINBECK

Penelope FITZGERALD   1916-
General

Jane AUSTEN

Beryl BAINBRIDGE

Rachel BILLINGTON

Anita BROOKNER

Isabel COLEGATE

Margaret DRABBLE

Margaret FORSTER

Penelope LIVELY

Amanda PRANTERA

Emma TENNANT

Ian FLEMING   1908-64
Adventure

Eric AMBLER

George BROWN

James FOLLETT

Brian FREEMANTLE

John GARDNER

Adam HALL

James LEASOR

Gavin LYALL

J.K. MAYO

Kate FLYNN   1936-
also writes as Judith SAXTON & Judy TURNER
Family Stories

Lyn ANDREWS

Anne BAKER

Catherine COOKSON

Josephine COX

Zoe FAIRBAIRNS

Helen FORRESTER

Ruth HAMILTON

Audrey HOWARD

Joan JONKER
Elizabeth MURPHY
Mary Jane STAPLES

James FOLLETT   1939-
Adventure
Desmond BAGLEY
George BROWN
Daniel EASTERMAN
Ian FLEMING
Jack GERSON
William HAGGARD
John HARRIS
Robert LUDLUM
Alistair MACLEAN
Craig THOMAS
Glover WRIGHT

Ken FOLLETT   1949-
Adventure
Desmond BAGLEY
Lionel DAVIDSON
Nelson DE MILLE
Frederick FORSYTH
Clare FRANCIS
Palma HARCOURT
Jack HIGGINS
Andrew MACALLAN
Alistair MACLEAN
Gerald SEYMOUR
Wilbur SMITH
Craig THOMAS

Bryan FORBES   1926-
Adventure
Len DEIGHTON
Clive EGLETON
John LE CARRÉ
Tim SEBASTIAN

Colin FORBES
Adventure
Ted ALLBEURY
Evelyn ANTHONY
Campbell ARMSTRONG
George BROWN
Tom CLANCY
Jon CLEARY
Clive EGLETON
Frederick FORSYTH
Palma HARCOURT
Geoffrey JENKINS
Andrew MACALLAN
John TRENHAILE

Ford Madox FORD   1873-1939
General
Joseph CONRAD
F. Scott FITZGERALD
Henry JAMES
Sinclair LEWIS
John O'HARA

Richard FORD US   1944-
General
Raymond CARVER
Pete DEXTER
William FAULKNER
Jim HARRISON
Garrison KEILLOR
Bobbie Ann MASON
Thomas McGUANE
John STEINBECK
William STYRON
Anne TYLER
John UPDIKE

C.S. FORESTER   1899-1966
Sea
Bernard CORNWELL
David DONACHIE
Raymond HARDIE
Alexander KENT
A.E. LANGSFORD
Nicholas MONSARRAT
Patrick O'BRIAN
C. Northcote PARKINSON
Dudley POPE
Showell STYLES
John WINTON
Richard WOODMAN

Helen FORRESTER   1919-
Family Stories
Lyn ANDREWS
Anne BAKER
Harry BOWLING
Kate FLYNN
Audrey HOWARD
Joan JONKER
Marie JOSEPH
Elizabeth MURPHY
Deirdre PURCELL
Marjorie QUARTON
Sarah SHEARS
Elizabeth WAITE

Larry FORRESTER
War
W.E.B. GRIFFIN
John HARRIS
Max HENNESSY
David MACE
Derek ROBINSON

E.M. FORSTER   1879-1970
General
F. Scott FITZGERALD
Graham GREENE
Henry JAMES
Ruth Prawer JHABVALA
Francis KING

H.G. WELLS
Edith WHARTON

Margaret FORSTER 1938-
General
Beryl BAINBRIDGE
Nina BAWDEN
Monica DICKENS
Margaret DRABBLE
Penelope FITZGERALD
Susan HILL
Elizabeth Jane HOWARD
Angela HUTH
Alison LURIE
Deborah MOGGACH

Frederick FORSYTH 1938-
Adventure
Ted ALLBEURY
Clive EGLETON
Ken FOLLETT
Colin FORBES
Jack HIGGINS
Derek LAMBERT
Robert LUDLUM
David MASON
John TRENHAILE

Alan Dean FOSTER US 1946-
Science Fiction
Piers ANTHONY
Greg BEAR
Orson Scott CARD
Terry PRATCHETT

Christopher FOWLER 1953-
Supernatural
Ramsey CAMPBELL
Nancy COLLINS
Stephen KING
Graham MASTERTON
Kim NEWMAN

John FOWLES 1926-
General
Peter ACKROYD
Melvyn BRAGG
Angela CARTER
Bruce CHATWIN
Lawrence DURRELL
William GOLDING
Christopher HOPE
D.H. LAWRENCE
Robert NYE
Salman RUSHDIE
Graham SWIFT
D.M. THOMAS
Barry UNSWORTH

Vanessa FOX
Glitz & Glamour
  Vera COWIE
  Alexandra THORNE
  Elizabeth VILLARS
  Penny VINCENZI

Janet FRAME   NZ   1924-
General
  David COOK
  Elizabeth JOLLEY
  Doris LESSING
  Paul SAYER
  Fay WELDON
  Antonia WHITE

Ronald FRAME   Sco   1953-
General
  Sebastian FAULKS
  Robert GODDARD
  Kazuo ISHIGURO
  Allan MASSIE
  Paul MICOU

Clare FRANCIS   1946-
Adventure
  Evelyn ANTHONY
  Richard COX
  Ken FOLLETT
  Geoffrey JENKINS

Duncan KYLE
Helen MACINNES

Dick FRANCIS   1920-
Crime
  David BRIERLEY
  Douglas CLARK
  Barry CORK
  Mark DANIEL
  Arthur DOUGLAS
  John FRANCOME
  Paul MYERS
  Richard PITMAN
  Martin RUSSELL
  Richard RUSSELL

John FRANCOME   1952-
Crime
  Barry CORK
  Mark DANIEL
  Dick FRANCIS
  Richard PITMAN
  Richard RUSSELL
  Douglas RUTHERFORD

Anthea FRASER
Crime
  Marian BABSON
  Elizabeth FERRARS
  June THOMSON
  Sara WOODS

Antonia FRASER   1932-
Crime
  Amanda CROSS
  Elizabeth GEORGE
  Jessica MANN
  Jennie MELVILLE
  Susan MOODY
  Anne MORICE
  STAYNES & STOREY
  Margaret YORKE

Caro FRASER Sco
General
  Nina BAWDEN
  Mavis CHEEK
  Mary HOCKING
  John MORTIMER
  Mary RYAN

Christine Marion FRASER Sco
Family Stories
  Emma BLAIR
  Margaret Thomson DAVIS
  Valerie GEORGESON
  Evelyn HOOD
  Susan HOWATCH
  Brenda JAGGER
  Gwen KIRKWOOD
  Anne MELVILLE
  Elvi RHODES
  Jessica STIRLING

  Anne VIVIS
  Jan WEBSTER

George Macdonald FRASER
Humour   1925-
  H.E. BATES
  Stewart ROSS
  Tom SHARPE
  Leslie THOMAS
  Peter TINNISWOOD

Sara FRASER
Family Stories
  Lyn ANDREWS
  Josephine COX
  Malcolm ROSS
  Mary Jane STAPLES
  Janet TANNER

Michael FRAYN   1933-
Humour
  Kingsley AMIS
  Guy BELLAMY
  Malcolm BRADBURY
  J.L. CARR
  Francis KING

Nicolas FREELING   1927-
Crime
- Colin DEXTER
- Mark HEBDEN
- H.R.F. KEATING
- Philip KERR
- Donna LEON
- Georges SIMENON

Cynthia FREEMAN   US 1915-88
Family Stories
- Charlotte Vale ALLEN
- Barbara Taylor BRADFORD
- Margaret PEMBERTON
- Belva PLAIN
- Danielle STEEL
- Nicola THORNE
- Helen VAN SLYKE

Brian FREEMANTLE   1936-
Adventure
- Ted ALLBEURY
- Ian FLEMING
- John GARDNER
- John LE CARRÉ
- Helen MACINNES
- Anthony PRICE

Celia FREMLIN   1914-
Crime
- Thomas H. COOK
- B.M. GILL
- Gerald HAMMOND
- Margaret YORKE

Marilyn FRENCH   US   1929-
General
- Lisa ALTHER
- Gail GODWIN
- Alice HOFFMAN
- Alison LURIE
- Ann OAKLEY
- Marge PIERCY
- Judith ROSSNER

Philip FRIEDMAN   US
Crime
- William J. COUGHLIN
- Alan M. DERSHOWITZ
- Dexter DIAS
- John GRISHAM
- Steve MARTINI
- Richard North PATTERSON
- Nancy Taylor ROSENBERG
- Scott TUROW

Alexander FULLERTON 1924-
Adventure
  Brian CALLISON
  Bernard CORNWELL
  Duncan HARDING
  Max HENNESSY
  Richard HOUGH
  Hammond INNES
  Philip McCUTCHAN
  Douglas REEMAN
  Douglas SCOTT
  Richard WOODMAN

Maggie FUREY
Fantasy
  David EDDINGS
  Robert JORDAN
  Mercedes LACKEY
  Tad WILLIAMS

Alan FURST
Adventure
  Lionel DAVIDSON
  Philip KERR
  Robert LITTELL
  Owen SELA

Frances FYFIELD 1948-
also writes as Frances HEGARTY
Crime
  Sarah CAUDWELL
  Natasha COOPER

  Patricia D. CORNWELL
  Martin EDWARDS
  Elizabeth GEORGE
  B.M. GILL
  P.D. JAMES
  Steve MARTINI
  Ann QUINTON
  Annette ROOME
  Minette WALTERS

Diana GABALDON US
Historical
  Philippa CARR
  Dorothy DUNNETT
  Barbara ERSKINE
  Reay TANNAHILL
  Patricia WENDORF

Elizabeth GAGE US 1943-
also writes as LaVyrle SPENCER
Glitz & Glamour
  Sally BEAUMAN
  Celia BRAYFIELD
  Sandra BROWN
  Julie BURCHILL
  Joan COLLINS
  Laramie DUNAWAY
  Olivia GOLDSMITH
  Judith GOULD
  June Flaum SINGER

Patrick GALE
General
  Guy BELLAMY
  Guy BURT
  Michael CARSON
  Alan HOLLINGHURST
  Paul MICOU
  Edmund WHITE

Stephen GALLAGHER   1954-
Supernatural
  Chaz BRENCHLEY
  Joe DONNELLY
  John FARRIS
  Steve HARRIS
  James HERBERT
  Peter JAMES
  Stephen KING
  Dean R. KOONTZ
  Graham MASTERTON
  Mark MORRIS
  Tim WILLOCKS
  T.M. WRIGHT

Paul GALLICO   1897-1976
General
  Richard ADAMS
  H.E. BATES
  Winston GRAHAM
  Nevil SHUTE

Janice GALLOWAY   1956-
General
  Amanda CRAIG
  Sally EMERSON
  A.L. KENNEDY
  Doris LESSING
  Agnes OWENS
  Mary WESLEY

John GALSWORTHY   1867-1933
General
  Phyllis BENTLEY
  R.F. DELDERFIELD
  Winston GRAHAM
  D.H. LAWRENCE
  J.B. PRIESTLEY
  Howard SPRING
  Hugh WALPOLE

Gabriel GARCIA MARQUEZ
General   Colombia   1928-
  Isabel ALLENDE
  Anthony BURGESS
  Angela CARTER
  Günter GRASS
  Salman RUSHDIE

Jane GARDAM   1928-
General

Hilary BAILEY

Nina BAWDEN

Amanda CRAIG

Susan HILL

Jennifer JOHNSTON

Joan LINGARD

Jane ROGERS

J.D. SALINGER

Muriel SPARK

William TREVOR

Mary WESLEY

Craig Shaw GARDNER   US
Fantasy

Robert ASPRIN

Dan McGIRT

Terry PRATCHETT

Christopher STASHEFF

Erle Stanley GARDNER   US
Crime   1889-1970

Raymond CHANDLER

George V. HIGGINS

Dell SHANNON

Rex STOUT

Ross THOMAS

Charles WILLEFORD

John GARDNER   1926-
Adventure

Eric AMBLER

Desmond BAGLEY

Ian FLEMING

Brian FREEMANTLE

William HAGGARD

Adam HALL

Palma HARCOURT

Jack HIGGINS

Gavin LYALL

Julian RATHBONE

Jonathan GASH   1933-
also writes as Jonathan GRANT
Crime

Robert BARNARD

Simon BRETT

W.J. BURLEY

Gerald HAMMOND

Tim HEALD

Peter LOVESEY

John MALCOLM

James MELVILLE

Frank PARRISH

Iain PEARS

Neville STEED

David WILLIAMS

Catherine GASKIN Ire 1929-
Historical

  Teresa CRANE

  Margaret ERSKINE

  Judith GLOVER

  Jane Aiken HODGE

  Susan HOWATCH

  Claire LORRIMER

  Pamela OLDFIELD

  Diane PEARSON

David GATES US 1947-
General

  Raymond CARVER

  Pete DEXTER

  Jim HARRISON

  Larry WATSON

Catherine GAVIN Sco 1907-
Historical

  Evelyn ANTHONY

  Winston GRAHAM

  Pamela HILL

  Olivia MANNING

  Charles WHITING

  Philippa WIAT

  Sarah WOODHOUSE

David A. GEMMELL 1948-
Fantasy

  Marion Zimmer BRADLEY

  Terry BROOKS

  Louise COOPER

  Dave DUNCAN

  David EDDINGS

  Mary GENTLE

  Stephen KING

  Michael MOORCOCK

  Michael Scott ROHAN

  Patrick TILLEY

  Margaret WEIS

Mary GENTLE 1956-
Science Fiction

  Storm CONSTANTINE

  Raymond E. FEIST

  David A. GEMMELL

  Colin GREENLAND

  Gwyneth JONES

  Ursula LE GUIN

  Sheri S. TEPPER

Catherine GEORGE
Romance

  Charlotte LAMB

  Audrey MANLEY-TUCKER

  Carole MORTIMER

  Jessica STEELE

Elizabeth GEORGE   US   1949-
Crime
   Patricia D. CORNWELL
   Amanda CROSS
   Antonia FRASER
   Frances FYFIELD
   Martha GRIMES
   P.D. JAMES
   Barbara VINE

Valerie GEORGESON
Historical
   Philippa CARR
   Christine Marion FRASER
   Sheila JANSEN
   Pamela OLDFIELD

Jack GERSON   Sco
Adventure
   Campbell ARMSTRONG
   James FOLLETT
   William HAGGARD
   John KATZENBACH
   J.K. MAYO

William GIBSON   US   1948-
Science Fiction
   John BRUNNER
   Philip K. DICK
   Kim Stanley ROBINSON

   Neal STEPHENSON
   Bruce STERLING
   John VARLEY

Ellen GILCHRIST   US   1935-
General
   Ellen DOUGLAS
   William FAULKNER
   Jane HAMILTON
   Bobbie Anne MASON
   Jane SMILEY

B.M. GILL   1921-
Crime
   W.J. BURLEY
   Anthea COHEN
   Celia FREMLIN
   Frances FYFIELD
   Patricia HIGHSMITH
   Julian SYMONS

Lesley GLAISTER   1956-
General
   Jenny DISKI
   Anne FINE
   A.L. KENNEDY
   Patrick McCABE
   Ian McEWAN
   Deborah MOGGACH
   Will SELF

Lesley GLAISTER (cont.)

    Graham SWIFT

    Marina WARNER

    Gillian WHITE

Judith GLOVER   1943-
Historical

    Margaret ERSKINE

    Catherine GASKIN

    Anne MELVILLE

    Pamela OLDFIELD

    Rosamunde PILCHER

    Judith SAXTON

Robert GODDARD   1954-
Adventure

    Jeffrey ARCHER

    Dirk BOGARDE

    John BUCHAN

    Susan CROSLAND

    Daphne DU MAURIER

    Ronald FRAME

    Winston GRAHAM

    Geoffrey HOUSEHOLD

    Graham HURLEY

    Piers Paul READ

Rumer GODDEN   1907-
General

    Dirk BOGARDE

    Monica DICKENS

    Elspeth HUXLEY

    Ruth Prawer JHABVALA

    Elizabeth JOLLEY

    Olivia MANNING

    John MASTERS

    John MORTIMER

    R.K. NARAYAN

    Vikram SETH

Gail GODWIN   1937-
Family Stories

    Marilyn FRENCH

    Belva PLAIN

    E. Annie PROULX

    Anne Rivers SIDDONS

    Helen VAN SLYKE

Marita GOLDEN   US
General

    Anita DESAI

    Nadine GORDIMER

    Toni MORRISON

    Alice WALKER

William GOLDING US   1911-93
General
Anthony BURGESS
Guy BURT
Albert CAMUS
John FOWLES
Graham GREENE
Ernest HEMINGWAY
Thomas KENEALLY
Barry UNSWORTH
Patrick WHITE

Olivia GOLDSMITH US
Glitz & Glamour
Pat BOOTH
Sandra BROWN
Shirley CONRAN
Elizabeth GAGE
Rona JAFFE
Judith KRANTZ
Jill MANSELL
Anne Rivers SIDDONS
Elizabeth VILLARS
Penny VINCENZI

Suzanne GOODWIN
Family Stories
Virginia ANDREWS
Brenda CLARKE
Josephine COX
Margaret GRAHAM

Maisie MOSCO
Elvi RHODES
Diana STAINFORTH
Jeanne WHITMEE

Nadine GORDIMER SA   1923-
General
Margaret ATWOOD
Lynne Reid BANKS
Nina BAWDEN
Andre BRINK
Brigid BROPHY
Joyce CARY
J.M. COETZEE
Marita GOLDEN
Doris LESSING
Alan PATON
Paul SCOTT
Patrick WHITE

Elizabeth GOUDGE   1900-84
General
Phyllis BENTLEY
Winston GRAHAM
Norah LOFTS
Miss READ
Anya SETON
Elswyth THANE

Laurence GOUGH   Can
Crime
  John HARVEY
  Elmore LEONARD
  Ed McBAIN
  William McILVANNEY
  Ted WOOD
  Eric WRIGHT

Judith GOULD   US   1952
Glitz & Glamour
  Jackie COLLINS
  Jilly COOPER
  Elizabeth GAGE
  Judith KRANTZ
  Jayne Ann KRENTZ
  Susan LEWIS
  Alexandra THORNE

Iris GOWER   1939-
Family Stories
  Donna BAKER
  Catherine COOKSON
  Josephine COX
  Elizabeth DAISH
  Margaret Thomson DAVIS
  Brenda JAGGER
  Marie JOSEPH
  Sheelagh KELLY
  Catrin MORGAN
  Elvi RHODES

  Grace THOMPSON
  Barbara WHITNELL

Sue GRAFTON   US   1940-
Crime
  Linda BARNES
  Liza CODY
  Patricia D. CORNWELL
  Amanda CROSS
  Karen KIJEWSKI
  Val McDERMID
  Susan MOODY
  Sara PARETSKY

Caroline GRAHAM   1931-
Crime
  Pat BURDEN
  Ann GRANGER
  Hazel HOLT
  Susan KELLY
  Jill McGOWN
  Ann QUINTON
  Nicholas RHEA
  Dorothy SIMPSON
  STAYNES & STOREY

Margaret GRAHAM   1945-
Family Stories
  Tessa BARCLAY
  Suzanne GOODWIN

Belva PLAIN

Pamela POPE

Denise ROBERTSON

Diana STAINFORTH

Rosie THOMAS

Anne WORBOYS

Janet LAURENCE

Betty ROWLANDS

John SHERWOOD

Margaret YORKE

Winston GRAHAM   1909-
General

R.F. DELDERFIELD

Daphne DU MAURIER

Robert GODDARD

Richard LLEWELLYN

Jonathan GRANT   1933-
also writes as Jonathan GASH
Historical

Philippa GREGORY

Connie MONK

Malcolm ROSS

T.R. WILSON

Winston GRAHAM   1909-
Historical

Anita BURGH

Alexander CORDELL

Catherine GAVIN

Cynthia HARROD-EAGLES

E.V. THOMPSON

Lesley GRANT-ADAMSON
Crime   1942-

Anthea COHEN

Sarah DUNANT

P.D. JAMES

Val McDERMID

Sara PARETSKY

Ruth RENDELL

Joan SMITH

Ann GRANGER   1939-
Crime

Catherine AIRD

M.C. BEATON

Pat BURDEN

Colin DEXTER

Caroline GRAHAM

Hazel HOLT

Günter GRASS Ger   1927-
General

Isabel ALLENDE

Heinrich BÖLL

Albert CAMUS

Gabriel GARCIA MARQUEZ

David GROSSMAN

Günter GRASS (cont.)

Franz KAFKA

Ben OKRI

Robert GRAVES   1895-1985
General

Gillian BRADSHAW

Anthony BURGESS

Lawrence DURRELL

Olivia MANNING

Allan MASSIE

Mary RENAULT

Gore VIDAL

Alasdair GRAY   Sco   1934-
General

Anne FINE

James KELMAN

Agnes OWENS

Salman RUSHDIE

Will SELF

Christine GREEN   1944-
Crime

Liza CODY

Anthea COHEN

Val McDERMID

Claire RAYNER

C.F. ROE

Graham GREENE   1904-91
General

Elizabeth BOWEN

E.M. FORSTER

William GOLDING

Aldous HUXLEY

George ORWELL

Alan PATON

Anthony POWELL

William TREVOR

Morris WEST

Angus WILSON

Colin GREENLAND   1954-
Fantasy

Mary GENTLE

Robert HOLDSTOCK

Mervyn PEAKE

Michael Scott ROHAN

John WHITBOURN

Colin GREENLAND   1954-
Science Fiction

C.J. CHERRYH

Ursula LE GUIN

Brian STABLEFORD

Sheri S. TEPPER

D.M. GREENWOOD
Crime

Kate CHARLES

Michael CLYNES

P.C. DOHERTY

Hazel HOLT

William KIENZLE

Ellis PETERS

Candace ROBB

John SHERWOOD

Barbara WHITEHEAD

Philippa GREGORY   1954-
Historical

Philippa CARR

Zoe FAIRBAIRNS

Jonathan GRANT

Rosalind LAKER

Kate SAUNDERS

Reay TANNAHILL

Lee F. GREGSON
Western

John BLAZE

J.T. EDSON

Zane GREY

Jack SCHAEFER

Anthony GREY
Adventure

Martin BOOTH

James CLAVELL

Eric LUSTBADER

Marc OLDEN

Zane GREY   US   1872-1939
Western

Max BRAND

Al CODY

Lee F. GREGSON

Louis L'AMOUR

Lauran PAINE

W.E.B. GRIFFIN
War

Peter ABRAHAMS

Harold COYLE

Larry FORRESTER

John HARRIS

Sven HASSEL

Graham HURLEY

Robert JACKSON

Derek ROBINSON

Terence STRONG

L.K. TRUSCOTT

Martha GRIMES US
Crime
   Simon BRETT
   Michael CLYNES
   P.C. DOHERTY
   Elizabeth GEORGE
   Gillian LINSCOTT
   Anne PERRY

John GRISHAM US   1955-
Crime
   Patricia D. CORNWELL
   William J. COUGHLIN
   Alan M. DERSHOWITZ
   Philip FRIEDMAN
   Steve MARTINI
   Richard North PATTERSON
   Nancy Taylor ROSENBERG
   Scott TUROW

David GROSSMAN Isr   1954-
General
   Günter GRASS
   Primo LEVI
   Amos OZ
   Chaim POTOK
   Salman RUSHDIE
   Isaac Bashevis SINGER

George GROSSMITH 1847-1912
Humour
   Beryl BAINBRIDGE
   Peter TINNISWOOD
   Keith WATERHOUSE
   P.G. WODEHOUSE

Nicholas GUILD
Adventure
   James CLAVELL
   Peter DRISCOLL
   Colin FALCONER
   Nicholas LUARD
   J.K. MAYO
   John TRENHAILE
   Elleston TREVOR

David GUTERSON US   1956-
General
   Ellen DOUGLAS
   Peter HOEG
   Harper LEE
   Cormac McCARTHY
   E. Annie PROULX

Rosa GUY US   1928-
General
   James BALDWIN
   Paule MARSHALL
   Terry McMILLAN

Toni MORRISON

Alice WALKER

William HAGGARD   1907-93
Adventure

Jeffrey ARCHER

Campbell ARMSTRONG

James FOLLETT

John GARDNER

Jack GERSON

Geoffrey HOUSEHOLD

Anthony PRICE

Arthur HAILEY   Can   1920-
Adventure

Jeffrey ARCHER

Peter BENCHLEY

Richard CONDON

Richard COX

Irwin SHAW

Sidney SHELDON

Wilbur SMITH

Leslie WALLER

Morris WEST

Joe HALDEMAN   US   1943-
Science Fiction

Brian W. ALDISS

Poul ANDERSON

J.G. BALLARD

Robert A. HEINLEIN

Adam HALL   1920-
also writes as Elleston TREVOR
Adventure

Ted ALLBEURY

Eric AMBLER

Evelyn ANTHONY

David BRIERLEY

Ian FLEMING

John GARDNER

Derek LAMBERT

Helen MACINNES

Owen SELA

James HALL   US
Crime

James Lee BURKE

Carl HIAASEN

Tony HILLERMAN

Elmore LEONARD

John D. MACDONALD

Rodney HALL   Aus   1935-
General

Peter CAREY

Thomas KENEALLY

David MALOUF

Patrick WHITE

Tim WINTON

Jane HAMILTON   US
General

  Ellen GILCHRIST

  Alice HOFFMAN

  Sue MILLER

  Alice MUNRO

  Jane SMILEY

  Anne TYLER

Ruth HAMILTON
Family Stories

  Lyn ANDREWS

  Harry BOWLING

  Rosemary ENRIGHT

  Kate FLYNN

  Audrey HOWARD

  Joan JONKER

  Pamela OLDFIELD

  Susan SALLIS

  Mary Jane STAPLES

  Kay STEPHENS

  Margaret THORNTON

James HAMILTON-PATERSON
General   1941-

  Peter ACKROYD

  John BANVILLE

  Ian COCHRANE

  Joseph CONRAD

  Louis DE BERNIÈRES

Dashiell HAMMETT US
Crime   1894-1961

  Stephen AMIDON

  Raymond CHANDLER

  James Hadley CHASE

  James ELLROY

  Loren D. ESTLEMAN

  Dan KAVANAGH

  Ross MACDONALD

  Walter MOSLEY

  Robert B. PARKER

  Ross THOMAS

Gerald HAMMOND   1926-
also writes as Arthur DOUGLAS
Crime

  Douglas CLARK

  Celia FREMLIN

  Jonathan GASH

  John Buxton HILTON

  Frank PARRISH

  John SHERWOOD

  Neville STEED

  Michael UNDERWOOD

  John WAINWRIGHT

  Margaret YORKE

Maeve HARAN   1950-
Family Stories

  Catherine ALLIOTT

  Charlotte BINGHAM

Sally BRAMPTON

Sarah HARRISON

Kathleen ROWNTREE

Diana STAINFORTH

Elizabeth WALKER

Palma HARCOURT
also writes as John PENN

Adventure

Ted ALLBEURY

Eric AMBLER

Clive EGLETON

Ken FOLLETT

Colin FORBES

John GARDNER

Geoffrey HOUSEHOLD

Helen MACINNES

Julian RATHBONE

Raymond HARDIE   Ire/US
Sea

C.S. FORESTER

Duncan HARDING

Alexander KENT

A.E. LANGSFORD

Patrick O'BRIAN

Dudley POPE

Richard WOODMAN

Duncan HARDING   1926-
is Charles WHITING also writes as Leo KESSLER

Sea

Alan EVANS

Alexander FULLERTON

Raymond HARDIE

Peter TONKIN

Paul HARDING
Crime

Kate CHARLES

Michael CLYNES

Lindsey DAVIS

P.C. DOHERTY

Elizabeth EYRE

Ellis PETERS

Candace ROBB

Peter TREMAYNE

Elizabeth HARRIS
General

Joan AIKEN

Barbara ERSKINE

Dinah LAMPITT

Barbara MICHAELS

John HARRIS   1916-91
also writes as Mark HEBDEN & Max HENNESSY

Adventure

James FOLLETT

Jack HIGGINS

John HARRIS (cont.)

    Christopher HYDE

    A.E. LANGSFORD

    Julian RATHBONE

John HARRIS   1916-91

also writes as Mark HEBDEN & Max HENNESSY

War

    Larry FORRESTER

    Sven HASSEL

    Richard HOUGH

    Robert JACKSON

    Leo KESSLER

    Nicholas MONSARRAT

    Douglas REEMAN

    Derek ROBINSON

    Douglas SCOTT

Robert HARRIS   1957-

Adventure

    David BRIERLEY

    Len DEIGHTON

    Philip KERR

    John LE CARRÉ

    Robert LITTELL

    Gerald SEYMOUR

Steve HARRIS

Supernatural

    Ramsey CAMPBELL

    Joe DONNELLY

    Stephen GALLAGHER

    James HERBERT

    Peter JAMES

    Philip RICKMAN

    John SAUL

Thomas HARRIS   US   1940-

Crime

    William BAYER

    Thomas H. COOK

    Joy FIELDING

    John KATZENBACH

    Jonathan KELLERMAN

    David L. LINDSEY

    Phillip M. MARGOLIN

    Ridley PEARSON

    John SANDFORD

    Tim WILLOCKS

    David WILTSE

Harry HARRISON   US   1925-

Science Fiction

    Douglas ADAMS

    Brian W. ALDISS

    Piers ANTHONY

    Tom HOLT

    Larry NIVEN

Terry PRATCHETT
Bob SHAW
John WYNDHAM

Jim HARRISON US   1937-
General
Raymond CARVER
Pete DEXTER
Richard FORD
David GATES
Ernest HEMINGWAY
Bobbie Ann MASON
Cormac McCARTHY
Thomas McGUANE
Larry McMURTRY
E. Annie PROULX
Larry WATSON

Ray HARRISON   1928-
Crime
Alanna KNIGHT
Gillian LINSCOTT
Peter LOVESEY
Amy MYERS
Anne PERRY
Kate ROSS
Julian SYMONS
M.J. TROW

Sarah HARRISON   1946-
General
Charlotte BINGHAM
Maeve HARAN
Susan HOWATCH
Susan ISAACS
Wendy PERRIAM
Rosie THOMAS
Barbara WHITNELL

Cynthia HARROD-EAGLES
Historical   1948-
Valerie ANAND
Evelyn ANTHONY
Pamela BELLE
Emma DRUMMOND
Barbara ERSKINE
Winston GRAHAM
Pamela HILL
Victoria HOLT
Rosalind LAKER
Judith M. RILEY
E.V. THOMPSON
Patricia WENDORF

Lilian HARRY
Family Stories
Elizabeth ELGIN
Rosemary ENRIGHT
Mary MINTON
Wendy ROBERTSON

Roy HART
Crime

W.J. BURLEY
Douglas CLARK
Reginald HILL
John Buxton HILTON
Alan HUNTER
Ruth RENDELL

Michael HARTLAND   1941-
Adventure

Larry BOND
George BROWN
John LE CARRÉ
James CLAVELL
Eric LUSTBADER

L.P. HARTLEY   1895-1972
General

Francis KING
D.H. LAWRENCE
Stanley MIDDLETON
J.B. PRIESTLEY
C.P. SNOW
Howard SPRING
Christina STEAD
Tim WINTON

John HARVEY   1938-
Crime

Robert BARNARD
Colin DEXTER
Laurence GOUGH
Mark HEBDEN
Reginald HILL
William McILVANNEY
Sheila RADLEY
Ian RANKIN
Mike RIPLEY
R.D. WINGFIELD

Sven HASSEL
War

Harold COYLE
W.E.B. GRIFFIN
John HARRIS
Leo KESSLER

Roy HATTERSLEY   1932-
General

Philip BOAST
Melvyn BRAGG
John MORTIMER
William TREVOR
A.N. WILSON

S.T. HAYMON 1918-
Crime
- P.D. JAMES
- Janet NEEL
- Jonathan ROSS
- STAYNES & STOREY
- June THOMSON
- Peter TURNBULL

Tim HEALD 1944-
Crime
- Simon BRETT
- Ruth Dudley EDWARDS
- Jonathan GASH
- Juliet HEBDEN
- Mark HEBDEN
- Frank PARRISH
- Neville STEED
- Colin WATSON

Juliet HEBDEN
Crime
- Michael DIBDIN
- Tim HEALD
- Mark HEBDEN
- Donna LEON
- Janwillem VAN DE WETERING

Mark HEBDEN 1916-91
also writes as John HARRIS & Max HENNESSY
Crime
- Robert BARNARD
- Nicolas FREELING
- John HARVEY
- Tim HEALD
- Juliet HEBDEN
- Alan HUNTER
- Roderic JEFFRIES
- H.R.F. KEATING
- Georges SIMENON
- John WAINWRIGHT

Frances HEGARTY 1948-
also writes as Frances FYFIELD
Crime
- Mary Higgins CLARK
- Jenny DISKI
- Domini HIGHSMITH
- Jonathan KELLERMAN
- Judith KELMAN
- Barbara VINE

Robert A. HEINLEIN US
Science Fiction 1907-88
- Brian W. ALDISS
- Isaac ASIMOV
- Ray BRADBURY
- Arthur C. CLARKE
- Philip K. DICK

Robert A. HEINLEIN (cont.)

Joe HALDEMAN

Jules VERNE

John WYNDHAM

Joseph HELLER   US   1923-
General

Saul BELLOW

Jon COHEN

John IRVING

Ken KESEY

Philip ROTH

Leslie THOMAS

John UPDIKE

William WHARTON

Ernest HEMINGWAY 1899-1961
General

Erskine CALDWELL

Truman CAPOTE

Joseph CONRAD

William FAULKNER

F. Scott FITZGERALD

William GOLDING

Jim HARRISON

Norman MAILER

John STEINBECK

William STYRON

Paul THEROUX

Max HENNESSY   1916-91
also writes as John HARRIS & Mark HEBDEN
War

Bernard CORNWELL

Alan EVANS

Larry FORRESTER

Alexander FULLERTON

John HARRIS

Christopher HYDE

Philip McCUTCHAN

Derek ROBINSON

Douglas SCOTT

John WINTON

Frank HERBERT   US   1920-86
Science Fiction

Brian W. ALDISS

Piers ANTHONY

Isaac ASIMOV

J.G. BALLARD

Ursula LE GUIN

Michael MOORCOCK

Jack VANCE

David WINGROVE

John WYNDHAM

James HERBERT   1943-
Supernatural

Ramsey CAMPBELL

Stephen GALLAGHER

Steve HARRIS

Peter JAMES

Stephen KING

Dean R. KOONTZ

Stephen LAWS

Bentley LITTLE

Guy N. SMITH

Peter STRAUB

Bernard TAYLOR

Clare DARCY

Emma DRUMMOND

Jane Aiken HODGE

Rosalind LAKER

Diana NORMAN

Kate ROSS

Sheila WALSH

Richard HERMAN   US   1939-
Adventure

Larry BOND

Dale BROWN

Stephen COONTS

Graham HURLEY

David MACE

Douglas TERMAN

Georgette HEYER   1904-74
Crime

Edmund CRISPIN

Gladys MITCHELL

Dorothy L. SAYERS

Josephine TEY

Georgette HEYER   1904-74
Historical

Jane AUSTEN

Elizabeth CHADWICK

Marion CHESNEY

Carl HIAASEN   US   1953-
Crime

Edna BUCHANAN

James HALL

Sara PARETSKY

Mike RIPLEY

Charles WILLEFORD

George V. HIGGINS   US   1939-
Crime

Lawrence BLOCK

James ELLROY

Erle Stanley GARDNER

Chester B. HIMES

Elmore LEONARD

Jim THOMPSON

Charles WILLEFORD

Jack HIGGINS   1939-
Adventure

Desmond BAGLEY

Tom CLANCY

Jack HIGGINS (cont.)

Harold COYLE
Ken FOLLETT
Frederick FORSYTH
John GARDNER
Duncan KYLE
Stephen LEATHER
Alistair MACLEAN
Gerald SEYMOUR
Craig THOMAS
Glover WRIGHT

Domini HIGHSMITH
General

Michael CLYNES
Barbara ERSKINE
Frances HEGARTY
Candace ROBB

Patricia HIGHSMITH US 1921-95
Crime

Anthea COHEN
Thomas H. COOK
Peter DICKINSON
B.M. GILL
Ruth RENDELL
Simon SHAW
Julian SYMONS
Barbara VINE
Minette WALTERS

Pamela HILL   Sco   1920-
Historical

Philippa CARR
Catherine GAVIN
Cynthia HARROD-EAGLES
Rosalind LAKER
Norah LOFTS
Edith PARGETER
Maureen PETERS
Jean PLAIDY
Philippa WIAT

Reginald HILL   1936-
Crime

Martin EDWARDS
Roy HART
John HARVEY
Bill JAMES
Bill KNOX
James McCLURE
Joyce PORTER
Jonathan ROSS
John WAINWRIGHT
Colin WATSON

Susan HILL   1942-
General

Joan AIKEN
Beryl BAINBRIDGE
Jane BRINDLE
Daphne DU MAURIER

Margaret FORSTER
Jane GARDAM
Jennifer JOHNSTON
Penelope LIVELY
Carol SHIELDS
William TREVOR

Chester B. HIMES   US   1909-84
Crime
George V. HIGGINS
Tom KAKONIS
Walter MOSLEY
Hillary WAUGH

Tony HILLERMAN   US   1925-
Crime
James Lee BURKE
James HALL
Eugene IZZI
David L. LINDSEY
Ed McBAIN
Walter SATTERTHWAIT

Mary HOCKING   1921-
General
Patricia ANGADI
Caro FRASER
Angela HUTH
Molly KEANE
Edith PARGETER
Barbara PYM
Mary WESLEY

John Buxton HILTON   1921-
Crime
W.J. BURLEY
John CREASEY
Lindsey DAVIS
Gerald HAMMOND
Roy HART
H.R.F. KEATING
Julian SYMONS
June THOMSON

Jane Aiken HODGE   1917-
Historical
Catherine GASKIN
Winston GRAHAM
Georgette HEYER
Isabelle HOLLAND
Victoria HOLT
Barbara MICHAELS
Jean PLAIDY

Peter HOEG Den   1957-
General
  David GUTERSON
  Stuart M. KAMINSKY
  E. Annie PROULX

Alice HOFFMAN US   1952-
General
  Lisa ALTHER
  Louise ERDRICH
  Marilyn FRENCH
  Jane HAMILTON
  Jack KEROUAC
  Alison LURIE
  Carson McCULLERS
  Alice MUNRO
  Carol SHIELDS
  Anita SHREVE
  Anne TYLER

Robert HOLDSTOCK   1948-
Fantasy
  Colin GREENLAND
  Keith ROBERTS
  Gene WOLFE

Isabelle HOLLAND US   1920-
Historical
  Philippa CARR
  Ursula CURTISS

Jane Aiken HODGE
Rosalind LAKER
Sharon PENMAN
Jean STUBBS
Phyllis A. WHITNEY

Alan HOLLINGHURST   1954-
General
  Michael CARSON
  Patrick GALE
  David LEAVITT
  Adam MARS-JONES
  Armistead MAUPIN
  Edmund WHITE

Hazel HOLT
Crime
  Pat BURDEN
  Caroline GRAHAM
  Ann GRANGER
  D.M. GREENWOOD
  Betty ROWLANDS
  John SHERWOOD
  Dorothy SIMPSON
  Minette WALTERS

Tom HOLT   1961-
Humour
  H.E. BATES
  E.F. BENSON

Colin DOUGLAS
Garrison KEILLOR
Tom SHARPE
Peter TINNISWOOD
Sue TOWNSEND
P.G. WODEHOUSE

Tom HOLT   1961-
Fantasy
Douglas ADAMS
Robert ASPRIN
Harry HARRISON
Grant NAYLOR
Terry PRATCHETT
Robert RANKIN

Victoria HOLT   1906-93
also writes as Philippa CARR & Jean PLAIDY
Historical
Madeleine BRENT
Catherine COULTER
Emma DRUMMOND
Cynthia HARROD-EAGLES
Jane Aiken HODGE
Harriet HUDSON
Sara HYLTON
Rosalind LAKER
Claire LORRIMER
Carola SALISBURY
Anya SETON

Winifred HOLTBY   1898-1935
General
Phyllis BENTLEY
Lettice COOPER
J.B. PRIESTLEY
Howard SPRING

Evelyn HOOD   Sco
Family Stories
Doris DAVIDSON
Margaret Thomson DAVIS
Christine Marion FRASER
Gwen KIRKWOOD
Maureen PETERS
Malcolm ROSS
Emma STIRLING
Nicola THORNE

Christopher HOPE   SA   1944-
General
Andre BRINK
John FOWLES
Alan PATON

Nick HORNBY   1957-
General
Kingsley AMIS
Guy BELLAMY
William BOYD

William HORWOOD 1944-
General
Richard ADAMS
Brian CARTER
Aeron CLEMENT
A.R. LLOYD
Brian PARVIN
Henry WILLIAMSON

Richard HOUGH 1922-
War
Alan EVANS
Alexander FULLERTON
John HARRIS
Robert JACKSON
Philip McCUTCHAN
Douglas SCOTT

Geoffrey HOUSEHOLD 1900-88
Adventure
Eric AMBLER
John BUCHAN
Robert GODDARD
William HAGGARD
Palma HARCOURT
Robert LITTELL
David MASON

Audrey HOWARD 1929-
Family Stories
Tessa BARCLAY
Emma BLAIR
Catherine COOKSON
Frank DELANEY
Kate FLYNN
Helen FORRESTER
Ruth HAMILTON
Marie JOSEPH
Beryl KINGSTON
Mary MACKIE
Connie MONK
Sue SULLY

Elizabeth Jane HOWARD 1923-
General
Rachel BILLINGTON
A.S. BYATT
Brenda CLARKE
Kathleen CONLON
Monica DICKENS
Margaret FORSTER
Susan HOWATCH
Brenda JAGGER
Elizabeth TAYLOR
Barbara VICTOR
Barbara WHITNELL

Susan HOWATCH 1940-
Family Stories
  Daphne DU MAURIER
  Zoe FAIRBAIRNS
  Christine Marion FRASER
  Catherine GASKIN
  Sarah HARRISON
  Elizabeth Jane HOWARD
  M.R. O'DONNELL
  Diane PEARSON
  Jean STUBBS
  Reay TANNAHILL

Christopher HUDSON
General
  Noel BARBER
  Dirk BOGARDE
  Louis DE BERNIÈRES
  J.G. FARRELL
  M.M. KAYE
  Francis KING
  W. Somerset MAUGHAM

Harriet HUDSON
also writes as Amy MYERS
Historical
  Victoria HOLT
  Sara HYLTON
  Caroline STICKLAND
  Patricia WENDORF

Alan HUNTER 1922-
Crime
  Ann CLEEVES
  Eileen DEWHURST
  Roy HART
  Mark HEBDEN
  Nicholas RHEA
  John WAINWRIGHT
  David WILLIAMS

Graham HURLEY
Adventure
  Dale BROWN
  Stephen COONTS
  Harold COYLE
  Clive CUSSLER
  Robert GODDARD
  W.E.B. GRIFFIN
  Richard HERMAN
  Terence STRONG
  L.K. TRUSCOTT

Angela HUTH
General
  Elizabeth BUCHAN
  A.S. BYATT
  Margaret FORSTER
  Mary HOCKING
  Angela LAMBERT
  Deborah MOGGACH

Shaun HUTSON
Supernatural
  Stephen KING
  Richard LAYMON
  Bentley LITTLE
  Graham MASTERTON
  Mark MORRIS
  Christopher PIKE
  Guy N. SMITH
  Whitley STRIEBER

Aldous HUXLEY   1894-1963
General
  Graham GREENE
  D.H. LAWRENCE
  George ORWELL
  Anthony POWELL
  Evelyn WAUGH

Elspeth HUXLEY   1907-
General
  Rumer GODDEN
  M.M. KAYE
  Doris LESSING
  Toni MORRISON

Christopher HYDE Can
Adventure
  John HARRIS
  Max HENNESSY

Geoffrey JENKINS
John KATZENBACH
Duncan KYLE

Sara HYLTON
Family Stories
  Madeleine BRENT
  Victoria HOLT
  Claire LORRIMER
  Barbara MICHAELS
  Margaret PEMBERTON
  Carola SALISBURY
  Elizabeth WALKER

Hammond INNES   1913-
Adventure
  Desmond BAGLEY
  Jon CLEARY
  Clive CUSSLER
  Lionel DAVIDSON
  Alexander FULLERTON
  Geoffrey JENKINS
  Duncan KYLE
  Alistair MACLEAN
  Douglas REEMAN
  Nevil SHUTE
  Elleston TREVOR

Michael INNES 1906-94
Crime
  Margery ALLINGHAM
  John Dickson CARR
  Edmund CRISPIN
  Gladys MITCHELL
  Dorothy L. SAYERS
  Josephine TEY
  Patricia WENTWORTH

John IRVING US 1942-
General
  Jonathan COE
  Robertson DAVIES
  J.P. DONLEAVY
  Joseph HELLER
  Ken KESEY
  Larry McMURTRY
  Irwin SHAW
  John UPDIKE

Susan ISAACS US 1943-
General
  Anabel DONALD
  Janet EVANOVICH
  Sarah HARRISON
  Elizabeth PETERS

Kazuo ISHIGURO Ja 1954-
General
  Russell BANKS
  Julian BARNES
  William BOYD
  Shusaku ENDO
  Ronald FRAME
  Ian McEWAN
  Yukio MISHIMA
  Timothy MO
  Haruki MURAKAMI
  Vladimir NABOKOV

Eugene IZZI US
Crime
  Lawrence BLOCK
  Lesley EGAN
  James ELLROY
  Loren D. ESTLEMAN
  Tony HILLERMAN
  Andrew VACHSS
  Charles WILLEFORD

Robert JACKSON
War
  W.E.B. GRIFFIN
  John HARRIS
  Richard HOUGH
  Derek ROBINSON
  Julian Jay SAVARIN
  Charles WHITING

Howard JACOBSON 1942-
General

William BOYD

Malcolm BRADBURY

Frederic RAPHAEL

Tom SHARPE

Rona JAFFE US
General

Lisa ALTHER

Olivia GOLDSMITH

Mary McCARTHY

Marge PIERCY

Carol SHIELDS

Brenda JAGGER 1936-86
Family Stories

Elizabeth ADLER

Aileen ARMITAGE

Brenda CLARKE

Christine Marion FRASER

Iris GOWER

Elizabeth Jane HOWARD

Sheelagh KELLY

Pamela OLDFIELD

Kay STEPHENS

Elizabeth VILLARS

Bill JAMES 1929-
Crime

Colin DEXTER

Martin EDWARDS

Reginald HILL

Dan KAVANAGH

James McCLURE

Ian RANKIN

Mark TIMLIN

Henry JAMES US 1843-1916
General

Joseph CONRAD

Ford Madox FORD

E.M. FORSTER

Edith WHARTON

P.D. JAMES 1920-
Crime

Amanda CROSS

Colin DEXTER

Michael DIBDIN

Peter DICKINSON

Frances FYFIELD

Elizabeth GEORGE

Lesley GRANT-ADAMSON

S.T. HAYMON

Jonathan KELLERMAN

Ruth RENDELL

Dorothy SIMPSON

Peter JAMES
Supernatural

Joe DONNELLY

Stephen GALLAGHER

Steve HARRIS

James HERBERT

Stephen KING

Bernard TAYLOR

Tim WILSON

Robin JAMES
War

Doug ARMSTRONG

Peter CAVE

Shaun CLARKE

David MONNERY

Sheila JANSEN
Family Stories

Anne BAKER

Catherine COOKSON

Valerie GEORGESON

James MITCHELL

Elizabeth JEFFREY
Historical

Lena KENNEDY

Beryl KINGSTON

Peter LING

Sarah SHEARS

Roderic JEFFRIES   1926-
Crime

Michael BOND

Mark HEBDEN

Magdalen NABB

Michael PEARCE

Julian SYMONS

John WAINWRIGHT

Geoffrey JENKINS   Ire   1914-
Adventure

Desmond BAGLEY

Brian CALLISON

Jon CLEARY

Colin FORBES

Clare FRANCIS

Christopher HYDE

Hammond INNES

Alistair MACLEAN

Douglas REEMAN

Nevil SHUTE

Wilbur SMITH

Charles WHITING

Gary JENNINGS   US   1928-
Adventure

James CLAVELL

Nelson DE MILLE

Nicholas LUARD

Linda Lay SHULER

Ruth Prawer JHABVALA US
General   1927-
  Margaret ATWOOD
  Anita DESAI
  J.G. FARRELL
  E.M. FORSTER
  Rumer GODDEN
  John MASTERS
  V.S. NAIPAUL
  Paul SCOTT

Pamela Hansford JOHNSON
General   1912-81
  Ivy COMPTON-BURNETT
  Olivia MANNING
  C.P. SNOW
  Muriel SPARK

Jennifer JOHNSTON Ire 1930-
General
  Alice Thomas ELLIS
  Jane GARDAM
  Susan HILL
  Molly KEANE
  Joan LINGARD
  Iris MURDOCH
  Edna O'BRIEN
  Flann O'BRIEN
  William TREVOR

Elizabeth JOLLEY Aus   1923-
General
  Angela CARTER
  Janet FRAME
  Rumer GODDEN
  Hilary MANTEL
  V.S. NAIPAUL

Gwyneth JONES   1952-
Science Fiction
  Mary GENTLE
  Ursula LE GUIN
  Paul J. McAULEY
  Joanna RUSS
  Neal STEPHENSON
  John VARLEY
  Ian WATSON

Erica JONG US   1942-
Glitz & Glamour
  Jackie COLLINS
  Laramie DUNAWAY
  Marge PIERCY
  Alexandra THORNE

Joan JONKER
Family Stories
  Anne BAKER
  Kate FLYNN
  Helen FORRESTER
  Ruth HAMILTON

Penny JORDAN   1946-
Romance
  Lindsay ARMSTRONG
  Barbara CARTLAND
  Jayne Ann KRENTZ
  Charlotte LAMB
  Anne MATHER
  Carole MORTIMER
  Betty NEELS
  Jessica STEELE
  Elizabeth WALKER
  Anne WEALE
  Sally WENTWORTH

Robert JORDAN   US   1948-
Fantasy
  Terry BROOKS
  Louise COOPER
  Gordon R. DICKSON
  Raymond E. FEIST
  Maggie FUREY
  Morgan LLYWELYN
  Melanie RAWN
  Tad WILLIAMS

Marie JOSEPH
Family Stories
  Tessa BARCLAY
  Catherine COOKSON
  Josephine COX
  Margaret Thomson DAVIS
  Helen FORRESTER
  Iris GOWER
  Audrey HOWARD
  Lena KENNEDY
  Mary MINTON
  Catrin MORGAN
  Maisie MOSCO

James JOYCE   Ire   1882-1941
General
  D.H. LAWRENCE
  Vladimir NABOKOV
  Flann O'BRIEN

Franz KAFKA   Austria   1883-1924
General
  Heinrich BÖLL
  Albert CAMUS
  Günter GRASS
  Arthur KOESTLER
  Paul SAYER

Tom KAKONIS US
Crime
- James Lee BURKE
- Robert CAMPBELL
- Chester B. HIMES
- Michael PEARCE
- Charles WILLEFORD

Stuart M. KAMINSKY US 1934-
General
- Andrew COBURN
- Peter HOEG
- Philip KERR
- James McCLURE

John KATZENBACH
Adventure
- Jack GERSON
- Thomas HARRIS
- Christopher HYDE
- David WILTSE

Dan KAVANAGH 1946-
also writes as Julian BARNES
Crime
- Dashiell HAMMETT
- Bill JAMES
- Mike RIPLEY
- Mark TIMLIN

Guy Gavriel KAY Can 1954-
Fantasy
- Storm CONSTANTINE
- Patricia KENNEALY
- Michael Scott ROHAN
- J.R.R. TOLKIEN
- Janny WURTS

M.M. KAYE 1908-
General
- Colin DE SILVA
- Winston GRAHAM
- Christopher HUDSON
- Elspeth HUXLEY
- John MASTERS
- Gita MEHTA
- Diane PEARSON
- Mary STEWART

Molly KEANE Ire 1904-96
General
- Maeve BINCHY
- Elizabeth BOWEN
- Kathleen CONLON
- Alice Thomas ELLIS
- Mary HOCKING
- Jennifer JOHNSTON
- Flann O'BRIEN
- Barbara PYM
- William TREVOR

H.R.F. KEATING 1926-
Crime
  John Dickson CARR
  Nicolas FREELING
  Mark HEBDEN
  John Buxton HILTON
  James MELVILLE
  Georges SIMENON
  Michael UNDERWOOD
  John WAINWRIGHT

Garrison KEILLOR US 1942-
Humour
  H.E. BATES
  Dan BINCHY
  Ethan CANIN
  Harry CAULEY
  Richard FORD
  Tom HOLT
  William KENNEDY
  Sinclair LEWIS
  Gloria NAYLOR

Faye KELLERMAN US 1952-
Crime
  Patricia D. CORNWELL
  Joy FIELDING
  Ed McBAIN
  Val McDERMID
  T. Jefferson PARKER

Jonathan KELLERMAN US
Crime 1949-
  Stephen AMIDON
  Mary Higgins CLARK
  Patricia D. CORNWELL
  Joy FIELDING
  Thomas HARRIS
  Frances HEGARTY
  P.D. JAMES
  Judith KELMAN
  Elmore LEONARD
  Ed McBAIN
  T. Jefferson PARKER
  Ridley PEARSON

Sheelagh KELLY
Family Stories
  Emma BLAIR
  Barbara Taylor BRADFORD
  Iris GOWER
  Brenda JAGGER
  Sheelagh KELLY
  Adam KENNEDY
  Genevieve LYONS
  Deirdre PURCELL
  Elvi RHODES
  Ann Victoria ROBERTS

Susan KELLY
Crime

Natasha COOPER
Caroline GRAHAM
Janet NEEL
Dell SHANNON
John SHERWOOD
Veronica STALLWOOD

James KELMAN   Sco   1946-
General

Roddy DOYLE
Alasdair GRAY
A.L. KENNEDY
William McILVANNEY
Agnes OWENS
David STOREY
Irvine WELSH

Judith KELMAN
General

Mary Higgins CLARK
Joy FIELDING
Frances HEGARTY
Jonathan KELLERMAN
Barbara MICHAELS
Anita SHREVE

Thomas KENEALLY   Aus   1935-
General

William BOYD
Malcolm BRADBURY
Andre BRINK
Peter CAREY
E.L. DOCTOROW
William GOLDING
Rodney HALL
David MALOUF
Brian MOORE
Barry UNSWORTH
Patrick WHITE

Patricia KENNEALY   US   1946
from 1993 known as KENNEALY-MORRISON
Fantasy

Marion Zimmer BRADLEY
Storm CONSTANTINE
Guy Gavriel KAY
Melanie RAWN

A.L. KENNEDY   Sco   1965-
General

Amanda CRAIG
Roddy DOYLE
Janice GALLOWAY
Lesley GLAISTER
James KELMAN

Adam KENNEDY
Family Stories
  Barbara Taylor BRADFORD
  Dominick DUNNE
  Sheelagh KELLY
  Beryl KINGSTON
  Belva PLAIN
  Anne Rivers SIDDONS

Lena KENNEDY   d. 1986
Family Stories
  Anne BAKER
  Donna BAKER
  Philip BOAST
  Patricia BURNS
  Josephine COX
  Elizabeth JEFFREY
  Marie JOSEPH
  Peter LING
  Maisie MOSCO
  Elvi RHODES

William KENNEDY   US   1928-
General
  John CHEEVER
  Pete DEXTER
  E.L. DOCTOROW
  Garrison KEILLOR
  John STEINBECK
  Irvine WELSH

Alexander KENT   1924-
also writes as Douglas REEMAN
Sea
  Bernard CORNWELL
  David DONACHIE
  C.S. FORESTER
  Raymond HARDIE
  A.E. LANGSFORD
  Philip McCUTCHAN
  Patrick O'BRIAN
  C. Northcote PARKINSON
  Dudley POPE
  Richard WOODMAN

Jack KEROUAC   US   1922-69
General
  Albert CAMUS
  Alice HOFFMAN
  Jay McINERNEY
  Larry McMURTRY

Katherine KERR   US   1944-
Fantasy
  Louise COOPER
  Anne McCAFFREY
  Andre NORTON
  Margaret WEIS
  Jonathan WYLIE

Philip KERR Sco 1956-
Adventure
  Len DEIGHTON
  Nicolas FREELING
  Alan FURST
  Robert HARRIS
  Stuart M. KAMINSKY
  Donna LEON
  James McCLURE
  Nigel WEST

Ken KESEY US 1935-
General
  David COOK
  Joseph HELLER
  John IRVING
  Larry McMURTRY
  Paul SAYER

Leo KESSLER 1926-
also writes as Charles WHITING &
                Duncan HARDING
War
  Harold COYLE
  John HARRIS
  Sven HASSEL
  L.K. TRUSCOTT

William KIENZLE US 1928-
Crime
  Michael CLYNES
  P.C. DOHERTY

D.M. GREENWOOD
Candace ROBB

Karen KIJEWSKI US
Crime
  Linda BARNES
  Liza CODY
  Sue GRAFTON
  Susan MOODY
  Sara PARETSKY

Garry D. KILWORTH 1941-
Fantasy
  Richard ADAMS
  Jean M. AUEL
  Marion Zimmer BRADLEY
  David EDDINGS
  Linda Lay SHULER
  Tad WILLIAMS

Francis KING 1923-
General
  Heinrich BÖLL
  E.M. FORSTER
  Michael FRAYN
  L.P. HARTLEY
  Christopher HUDSON
  Stanley MIDDLETON

Stephen KING US 1947-
Fantasy

  Orson Scott CARD

  Stephen DONALDSON

  Christopher FOWLER

  David A. GEMMELL

Stephen KING US 1947-
Supernatural

  Ramsey CAMPBELL

  John FARRIS

  Stephen GALLAGHER

  James HERBERT

  Shaun HUTSON

  Peter JAMES

  Dean R. KOONTZ

  Richard LAYMON

  Dan SIMMONS

Beryl KINGSTON
Family Stories

  Emma BLAIR

  Philip BOAST

  Rose BOUCHERON

  Harry BOWLING

  Patricia BURNS

  Elaine CROWLEY

  Audrey HOWARD

  Elizabeth JEFFREY

  Adam KENNEDY

  James MITCHELL

  Claire RAYNER

  Ann Victoria ROBERTS

  Malcolm ROSS

Gwen KIRKWOOD
Family Stories

  Doris DAVIDSON

  Christine Marion FRASER

  Evelyn HOOD

  Mary E. PEARCE

Alanna KNIGHT Sco
Crime

  Gwendoline BUTLER

  Ray HARRISON

  Gillian LINSCOTT

  Peter LOVESEY

  Amy MYERS

  Anne PERRY

Bill KNOX Sco 1928-
Crime

  M.C. BEATON

  Reginald HILL

  Ian RANKIN

  Peter TURNBULL

  John WAINWRIGHT

Arthur KOESTLER Hu 1905-83
General
  Andre BRINK
  Franz KAFKA
  George ORWELL
  Alexander SOLZHENITSYN

Dean R. KOONTZ US 1945-
Supernatural
  Jonathan AYCLIFFE
  Ramsey CAMPBELL
  Michael CRICHTON
  Stephen GALLAGHER
  James HERBERT
  Stephen KING
  Richard LAYMON
  Robert McCAMMON
  John SAUL
  Dan SIMMONS
  Peter STRAUB
  Whitley STRIEBER
  Tim WILLOCKS

Judith KRANTZ US 1928-
Glitz & Glamour
  Pat BOOTH
  Freda BRIGHT
  Jacqueline BRISKIN
  Jackie COLLINS
  Jilly COOPER
  Julie ELLIS

  Olivia GOLDSMITH
  Judith GOULD
  Harold ROBBINS
  June Flaum SINGER
  Penny VINCENZI

Jayne Ann KRENTZ US 1948-
Glitz & Glamour
  Sandra BROWN
  Judith GOULD
  Penny JORDAN
  Judith McNAUGHT
  LaVyrle SPENCER

Milan KUNDERA Cz 1929-
General
  Isabel ALLENDE
  Sebastian FAULKS
  Ben OKRI
  Evelyn WAUGH

Hanif KUREISHI 1954-
General
  Farrukh DHONDY
  Armistead MAUPIN
  Gita MEHTA
  Timothy MO

Duncan KYLE   1930-
Adventure
  Desmond BAGLEY
  John BUCHAN
  Jon CLEARY
  Lionel DAVIDSON
  Clare FRANCIS
  Jack HIGGINS
  Christopher HYDE
  Hammond INNES
  James LEASOR
  Robert LUDLUM
  Alistair MACLEAN
  Glover WRIGHT

Lynda LA PLANTE
General
  Pat BOOTH
  Celia BRAYFIELD
  Martina COLE
  Julie ELLIS
  Michael MOLLOY

Sara LACEY
Crime
  Liza CODY
  Anabel DONALD
  Janet EVANOVICH
  Janet LAURENCE

Louis L'AMOUR   US   1908-88
Western
  Max BRAND
  Matt CHISHOLM
  Al CODY
  Jess CODY
  J.T. EDSON
  Zane GREY
  Chuck MARTIN
  Nelson NYE
  Clint OGDEN
  T.C. OLSEN
  Lauran PAINE
  Gary PAULSEN
  Jack SCHAEFER
  Bill WADE

Mercedes LACKEY   US
Fantasy
  Marion Zimmer BRADLEY
  C.J. CHERRYH
  Maggie FUREY
  Anne McCAFFREY
  R.A. SALVATORE

Rosalind LAKER
Historical
  Pamela BELLE
  Winston GRAHAM
  Philippa GREGORY
  Cynthia HARROD-EAGLES
  Georgette HEYER

Rosalind LAKER (cont.)

Pamela HILL

Isabelle HOLLAND

Victoria HOLT

Norah LOFTS

Jean PLAIDY

Cynthia S. ROBERTS

E.V. THOMPSON

Charlotte LAMB   1937-
Romance

Iris BROMIGE

Joyce DINGWELL

Jane DONNELLY

Catherine GEORGE

Penny JORDAN

Audrie MANLEY-TUCKER

Anne MATHER

Carole MORTIMER

Betty NEELS

Jessica STEELE

Kay THORPE

Sally WENTWORTH

Angela LAMBERT
General

Hilary BAILEY

Angela HUTH

Hilary MANTEL

Deborah MOGGACH

Edna O'BRIEN

Kate SAUNDERS

Joanna TROLLOPE

Derek LAMBERT   1929-
Adventure

Jon CLEARY

Robert ELEGANT

Frederick FORSYTH

Adam HALL

Robert LUDLUM

Dinah LAMPITT   1939-
Historical

Philippa CARR

Barbara ERSKINE

Elizabeth HARRIS

Diana NORMAN

Kathleen ROWNTREE

A.E. LANGSFORD
Sea

C.S. FORESTER

Raymond HARDIE

John HARRIS

Alexander KENT

Nicholas MONSARRAT

Douglas SCOTT

Peter TONKIN

Emma LATHEN US
Crime
  Amanda CROSS
  Jane DENTINGER
  Elizabeth FERRARS
  Anne MORICE
  Emma PAGE

Janet LAURENCE   1937-
Crime
  Jane DENTINGER
  Ann GRANGER
  Sara LACEY
  Amy MYERS
  C.F. ROE
  Annette ROOME
  John SHERWOOD
  David WILLIAMS

D.H. LAWRENCE   1885-1930
General
  Stan BARSTOW
  Melvyn BRAGG
  John FOWLES
  John GALSWORTHY
  L.P. HARTLEY
  Aldous HUXLEY
  James JOYCE
  Richard LLEWELLYN
  Alan SILLITOE

Christina STEAD
David STOREY

Stephen LAWS
Fantasy
  Jonathan AYCLIFFE
  Joe DONNELLY
  James HERBERT
  Philip RICKMAN
  Tim WILSON

Richard LAYMON US
Supernatural
  Shaun HUTSON
  Stephen KING
  Dean R. KOONTZ
  Bentley LITTLE
  Christopher PIKE
  Guy N. SMITH
  Peter STRAUB
  Bernard TAYLOR
  Tim WILLOCKS
  T.M. WRIGHT

John LE CARRÉ   1931-
Adventure
  David BRIERLEY
  Richard CONDON
  Lionel DAVIDSON
  Len DEIGHTON

John LE CARRÉ (cont.)

Clive EGLETON
Bryan FORBES
Brian FREEMANTLE
Robert HARRIS
Michael HARTLAND
Robert LITTELL
Anthony PRICE
Julian Jay SAVARIN
John TRENHAILE

Ursula LE GUIN   US   1929-
Science Fiction

Mary GENTLE
Colin GREENLAND
Frank HERBERT
Gwyneth JONES
Andre NORTON
Joanna RUSS
Robert SILVERBERG
Sheri S. TEPPER
Gene WOLFE

James LEASOR   1923-
Adventure

Ian FLEMING
Duncan KYLE
Stephen LEATHER
Andrew MACALLAN

Stephen LEATHER
Adventure

Larry BOND
Tom CLANCY
Gavin ESLER
Jack HIGGINS
James LEASOR
David MASON
John TRENHAILE

David LEAVITT   US
General

Michael CARSON
Alan HOLLINGHURST
Adam MARS-JONES
Edmund WHITE

Harper LEE   US   1926-
General

David GUTERSON
Bobbie Ann MASON
Carson McCULLERS
Joyce Carol OATES
John STEINBECK
Larry WATSON

Rupert LEGGE
Glitz & Glamour

Sally BEAUMAN
Julie BURCHILL

Jilly COOPER

Laramie DUNAWAY

Fiona WALKER

Rosamond LEHMANN   1901-90

General

Elizabeth BOWEN

Olivia MANNING

Iris MURDOCH

Elizabeth TAYLOR

Rebecca WEST

Antonia WHITE

Virginia WOOLF

Annie LEITH   1937-

also writes as Anita BURGH

General

H.E. BATES

E. F. BENSON

Vernon COLEMAN

E.M. DELAFIELD

Kathleen ROWNTREE

Stanislaw LEM   Pol   1921-

Science Fiction

Arthur C. CLARKE

Philip K. DICK

Larry NIVEN

Bob SHAW

Elizabeth LEMARCHAND 1906-

Crime

Catherine AIRD

Marian BABSON

Pat BURDEN

Agatha CHRISTIE

Ngaio MARSH

Anne MORICE

Patricia MOYES

Emma PAGE

Patricia WENTWORTH

Donna LEON

Crime

Sarah CAUDWELL

Michael DIBDIN

Nicholas FREELING

Juliet HEBDEN

Philip KERR

Elmore LEONARD   US   1925-

Crime

Lawrence BLOCK

James Lee BURKE

James ELLROY

Loren D. ESTLEMAN

Laurence GOUGH

James HALL

George V. HIGGINS

Jonathan KELLERMAN

Elmore LEONARD (cont.)

   Ross MACDONALD

   Ed McBAIN

   Robert B. PARKER

   Charles WILLEFORD

Doris LESSING   1919-

General

   Joyce CARY

   Janet FRAME

   Janice GALLOWAY

   Nadine GORDIMER

   Elspeth HUXLEY

   Candia McWILLIAM

   Penelope MORTIMER

   Iris MURDOCH

   Joyce Carol OATES

   Alan PATON

   Paul SCOTT

   Muriel SPARK

Kathy LETTE   Aus

Glitz & Glamour

   Sally BRAMPTON

   Laramie DUNAWAY

   Sue TOWNSEND

   Fiona WALKER

Primo LEVI It   1917-87

General

   David GROSSMAN

   Amos OZ

   Isaac Bashevis SINGER

   Alexander SOLZHENITSYN

C.S. LEWIS   1898-1963

Fantasy

   H.P. LOVECRAFT

   Mervyn PEAKE

   J.R.R. TOLKIEN

Sinclair LEWIS US   1885-1951

General

   William FAULKNER

   F. Scott FITZGERALD

   Ford Madox FORD

   Garrison KEILLOR

   Paul MICOU

Susan LEWIS

Glitz & Glamour

   Sally BEAUMAN

   Shirley CONRAN

   Vera COWIE

   Judith GOULD

David L. LINDSEY US
Crime
  William BAYER
  James Lee BURKE
  Thomas H. COOK
  Thomas HARRIS
  Tony HILLERMAN
  Michael PEARCE
  John SANDFORD
  David WILTSE

Peter LING
Family Stories
  Noel BARBER
  Philip BOAST
  Harry BOWLING
  Elizabeth DARRELL
  Elizabeth JEFFREY
  Lena KENNEDY
  Lewis ORDE
  Patricia SHAW
  Mary Jane STAPLES
  Dee WILLIAMS

Joan LINGARD Ire
General
  Anne FINE
  Jane GARDAM
  Jennifer JOHNSTON
  Deborah MOGGACH

Gillian LINSCOTT
Crime
  Martha GRIMES
  Ray HARRISON
  Alanna KNIGHT
  Gwen MOFFAT
  M.J. TROW

Robert LITTELL US   1935-
Adventure
  Eric AMBLER
  Len DEIGHTON
  Alan FURST
  Robert HARRIS
  Geoffrey HOUSEHOLD
  John LE CARRÉ
  Owen SELA
  Christopher SHERLOCK

Bentley LITTLE US   1935-
Supernatural
  James HERBERT
  Shaun HUTSON
  Richard LAYMON
  Mark MORRIS
  Dan SIMMONS

Penelope LIVELY   1933-
General
  Nina BAWDEN
  Rachel BILLINGTON
  Anita BROOKNER
  A.S. BYATT
  Janice ELLIOTT
  Alice Thomas ELLIS
  Penelope FITZGERALD
  Susan HILL
  Deborah MOGGACH
  Gillian TINDALL

Caroline LLEWELLYN   Can
General
  Barbara MICHAELS
  Nora ROBERTS
  Mary STEWART
  Phyllis A. WHITNEY

Richard LLEWELLYN   Wales
General   1907-83
  Phyllis BENTLEY
  Alexander CORDELL
  A.J. CRONIN
  Winston GRAHAM
  D.H. LAWRENCE
  Howard SPRING
  Christina STEAD

Sam LLEWELLYN   1948-
Sea
  Bernard CORNWELL
  Philip McCUTCHAN
  Antony TREW
  John WINGATE

A.R. LLOYD   1927-
General
  Richard ADAMS
  Brian CARTER
  William HORWOOD
  Brian PARVIN
  Henry WILLIAMSON

Morgan LLYWELYN   Ire   1947-
Historical
  Valerie ANAND
  Robert JORDAN
  Diana NORMAN
  Edith PARGETER
  Sharon PENMAN
  Rosemary SUTCLIFF

David LODGE   1935-
General
  Kingsley AMIS
  Martin AMIS
  William BOYD
  Malcolm BRADBURY
  Jonathan COE

Colin DOUGLAS
Stanley MIDDLETON
John MORTIMER
Alan SILLITOE
Leslie THOMAS
Keith WATERHOUSE

Norah LOFTS   1904-83
General

Elizabeth CHADWICK
Elizabeth GOUDGE
Georgette HEYER
Pamela HILL
Rosalind LAKER
Jean PLAIDY
Marguerite STEEN

Claire LORRIMER   1921-
also writes as Patricia ROBINS
Family Stories

Charlotte Vale ALLEN
Catherine GASKIN
Victoria HOLT
Sara HYLTON
Jeanne WHITMEE
Barbara WHITNELL

H.P. LOVECRAFT US 1890-1937
Fantasy

Robert BLOCH
Ray BRADBURY
Ramsey CAMPBELL
August DERLETH
C.S. LEWIS
Brian LUMLEY
Mervyn PEAKE

Peter LOVESEY   1936-
Crime

Jonathan GASH
Ray HARRISON
Alanna KNIGHT
Anne PERRY
Julian SYMONS
M.J. TROW

Nicholas LUARD   1937-
Fantasy

Jean M. AUEL
Nicholas GUILD
Gary JENNINGS
Linda Lay SHULER
Wilbur SMITH

Russell LUCAS 1930-
General
- Amit CHAUDHURI
- Anita DESAI
- Gita MEHTA
- R.K. NARAYAN

Robert LUDLUM US 1927-
Adventure
- Ted ALLBEURY
- Geoffrey ARCHER
- George BROWN
- Victor CANNING
- Clive EGLETON
- James FOLLETT
- Frederick FORSYTH
- Duncan KYLE
- Derek LAMBERT
- Julian RATHBONE
- Lawrence SANDERS
- Sidney SHELDON

Brian LUMLEY 1937-
Fantasy
- Robert BLOCH
- August DERLETH
- H.P. LOVECRAFT
- Anne RICE

Alison LURIE US 1926-
General
- Nina BAWDEN
- Rachel BILLINGTON
- Anita BROOKNER
- Louise ERDRICH
- Margaret FORSTER
- Marilyn FRENCH
- Alice HOFFMAN
- Mary McCARTHY
- John O'HARA
- Jane ROGERS
- Carol SHIELDS
- Anne TYLER
- Robert James WALLER

Eric LUSTBADER US 1946-
Adventure
- Martin BOOTH
- George BROWN
- James CLAVELL
- Bryce COURTENAY
- Robert ELEGANT
- Colin FALCONER
- Anthony GREY
- Michael HARTLAND
- David MORRELL
- Christopher NICOLE
- Marc OLDEN
- Alan SAVAGE
- Dov SILVERMAN

Gavin LYALL 1932-
Adventure
Jon CLEARY
Len DEIGHTON
Ian FLEMING
John GARDNER
Alistair MACLEAN
Derek ROBINSON
Gerald SEYMOUR
Terence STRONG
Craig THOMAS

Genevieve LYONS
Historical
Evelyn ANTHONY
Maeve BINCHY
Teresa CRANE
Frank DELANEY
Sheelagh KELLY
Mary MINTON
M.R. O'DONNELL

Amin MAALOUF Lebanon
Adventure
James CLAVELL
Bryce COURTENAY
Daniel EASTERMAN
Julian RATHBONE
Alan SAVAGE

Andrew MACALLAN 1923-
Adventure
Desmond BAGLEY
Ken FOLLETT
Colin FORBES
James LEASOR

John D. MACDONALD US
Crime 1916-
Lawrence BLOCK
James M. CAIN
Raymond CHANDLER
James Hadley CHASE
James HALL
Gregory McDONALD
Charles WILLEFORD

Malcolm MACDONALD 1932-
also writes as M.R. O'DONNELL & Malcolm ROSS
Family Stories
Noel BARBER
Alexander CORDELL
R.F. DELDERFIELD
Winston GRAHAM
Adam KENNEDY
Malcolm ROSS
Caroline STICKLAND
Jessica STIRLING
Vivian STUART
Janet TANNER
E.V. THOMPSON
T.R. WILSON

Ross MACDONALD US 1915-83
Crime
  Lawrence BLOCK
  James Hadley CHASE
  Dashiell HAMMETT
  Elmore LEONARD
  Walter SATTERTHWAIT
  Ross THOMAS

David MACE
Adventure
  Larry BOND
  Stephen COONTS
  Larry FORRESTER
  Richard HERMAN

Helen MACINNES US 1907-85
Adventure
  Evelyn ANTHONY
  David BRIERLEY
  John BUCHAN
  Clare FRANCIS
  Brian FREEMANTLE
  Adam HALL
  Palma HARCOURT
  Anne STEVENSON
  Mary STEWART

Mary MACKIE
Family Stories
  Audrey HOWARD
  Connie MONK
  Judith SAXTON
  Sue SULLY

Alistair MACLEAN Sco 1923-87
Adventure
  Desmond BAGLEY
  Victor CANNING
  Clive CUSSLER
  Clive EGLETON
  James FOLLETT
  Ken FOLLETT
  Jack HIGGINS
  Hammond INNES
  Geoffrey JENKINS
  Duncan KYLE
  Gavin LYALL
  Nicholas MONSARRAT

Charlotte MACLEOD Can 1922-
Crime
  Robert BARNARD
  John SHERWOOD
  Neville STEED
  David WILLIAMS

Norman MAILER US 1923-
General
  Ernest HEMINGWAY
  John STEINBECK
  William STYRON
  John UPDIKE
  Tom WOLFE

John MALCOLM 1936-
Crime
  Jonathan GASH
  Iain PEARS
  Neville STEED
  Derek WILSON

David MALOUF Aus 1934-
General
  Peter CAREY
  Rodney HALL
  Thomas KENEALLY
  Morris WEST

Audrie MANLEY-TUCKER
Romance 1924-83
  Catherine GEORGE
  Charlotte LAMB
  Carole MORTIMER
  Jessica STEELE

Jessica MANN 1937-
Crime
  Antonia FRASER
  Mary McMULLEN
  Paul MYERS
  Margaret YORKE

Olivia MANNING 1908-80
General
  Lynne Reid BANKS
  Elizabeth BOWEN
  Lawrence DURRELL
  Catherine GAVIN
  Rumer GODDEN
  Robert GRAVES
  Pamela Hansford JOHNSON
  Rosamond LEHMANN
  Penelope MORTIMER
  Paul SCOTT
  Rebecca WEST
  Antonia WHITE

Jill MANSELL
Glitz & Glamour
  Catherine ALLIOTT
  Jilly COOPER
  Olivia GOLDSMITH
  Penny VINCENZI

Hilary MANTEL   1952-
General
   Hilary BAILEY
   Elizabeth JOLLEY
   Angela LAMBERT
   Deborah MOGGACH
   Mary WESLEY

Phillip M. MARGOLIN   US
Crime
   William BAYER
   Thomas HARRIS
   John SANDFORD
   Scott TUROW

Adam MARS-JONES   1954-
General
   Michael CARSON
   Alan HOLLINGHURST
   David LEAVITT
   Armistead MAUPIN
   Edmund WHITE

Ngaio MARSH   NZ   1895-1982
Crime
   Margery ALLINGHAM
   John Dickson CARR
   Agatha CHRISTIE
   Elizabeth FERRARS

   Elizabeth LEMARCHAND
   Gladys MITCHELL
   Anne MORICE
   Patricia MOYES
   Emma PAGE
   Dorothy L. SAYERS
   Dorothy SIMPSON
   Patricia WENTWORTH

Paule MARSHALL   Carib/US
General   1929-
   Rosa GUY
   Terry McMILLAN
   Gloria NAYLOR
   Alice WALKER

Sybil MARSHALL
General
   Margaret BACON
   Caroline BRIDGWOOD
   Nora NAISH
   Pamela OLDFIELD
   Mary E. PEARCE
   Ann PURSER
   Miss READ
   Susan SALLIS

Chuck MARTIN US 1891-1954
Western
  Jess CODY
  Louis L'AMOUR

George R. MARTIN US 1948-
Supernatural
  Nancy COLLINS
  Graham MASTERTON
  Anne RICE

Steve MARTINI US 1946-
Crime
  William J. COUGHLIN
  Philip FRIEDMAN
  Frances FYFIELD
  John GRISHAM
  Richard North PATTERSON
  Nancy Taylor ROSENBERG
  Scott TUROW

Bobbie Ann MASON US 1940-
General
  Raymond CARVER
  Richard FORD
  Ellen GILCHRIST
  Jim HARRISON
  Harper LEE
  Joyce Carol OATES

  Jane SMILEY
  Anne TYLER

David MASON 1951-
Adventure
  Jeffrey ARCHER
  Frederick FORSYTH
  Geoffrey HOUSEHOLD
  Stephen LEATHER

Allan MASSIE Sco 1938-
General
  Ronald FRAME
  Robert GRAVES
  Naomi MITCHISON
  Frederic RAPHAEL
  Piers Paul READ
  Mary RENAULT
  Rosemary SUTCLIFF
  Gore VIDAL

John MASTERS US 1914-83
General
  Amit CHAUDHURI
  James CLAVELL
  Colin DE SILVA
  J.G. FARRELL
  Rumer GODDEN
  Ruth Prawer JHABVALA
  M.M. KAYE

John MASTERS (cont.)

James A. MICHENER
V.S. NAIPAUL
R.K. NARAYAN
Paul SCOTT
Morris WEST

Graham MASTERTON   1946-
Supernatural

Ramsey CAMPBELL
Joe DONNELLY
Christopher FOWLER
Stephen GALLAGHER
Shaun HUTSON
George R. MARTIN
Robert McCAMMON
Mark MORRIS
Kim NEWMAN
John SAUL
Whitley STRIEBER
Dennis WHEATLEY

Anne MATHER
Romance

Lucilla ANDREWS
Joyce DINGWELL
Jane DONNELLY
Penny JORDAN
Charlotte LAMB
Judith McNAUGHT
Carole MORTIMER

Betty NEELS
Elizabeth SEIFERT
Jessica STEELE
Kay THORPE

W. Somerset MAUGHAM
General   1874-1965

Joseph CONRAD
Christopher HUDSON
Howard SPRING
Morris WEST

Armistead MAUPIN   US   1944-
General

Truman CAPOTE
Michael CARSON
Alan HOLLINGHURST
Hanif KUREISHI
Jay McINERNEY
Adam MARS-JONES

Julian MAY   US   1931-
Fantasy

Stephen DONALDSON
David EDDINGS
Michael MOORCOCK
Fred SABERHAGEN
Robert SILVERBERG
Patrick TILLEY
Gene WOLFE

J.K. MAYO   1914-
Adventure
  Eric AMBLER
  Peter DRISCOLL
  Ian FLEMING
  Jack GERSON
  Nicholas GUILD
  Elleston TREVOR

Paul J. McAULEY
Science Fiction
  Brian W. ALDISS
  Greg BEAR
  Greg EGAN
  Gwyneth JONES

Ed McBAIN   US   1926-
Crime
  John Newton CHANCE
  James Hadley CHASE
  K.C. CONSTANTINE
  William DIEHL
  Lesley EGAN
  Laurence GOUGH
  Tony HILLERMAN
  Faye KELLERMAN
  Jonathan KELLERMAN
  Elmore LEONARD
  Dell SHANNON
  Janwillem VAN DE WETERING

Brenda McBRYDE
Family Stories
  Harry BOWLING
  Sarah SHEARS
  Dee WILLIAMS

Patrick McCABE   Ire   1955-
General
  Guy BURT
  Bruce CHATWIN
  Roddy DOYLE
  Lesley GLAISTER
  Paul MICOU
  Will SELF

Anne McCAFFREY   US   1926-
Fantasy
  Marion Zimmer BRADLEY
  C.J. CHERRYH
  David EDDINGS
  Raymond E. FEIST
  Katherine KERR
  Mercedes LACKEY
  Andre NORTON
  Melanie RAWN
  Christopher STASHEFF
  Sheri S. TEPPER
  Margaret WEIS
  Janny WURTS

Robert McCAMMON US
Supernatural
  Jonathan AYCLIFFE
  John FARRIS
  Dean R. KOONTZ
  Graham MASTERTON

Cormac McCARTHY US
General
  Saul BELLOW
  William FAULKNER
  David GUTERSON
  Jim HARRISON
  Thomas McGUANE
  E. Annie PROULX
  J.D. SALINGER
  Larry WATSON

Mary McCARTHY US   1912-
General
  Rona JAFFE
  Alison LURIE
  Edna O'BRIEN
  Flannery O'CONNOR
  William WHARTON

James McCLURE SA   1939-
Crime
  Michael DIBDIN
  Reginald HILL

  Bill JAMES
  Stuart M. KAMINSKY
  Philip KERR
  James MELVILLE
  Magdalen NABB
  Michael PEARCE

Carson McCULLERS US
General   1917-67
  Erskine CALDWELL
  Truman CAPOTE
  F. Scott FITZGERALD
  Alice HOFFMAN
  Harper LEE
  Flannery O'CONNOR
  J.D. SALINGER

Colleen McCULLOUGH Aus
General   1937-
  John Gordon DAVIS
  Marguerite STEEN
  Vivian STUART
  Eileen TOWNSEND

Philip McCUTCHAN   1920-
Sea
  Brian CALLISON
  Alexander FULLERTON
  Max HENNESSY
  Richard HOUGH

Alexander KENT
Sam LLEWELLYN
Dudley POPE
Douglas REEMAN
Peter TONKIN
Antony TREW
John WINGATE
John WINTON
Richard WOODMAN

Val McDERMID   Sco
Crime
Liza CODY
Sarah DUNANT
Martin EDWARDS
Sue GRAFTON
Lesley GRANT-ADAMSON
Christine GREEN
Faye KELLERMAN
Marcia MULLER
Sara PARETSKY
Joan SMITH

Gregory McDONALD US 1937-
Crime
Raymond CHANDLER
John D. MACDONALD
Walter SATTERTHWAIT
Neville STEED

Ian McEWAN   1948-
General
Martin AMIS
Paul BAILEY
Iain BANKS
Julian BARNES
Ian COCHRANE
David COOK
Lesley GLAISTER
Kazuo ISHIGURO
Brian MOORE
Piers Paul READ
Graham SWIFT
Colin THUBRON

John McGAHERN   Ire   1934-
General
John BANVILLE
Brian MOORE
V.S. PRITCHETT
William TREVOR

Dan McGIRT   US   1967-
Fantasy
Robert ASPRIN
Craig Shaw GARDNER
Terry PRATCHETT
Robert RANKIN
Christopher STASHEFF

Jill McGOWN   1947-
Crime
   Caroline GRAHAM
   Jennie MELVILLE
   Janet NEEL
   Ann QUINTON
   STAYNES & STOREY

Thomas McGUANE US   1939-
General
   Pete DEXTER
   Richard FORD
   Jim HARRISON
   Cormac McCARTHY
   Larry McMURTRY

William McILVANNEY Sco 1936-
Crime
   Melvyn BRAGG
   Laurence GOUGH
   John HARVEY
   James KELMAN
   C.F. ROE
   Peter TURNBULL

Jay McINERNEY US   1955-
General
   Louis DE BERNIÈRES
   Jack KEROUAC
   Armistead MAUPIN

   Philip ROTH
   J.D. SALINGER
   Tom WOLFE

Hilda McKENZIE Wales
Family Stories
   Catrin COLLIER
   Mary MINTON
   Lynda PAGE
   Janet TANNER
   Rosie THOMAS

Terry McMILLAN US   1951-
General
   Rosa GUY
   Paule MARSHALL
   Toni MORRISON
   Gloria NAYLOR
   Alice WALKER

Mary McMULLEN US   1920-86
Crime
   Mary Higgins CLARK
   Ursula CURTISS
   Jessica MANN
   Martin RUSSELL
   Margaret YORKE

Larry McMURTRY   US   1936-
General
  Jim HARRISON
  John IRVING
  Jack KEROUAC
  Ken KESEY
  Thomas McGUANE
  Marge PIERCY

Judith McNAUGHT   US   1944-
Romance
  Catherine COULTER
  Jayne Ann KRENTZ
  Anne MATHER
  Betty NEELS
  LaVyrle SPENCER
  Kay THORPE

Elisabeth McNEILL   Sco   1931-
Family Stories
  Emma BLAIR
  Teresa CRANE
  Elvi RHODES
  Sarah SHEARS
  Agnes SHORT

Candia McWILLIAM   Sco   1955-
General
  A.S. BYATT
  Sally EMERSON

  Doris LESSING
  Jane ROGERS
  Marina WARNER

Gita MEHTA   Ind
General
  Amit CHAUDHURI
  M.M. KAYE
  Hanif KUREISHI
  Russell LUCAS
  R.K. NARAYAN
  Michael ONDAATJE
  Salman RUSHDIE

Anne MELVILLE   1926-
Family Stories
  Christine Marion FRASER
  Judith GLOVER
  Pamela OLDFIELD
  Claire RAYNER
  Sarah SHEARS

James MELVILLE   1931-
Crime
  Jonathan GASH
  H.R.F. KEATING
  James McCLURE
  Eric WRIGHT

Jennie MELVILLE
also writes as Gwendoline BUTLER
Crime

Natasha COOPER

Antonia FRASER

Jill McGOWN

Iain PEARS

Ann QUINTON

Patricia WENTWORTH

Mary MELWOOD
Family Stories

Miss READ

D.E. STEVENSON

Essie SUMMERS

Angela THIRKELL

Barbara MICHAELS   US   1927-
also writes as Elizabeth PETERS
General

Virginia ANDREWS

Jane BRINDLE

Mary Higgins CLARK

Virginia COFFMAN

Dorothy EDEN

Elizabeth HARRIS

Jane Aiken HODGE

Sara HYLTON

Judith KELMAN

Caroline LLEWELLYN

Mary STEWART

Mary WILLIAMS

Daoma WINSTON

James A. MICHENER   US 1907-
General

Noel BARBER

Robert ELEGANT

John MASTERS

Vikram SETH

Leon URIS

Gore VIDAL

Herman WOUK

Paul MICOU   US   1959-
General

William BOYD

Ronald FRAME

Patrick GALE

Sinclair LEWIS

Patrick McCABE

J.D. SALINGER

Evelyn WAUGH

Tom WOLFE

Stanley MIDDLETON   1919-
General

Stan BARSTOW

Melvyn BRAGG

William COOPER

L.P. HARTLEY

Francis KING

David LODGE

Alan SILLITOE

David STOREY

Tony WARREN

Sue MILLER US   1943-
General
  Ethan CANIN

  Jon COHEN

  Jane HAMILTON

  Lorrie MOORE

  Mary McGarry MORRIS

  Marge PIERCY

  Anne TYLER

Mary MINTON
Family Stories
  Maeve BINCHY

  Brenda CLARKE

  Pamela EVANS

  Lilian HARRY

  Marie JOSEPH

  Genevieve LYONS

  Hilda McKENZIE

  Pamela POPE

  Malcolm ROSS

  Jessica STIRLING

  Anne WORBOYS

Yukio MISHIMA Ja   1925-70
General
  Russell BANKS

  Shusaku ENDO

  Kazuo ISHIGURO

  Haruki MURAKAMI

Gladys MITCHELL   1901-83
Crime
  Margery ALLINGHAM

  John Dickson CARR

  Agatha CHRISTIE

  Edmund CRISPIN

  Georgette HEYER

  Michael INNES

  Ngaio MARSH

  Gwen MOFFAT

  John SHERWOOD

  Patricia WENTWORTH

James MITCHELL   1926-
General
  Hilary BAILEY

  Sheila JANSEN

  Beryl KINGSTON

  Kenneth ROYCE

Naomi MITCHISON Sco 1897-
Historical
    Dorothy DUNNETT
    Alan MASSIE
    Edith PARGETER
    Mary RENAULT
    Rosemary SUTCLIFF

Nancy MITFORD 1904-73
Humour
    Sally BRAMPTON
    Helen MUIR
    Nora NAISH
    Evelyn WAUGH

Timothy MO 1953-
General
    Julian BARNES
    Kazuo ISHIGURO
    Hanif KUREISHI
    Caryl PHILLIPS

Gwen MOFFAT 1924-
Crime
    Gillian LINSCOTT
    Gladys MITCHELL
    Betty ROWLANDS
    John SHERWOOD
    Patricia WENTWORTH

Deborah MOGGACH 1948-
General
    Patricia ANGADI
    Rachel BILLINGTON
    Alice Thomas ELLIS
    Margaret FORSTER
    Lesley GLAISTER
    Angela HUTH
    Angela LAMBERT
    Joan LINGARD
    Penelope LIVELY
    Hilary MANTEL
    Gillian TINDALL
    Gillian WHITE

Michael MOLLOY 1940-
General
    Martina COLE
    Lynda LA PLANTE
    James PATTINSON
    Mark TIMLIN

Connie MONK
Family Stories
    Philip BOAST
    Jonathan GRANT
    Audrey HOWARD
    Mary MACKIE
    Eileen STAFFORD
    Jessica STIRLING
    Dee WILLIAMS

David MONNERY
War
  Peter ABRAHAMS
  Doug ARMSTRONG
  Peter CAVE
  Shaun CLARKE
  Robin JAMES

Nicholas MONSARRAT 1910-79
Sea
  C.S. FORESTER
  John HARRIS
  A.E. LANGSFORD
  Alistair MACLEAN
  Nevil SHUTE

Susan MOODY
Crime
  Linda BARNES
  Liza CODY
  Antonia FRASER
  Sue GRAFTON
  Karen KIJEWSKI
  Sara PARETSKY
  Mike RIPLEY
  Barbara VINE

Michael MOORCOCK 1939-
Fantasy
  Piers ANTHONY
  Ray BRADBURY
  Samuel R. DELANY
  Philip José FARMER
  David A. GEMMELL
  Frank HERBERT
  Julian MAY
  Christopher PRIEST
  Bob SHAW
  Gene WOLFE

Brian MOORE Can 1921-
General
  Martin AMIS
  Paul BAILEY
  William BOYD
  David COOK
  Thomas KENEALLY
  Ian McEWAN
  John McGAHERN
  Paul THEROUX
  D.M. THOMAS
  William TREVOR
  Barry UNSWORTH
  Tim WINTON

Lorrie MOORE US 1957-
General
  Louise ERDRICH
  Sue MILLER
  Mary McGarry MORRIS
  Paul SAYER
  Anne TYLER

Catrin MORGAN Wales
Family Stories
  Catrin COLLIER
  Iris GOWER
  Marie JOSEPH
  Jessica STIRLING

Anne MORICE 1918-
Crime
  Pat BURDEN
  Jane DENTINGER
  Antonia FRASER
  Emma LATHEN
  Elizabeth LEMARCHAND
  Ngaio MARSH
  David WILLIAMS
  Sara WOODS
  Margaret YORKE

David MORRELL Can
Adventure
  Eric LUSTBADER
  Alan SAVAGE

  Dov SILVERMAN
  Richard STARK
  Douglas TERMAN

Mark MORRIS
Supernatural
  Joe DONNELLY
  Stephen GALLAGHER
  Shaun HUTSON
  Bentley LITTLE
  Graham MASTERTON
  Kim NEWMAN
  Philip RICKMAN
  Tim WILSON

Mary McGarry MORRIS US
General 1947-
  Ethan CANIN
  Jon COHEN
  Sue MILLER
  Lorrie MOORE

Toni MORRISON US 1931-
General
  Lisa ALTHER
  James BALDWIN
  E.L. DOCTOROW
  Buchi EMECHETA
  Marita GOLDEN
  Rosa GUY

Elspeth HUXLEY

Terry McMILLAN

Judith ROSSNER

Alice WALKER

Carole MORTIMER   c. 1960-
Romance

Lindsay ARMSTRONG

Joyce DINGWELL

Jane DONNELLY

Catherine GEORGE

Penny JORDAN

Charlotte LAMB

Audrie MANLEY-TUCKER

Anne MATHER

Betty NEELS

Jessica STEELE

Kay THORPE

Sally WENTWORTH

John MORTIMER   1923-
Humour

Malcolm BRADBURY

Caro FRASER

Rumer GODDEN

Roy HATTERSLEY

David LODGE

Frederic RAPHAEL

Keith WATERHOUSE

Penelope MORTIMER   1918-
General

Beryl BAINBRIDGE

Margaret DRABBLE

Doris LESSING

Olivia MANNING

Edna O'BRIEN

Muriel SPARK

Doris MORTMAN   US
Family Stories

Barbara DELINSKY

Lewis ORDE

Margaret PEMBERTON

Belva PLAIN

Maisie MOSCO
Family Stories

Charlotte Vale ALLEN

Lyn ANDREWS

Donna BAKER

Louise BRINDLEY

Josephine COX

Rosemary ENRIGHT

Suzanne GOODWIN

Marie JOSEPH

Lena KENNEDY

Claire RAYNER

Jessica STIRLING

Elizabeth WAITE

Walter MOSLEY US
Crime
  Raymond CHANDLER
  James ELLROY
  Dashiell HAMMETT
  Chester B. HIMES
  Charles WILLEFORD

Patricia MOYES 1923-
Crime
  Margery ALLINGHAM
  Marian BABSON
  Elizabeth LEMARCHAND
  Ngaio MARSH
  Betty ROWLANDS

Helen MUIR 1937-
Humour
  Mavis CHEEK
  Nancy MITFORD
  Sue TOWNSEND
  Nigel WILLIAMS

Marcia MULLER US 1944-
Crime
  Linda BARNES
  Liza CODY
  Val McDERMID
  Sara PARETSKY

Alice MUNRO Can 1931-
General
  Edna O'BRIEN
  Jane HAMILTON
  Alice HOFFMAN
  Anne TYLER

Neil MUNRO Sco 1864-1930
Historical
  D.K. BROSTER
  Elizabeth BYRD
  Sharon PENMAN
  Nigel TRANTER

Haruki MURAKAMI Ja
General
  Russell BANKS
  Shusaku ENDO
  Kazuo ISHIGURO
  Yukio MISHIMA

Iris MURDOCH 1919-
General
  Joan AIKEN
  Elizabeth BOWEN
  Brigid BROPHY
  Jennifer JOHNSTON
  Rosamond LEHMANN
  Doris LESSING
  Joyce Carol OATES

Bernice RUBENS

Muriel SPARK

Emma TENNANT

Angus WILSON

Virginia WOOLF

Elizabeth MURPHY
Family Stories

Anne BAKER

Kate FLYNN

Helen FORRESTER

Nicola THORNE

Margaret THORNTON

Amy MYERS
also writes as Harriet HUDSON
Crime

Ray HARRISON

Alanna KNIGHT

Janet LAURENCE

Anne PERRY

Julian SYMONS

M.J. TROW

Paul MYERS   1932-
Crime

Dick FRANCIS

Jessica MANN

Ann QUINTON

Kenneth ROYCE

Richard RUSSELL

Magdalen NABB   1947-
Crime

Marian BABSON

Michael DIBDIN

Roderic JEFFRIES

James McCLURE

Michael PEARCE

Vladimir NABOKOV   Rus
General   1899-1977

Kazuo ISHIGURO

James JOYCE

Alexander SOLZHENITSYN

John UPDIKE

V.S. NAIPAUL   Carib   1932-
General

Chinua ACHEBE

Saul BELLOW

David DABYDEEN

Ruth Prawer JHABVALA

Elizabeth JOLLEY

John MASTERS

Vikram SETH

Paul THEROUX

Patrick WHITE

Nora NAISH
General
  Marika COBBOLD
  Sybil MARSHALL
  Nancy MITFORD
  Ann PURSER
  Kathleen ROWNTREE
  Joanna TROLLOPE
  Mary WESLEY

R.K. NARAYAN Ind 1906-
General
  Amit CHAUDHURI
  Anita DESAI
  Rumer GODDEN
  Russell LUCAS
  John MASTERS
  Gita MEHTA
  Vikram SETH

Gloria NAYLOR US 1950-
General
  Ellen DOUGLAS
  Garrison KEILLOR
  Paule MARSHALL
  Terry McMILLAN
  Alice WALKER

Grant NAYLOR
Science Fiction
  Douglas ADAMS
  Robert ASPRIN
  Tom HOLT
  Terry PRATCHETT
  Robert RANKIN

Janet NEEL
Crime
  Natasha COOPER
  S.T. HAYMON
  Susan KELLY
  Jill McGOWN
  Jonathan ROSS
  Dorothy SIMPSON

Betty NEELS 1909-
Romance
  Penny JORDAN
  Charlotte LAMB
  Anne MATHER
  Judith McNAUGHT
  Carole MORTIMER
  Jessica STEELE
  Anne WEALE
  Sally WENTWORTH

Kim NEWMAN 1959-
Supernatural
  Jonathan AYCLIFFE
  J.G. BALLARD
  Joe DONNELLY
  Christopher FOWLER
  Graham MASTERTON
  Mark MORRIS
  Philip RICKMAN

Christopher NICOLE 1930-
also writes as Alan SAVAGE
Adventure
  Martin BOOTH
  James CLAVELL
  Colin FALCONER
  Eric LUSTBADER
  Marc OLDEN

Larry NIVEN US 1938-
Science Fiction
  Isaac ASIMOV
  Arthur C. CLARKE
  Harry HARRISON
  Stanislaw LEM
  Frederik POHL
  Kim Stanley ROBINSON

David NOBBS 1935-
Humour
  Kingsley AMIS
  H.E. BATES
  Guy BELLAMY
  J.L. CARR
  Roy CLARKE
  Colin DOUGLAS
  Roddy DOYLE
  Tom HOLT
  Leslie THOMAS
  Peter TINNISWOOD
  Keith WATERHOUSE
  Nigel WILLIAMS
  P.G. WODEHOUSE

Diana NORMAN 1935-
Historical
  Evelyn ANTHONY
  Pamela BELLE
  D.K. BROSTER
  Philippa CARR
  Georgette HEYER
  Dinah LAMPITT
  Morgan LLYWELYN
  Maureen PETERS
  Jean PLAIDY
  Stewart ROSS
  Rosemary SUTCLIFF
  Connie WILLIS

Andre NORTON US 1912-
Fantasy
  Katherine KERR
  Ursula LE GUIN
  Anne McCAFFREY
  Sheri S. TEPPER
  Janny WURTS

Nelson NYE US 1907-
Western
  Max BRAND
  J.T. EDSON
  Louis L'AMOUR

Robert NYE 1939-
General
  Peter ACKROYD
  Bruce CHATWIN
  John FOWLES
  Barry UNSWORTH

Patrick O'BRIAN Ire 1914-
Sea
  Joseph CONRAD
  Bernard CORNWELL
  David DONACHIE
  C.S. FORESTER
  Raymond HARDIE
  Alexander KENT
  C. Northcote PARKINSON

  Dudley POPE
  Douglas REEMAN
  Showell STYLES
  Richard WOODMAN

Edna O'BRIEN Ire 1932-
General
  Lynne Reid BANKS
  Clare BOYLAN
  Brigid BROPHY
  Margaret DRABBLE
  Nell DUNN
  Alice Thomas ELLIS
  Jennifer JOHNSTON
  Angela LAMBERT
  Mary McCARTHY
  Penelope MORTIMER
  Alice MUNRO
  Joyce Carol OATES
  Fay WELDON

Flann O'BRIEN Ire
Humour
  J.P. DONLEAVY
  Jennifer JOHNSTON
  James JOYCE
  Molly KEANE

Flannery O'CONNOR US
General
  Mary McCARTHY
  Carson McCULLERS
  J.D. SALINGER

M.R. O'DONNELL 1932-
also writes as Malcolm MACDONALD &
                          Malcolm ROSS
Family Stories
  Maeve BINCHY
  J.G. FARRELL
  Susan HOWATCH
  Genevieve LYONS

John O'HARA US 1905-70
General
  John CHEEVER
  F. Scott FITZGERALD
  Ford Madox FORD
  Alison LURIE

Gilda O'NEILL
Historical
  Philip BOAST
  Harry BOWLING
  Martina COLE
  Pamela EVANS
  Pamela OLDFIELD
  Mary Jane STAPLES

Jeanne WHITMEE
Dee WILLIAMS

Ann OAKLEY 1944-
General
  Lisa ALTHER
  Guy BELLAMY
  Marilyn FRENCH
  Judith ROSSNER

Joyce Carol OATES US 1938-
General
  Jenny DISKI
  Harper LEE
  Doris LESSING
  Bobbie Ann MASON
  Iris MURDOCH
  Edna O'BRIEN
  V.S. PRITCHETT

Clint OGDEN Ire 1924-
Western
  Louis L'AMOUR
  T.C. OLSEN
  Lauran PAINE

Ben OKRI Nigeria 1959-
General
  Chinua ACHEBE
  David DABYDEEN
  Günter GRASS
  Milan KUNDERA
  Caryl PHILLIPS
  Wole SOYINKA

Marc OLDEN
Adventure
  Martin BOOTH
  Anthony GREY
  Eric LUSTBADER
  Christopher NICOLE
  Alan SAVAGE

Pamela OLDFIELD 1931-
Family Stories
  Charlotte Vale ALLEN
  Tessa BARCLAY
  Rosemary ENRIGHT
  Catherine GASKIN
  Valerie GEORGESON
  Judith GLOVER
  Ruth HAMILTON
  Brenda JAGGER
  Sybil MARSHALL
  Anne MELVILLE
  Gilda O'NEILL

  Mary E. PEARCE
  Jeanne WHITMEE
  Sarah WOODHOUSE

T.C. OLSEN US 1932-
Western
  Jess CODY
  Louis L'AMOUR
  Clint OGDEN
  Lauran PAINE
  Gary PAULSEN

Michael ONDAATJE Can 1943-
General
  Gita MEHTA
  Salman RUSHDIE
  Colin THUBRON
  Marianne WIGGINS

Lewis ORDE
Family Stories
  Peter LING
  Doris MORTMAN
  Belva PLAIN
  Anne Rivers SIDDONS
  Rosie THOMAS
  Judy TURNER

Roger ORMEROD 1920-
Crime
   W.J. BURLEY
   Colin DEXTER
   Elizabeth FERRARS
   Nicholas RHEA
   Michael UNDERWOOD

George ORWELL 1903-50
General
   Anthony BURGESS
   Graham GREENE
   Aldous HUXLEY
   Arthur KOESTLER

Agnes OWENS
General
   Janice GALLOWAY
   Alisdair GRAY
   James KELMAN
   Irvine WELSH

Amos OZ Isr 1939-
General
   David GROSSMAN
   Primo LEVI
   Chaim POTOK
   Isaac Bashevis SINGER

Emma PAGE
Crime
   Pat BURDEN
   Jane DENTINGER
   Emma LATHEN
   Elizabeth LEMARCHAND
   Ngaio MARSH
   Sara WOODS

Lynda PAGE
Family Stories
   Hilda McKENZIE
   Mary Jane STAPLES
   Kay STEPHENS
   Margaret THORNTON

Lauran PAINE US 1916-
Western
   Zane GREY
   Louis L'AMOUR
   Clint OGDEN
   T.C. OLSEN

Elizabeth PALMER 1942-
General
   Katie FFORDE
   Barbara PYM
   May SARTON
   Titia SUTHERLAND
   Elizabeth TAYLOR
   Joanna TROLLOPE

Frank PALMER
Crime

Sheila RADLEY

Peter TURNBULL

Sara PARETSKY   US   1947-
Crime

Linda BARNES

James Lee BURKE

Liza CODY

Sue GRAFTON

Lesley GRANT-ADAMSON

Carl HIAASEN

Karen KIJEWSKI

Val McDERMID

Susan MOODY

Marcia MULLER

Robert B. PARKER

Joan SMITH

Edith PARGETER   1913-95
also writes as Ellis PETERS
Historical

Valerie ANAND

Pamela HILL

Mary HOCKING

Morgan LLYWELYN

Naomi MITCHISON

Sharon PENMAN

Jean PLAIDY

Judith M. RILEY

Rosemary SUTCLIFF

Nigel TRANTER

Robert B. PARKER   US   1932-
Crime

Lawrence BLOCK

Raymond CHANDLER

James Hadley CHASE

Andrew COBURN

Liza CODY

Dashiell HAMMETT

Elmore LEONARD

Ed McBAIN

Sara PARETSKY

T. Jefferson PARKER
Crime

M.C. BEATON

Faye KELLERMAN

Jonathan KELLERMAN

Ridley PEARSON

Una-Mary PARKER   1930-
Glitz & Glamour

Sally BEAUMAN

Fiona BULLEN

Julie ELLIS

Shirley ESKAPA

LaVyrle SPENCER

Danielle STEEL

C. Northcote PARKINSON
Sea   1909-93
   C.S. FORESTER
   Alexander KENT
   Patrick O'BRIAN
   Richard WOODMAN

Frank PARRISH   Sco   1929-
Crime
   Marion BABSON
   Jonathan GASH
   Gerald HAMMOND
   Tim HEALD

Brian PARVIN
General
   Brian CARTER
   Aeron CLEMENT
   William HORWOOD
   A.R. LLOYD
   Henry WILLIAMSON

Alan PATON   SA   1903-88
General
   James BALDWIN
   Andre BRINK
   J.M. COETZEE
   Nadine GORDIMER
   Graham GREENE
   Christopher HOPE
   Doris LESSING

Richard North PATTERSON
Crime
   Dexter DIAS
   William DIEHL
   Philip FRIEDMAN
   John GRISHAM
   Steve MARTINI
   Scott TUROW

James PATTINSON
Crime
   John Newton CHANCE
   Martina COLE
   Michael MOLLOY
   Joyce PORTER

Gary PAULSEN   US   1939-
Western
   Louis L'AMOUR
   T.C. OLSEN

Mervyn PEAKE   1911-68
Fantasy
   Colin GREENLAND
   C.S. LEWIS
   H.P. LOVECRAFT
   J.R.R. TOLKIEN
   Gene WOLFE

Mary E. PEARCE 1932-
Family Stories
  Iris BROMIGE
  Catherine COOKSON
  Monica DICKENS
  Gwen KIRKWOOD
  Sybil MARSHALL
  Pamela OLDFIELD
  Diane PEARSON
  Miss READ
  Sarah SHEARS
  Margaret SUNLEY
  Anne WORBOYS

Michael PEARCE
Crime
  Lindsey DAVIS
  Roderic JEFFRIES
  Tom KAKONIS
  James McCLURE
  Magdalen NABB

Iain PEARS 1955-
Crime
  Simon BRETT
  Gwendoline BUTLER
  Jonathan GASH
  John MALCOLM
  Jennie MELVILLE
  Neville STEED
  Derek WILSON

Diane PEARSON 1931-
Historical
  Catherine GASKIN
  Susan HOWATCH
  M.M. KAYE
  Mary E. PEARCE
  Ann Victoria ROBERTS
  Jean STUBBS

Ridley PEARSON US 1953-
Crime
  Patricia D. CORNWELL
  Thomas HARRIS
  Jonathan KELLERMAN
  T. Jefferson PARKER
  Lawrence SANDERS
  John SANDFORD
  David WILTSE

Margaret PEMBERTON 1943-
Historical
  Cynthia FREEMAN
  Sara HYLTON
  Doris MORTMAN
  Belva PLAIN
  Danielle STEEL
  Nicola THORNE

Sharon PENMAN US
Historical
Valerie ANAND
Pamela BELLE
Dorothy DUNNETT
Isabelle HOLLAND
Morgan LLYWELYN
Neil MUNRO
Edith PARGETER
Judith M. RILEY
Mary STEWART
Nigel TRANTER

Anne PERRY 1938-
Crime
Gwendoline BUTLER
P.C. DOHERTY
Martha GRIMES
Ray HARRISON
Georgette HEYER
Alanna KNIGHT
Peter LOVESEY
Amy MYERS
Ellis PETERS
M.J. TROW

John PENN
also writes as Palma HARCOURT
Crime
Catherine AIRD
W.J. BURLEY
Colin DEXTER
Elizabeth FERRARS
Ann QUINTON
John WAINWRIGHT

Elizabeth PETERS US 1927-
also writes as Barbara MICHAELS
General
Lilian Jackson BRAUN
Mavis CHEEK
Susan ISAACS
Mary STEWART
Phyllis A. WHITNEY
Mary WILLIAMS

Wendy PERRIAM 1940-
General
Clare BOYLAN
Carol CLEWLOW
Sarah HARRISON
Alison Scott SKELTON
Fay WELDON

Ellis PETERS 1913-95
also writes as Edith PARGETER
Crime
Kate CHARLES
Michael CLYNES
Lindsey DAVIS
P.C. DOHERTY
Elizabeth EYRE
D.M. GREENWOOD

Ellis PETERS (cont.)

   Paul HARDING

   Anne PERRY

   Candace ROBB

   Kate SEDLEY

   Peter TREMAYNE

   Derek WILSON

Maureen PETERS   Wales   1935-
Historical

   Pamela HILL

   Evelyn HOOD

   Diana NORMAN

   Philippa WIAT

Caryl PHILLIPS   Carib   1958-
General

   Chinua ACHEBE

   David DABYDEEN

   Timothy MO

   Ben OKRI

   Wole SOYINKA

Marge PIERCY   US   1936-
General

   Lisa ALTHER

   Dominick DUNNE

   Marilyn FRENCH

   Rona JAFFE

   Erica JONG

   Larry McMURTRY

   Sue MILLER

   Erin PIZZEY

   Jane SMILEY

   Anne TYLER

Christopher PIKE   US
Supernatural

   Shaun HUTSON

   Richard LAYMON

   John SAUL

   Guy N. SMITH

Rosamunde PILCHER   1924-
General

   Maeve BINCHY

   Iris BROMIGE

   Katie FFORDE

   Judith GLOVER

   Miss READ

   Kathleen ROWNTREE

   Susan SALLIS

   May SARTON

   Sue SULLY

   Titia SUTHERLAND

   Eileen TOWNSEND

   Joanna TROLLOPE

Richard PITMAN
Crime
Barry CORK
Mark DANIEL
Dick FRANCIS
John FRANCOME
Richard RUSSELL

Erin PIZZEY   1939-
Family Stories
Maeve BINCHY
Shirley CONRAN
Marge PIERCY
Judith SAXTON

Jean PLAIDY   1906-93
also writes as Victoria HOLT & Philippa CARR
Historical
Valerie ANAND
Evelyn ANTHONY
Dorothy DUNNETT
Pamela HILL
Jane Aiken HODGE
Rosalind LAKER
Norah LOFTS
Diana NORMAN
Edith PARGETER
Jean STUBBS
Nigel TRANTER
Philippa WIAT

Belva PLAIN   US   1918-
Family Stories
Janice Young BROOKS
Teresa CRANE
Barbara DELINSKY
Cynthia FREEMAN
Gail GODWIN
Margaret GRAHAM
Adam KENNEDY
Doris MORTMAN
Lewis ORDE
Margaret PEMBERTON
Claire RAYNER
Danielle STEEL
Rosie THOMAS

Frederik POHL   US   1919-
Science Fiction
Isaac ASIMOV
Greg BEAR
C.J. CHERRYH
Arthur C. CLARKE
Larry NIVEN
John WYNDHAM

Dudley POPE   1925-
Sea
David DONACHIE
C.S. FORESTER
Raymond HARDIE
Alexander KENT

Dudley POPE (cont.)

    Philip McCUTCHAN

    Patrick O'BRIAN

    Showell STYLES

    John WINGATE

    Richard WOODMAN

Pamela POPE
Family Stories

    Margaret GRAHAM

    Mary MINTON

    Jeanne WHITMEE

    Barbara WHITNELL

Joyce PORTER   1924-
Crime

    Sarah CAULDWELL

    Reginald HILL

    James PATTINSON

    Colin WATSON

Chaim POTOK   US   1929-
General

    Saul BELLOW

    David GROSSMAN

    Amos OZ

    Isaac Bashevis SINGER

Anthony POWELL   1905-
General

    Isabel COLEGATE

    Graham GREENE

    Aldous HUXLEY

    J.B. PRIESTLEY

    C.P. SNOW

    Evelyn WAUGH

    Henry WILLIAMSON

Amanda PRANTERA   1942-
General

    J.M. COETZEE

    Amanda CRAIG

    Penelope FITZGERALD

    Barbara TRAPIDO

    Barry UNSWORTH

    Marina WARNER

Terry PRATCHETT   1948-
Fantasy

    Douglas ADAMS

    Piers ANTHONY

    Robert ASPRIN

    Alan Dean FOSTER

    Craig Shaw GARDNER

    Harry HARRISON

    Tom HOLT

    Dan McGIRT

    Grant NAYLOR

Robert RANKIN

Christopher STASHEFF

Anthony PRICE   1928-
Adventure

Lionel DAVIDSON

Len DEIGHTON

Clive EGLETON

Brian FREEMANTLE

William HAGGARD

John LE CARRÉ

Julian RATHBONE

Christopher PRIEST   1943-
Science Fiction

J.G. BALLARD

Iain M. BANKS

Philip K. DICK

Michael MOORCOCK

Keith ROBERTS

Kurt VONNEGUT

Connie WILLIS

J.B. PRIESTLEY   1894-1984
General

Thomas ARMSTRONG

Phyllis BENTLEY

A.J. CRONIN

R.F. DELDERFIELD

John GALSWORTHY

L.P. HARTLEY

Winifred HOLTBY

Anthony POWELL

C.P. SNOW

Howard SPRING

Hugh WALPOLE

Angus WILSON

V.S. PRITCHETT   1900-
General

William BOYD

John McGAHERN

Joyce Carol OATES

William TREVOR

E. Annie PROULX   US/Can
General

Margaret ATWOOD

Louise ERDRICH

Gail GODWIN

David GUTERSON

Jim HARRISON

Peter HOEG

Cormac McCARTHY

Carol SHIELDS

Jane SMILEY

Deirdre PURCELL
Family Stories
Maeve BINCHY
Frank DELANEY
Helen FORRESTER
Sheelagh KELLY
Marjorie QUARTON
Elvi RHODES
Mary RYAN
Susan SALLIS
Janet TANNER

Ann PURSER
General
Marika COBBOLD
Sybil MARSHALL
Nora NAISH
Miss READ
Kathleen ROWNTREE
Barbara VICTOR

Barbara PYM   1913-80
General
Jane AUSTEN
A.L. BARKER
Anita BROOKNER
Janice ELLIOTT
Alice Thomas ELLIS
Julian FANE
Mary HOCKING
Molly KEANE

Elizabeth PALMER
May SARTON
Elizabeth TAYLOR
Emma TENNANT

Marjorie QUARTON
Family Stories
Helen FORRESTER
Deirdre PURCELL
Denise ROBERTSON
Wendy ROBERTSON
Margaret SUNLEY

Ann QUINTON
Crime
M.C. BEATON
W.J. BURLEY
Eileen DEWHURST
Frances FYFIELD
Caroline GRAHAM
Jill McGOWN
Jennie MELVILLE
Paul MYERS
John PENN
Sheila RADLEY

Sheila RADLEY   1928-
Crime
Eileen DEWHURST
John HARVEY

Frank PALMER
Ann QUINTON
C.F. ROE
Jonathan ROSS
Betty ROWLANDS
Dorothy SIMPSON
June THOMSON
Peter TURNBULL
R.D. WINGFIELD

Ian RANKIN Sco
Crime
Colin DEXTER
John HARVEY
Bill JAMES
Bill KNOX
Peter TURNBULL
R.D. WINGFIELD

Robert RANKIN
Science Fiction
Douglas ADAMS
Robert ASPRIN
Tom HOLT
Dan McGIRT
Grant NAYLOR
Terry PRATCHETT
Robert SHECKLEY

Frederic RAPHAEL US 1931-
General
Howard JACOBSON
Allan MASSIE
John MORTIMER
Piers Paul READ
C.P. SNOW

Julian RATHBONE 1935-
Adventure
Lionel DAVIDSON
John GARDNER
Palma HARCOURT
John HARRIS
Robert LUDLUM
Amin MAALOUF
Anthony PRICE
Craig THOMAS

Melanie RAWN US 1953-
Fantasy
Marion Zimmer BRADLEY
Terry BROOKS
Louise COOPER
David EDDINGS
Raymond E. FEIST
Robert JORDAN
Patricia KENNEALY
Anne McCAFFREY
Margaret WEIS
Tad WILLIAMS

Claire RAYNER 1931-
Family Stories
  Winston GRAHAM
  Christine GREEN
  Beryl KINGSTON
  Anne MELVILLE
  Maisie MOSCO
  Belva PLAIN
  Judith SAXTON
  Patricia WENDORF

Miss READ 1913-
Family Stories
  Lucilla ANDREWS
  E.M. DELAFIELD
  Jane DUNCAN
  Elizabeth GOUDGE
  Sybil MARSHALL
  Mary MELWOOD
  Mary E. PEARCE
  Rosamunde PILCHER
  Ann PURSER
  Sarah SHEARS
  D.E. STEVENSON
  Angela THIRKELL

Piers Paul READ 1941-
General
  Paul BAILEY
  Robert GODDARD
  Allan MASSIE

  Ian McEWAN
  Frederic RAPHAEL
  Paul THEROUX
  Angus WILSON

Douglas REEMAN 1924-
also writes as Alexander KENT
Sea
  Brian CALLISON
  Bernard CORNWELL
  Alexander FULLERTON
  John HARRIS
  Hammond INNES
  Geoffrey JENKINS
  Philip McCUTCHAN
  Patrick O'BRIAN
  Douglas SCOTT
  Antony TREW
  Charles WHITING
  John WINGATE
  John WINTON

Erich Maria REMARQUE Ger
General 1898-1970
  Pat BARKER
  Sebastian FAULKS
  Paul WATKINS
  William WHARTON
  Henry WILLIAMSON

Mary RENAULT 1905-83
Historical
Gillian BRADSHAW
Dorothy DUNNETT
Robert GRAVES
Allan MASSIE
Naomi MITCHISON
Rosemary SUTCLIFF
Gore VIDAL

Ruth RENDELL 1930-
also writes as Barbara VINE
Crime
Patricia D. CORNWELL
Colin DEXTER
Michael DIBDIN
Lesley GRANT-ADAMSON
Roy HART
Patricia HIGHSMITH
P.D. JAMES
Peter ROBINSON
Dorothy SIMPSON
June THOMSON
Minette WALTERS
R.D. WINGFIELD

Nicholas RHEA
Crime
Caroline GRAHAM
Alan HUNTER

Roger ORMEROD
M.J. TROW
John WAINWRIGHT

Elvi RHODES c. 1930-
Family Stories
Lyn ANDREWS
Aileen ARMITAGE
Catherine COOKSON
Elaine CROWLEY
Christine Marion FRASER
Suzanne GOODWIN
Iris GOWER
Sheelagh KELLY
Lena KENNEDY
Elisabeth McNEILL
Deirdre PURCELL
Susan SALLIS

Anne RICE US 1941-
Supernatural
Nancy COLLINS
Storm CONSTANTINE
John FARRIS
Brian LUMLEY
George R. MARTIN
Dan SIMMONS

Philip RICKMAN
Supernatural

Jonathan AYCLIFFE

Joe DONNELLY

Steve HARRIS

Stephen LAWS

Mark MORRIS

Kim NEWMAN

Dennis WHEATLEY

Tim WILSON

Judith M. RILEY
Historical

Valerie ANAND

Pamela BELLE

Dorothy DUNNETT

Cynthia HARROD-EAGLES

Edith PARGETER

Sharon PENMAN

Philippa WIAT

Mike RIPLEY   1952-
Crime

Simon BRETT

John HARVEY

Carl HIAASEN

Dan KAVANAGH

Susan MOODY

Walter SATTERTHWAIT

Mark TIMLIN

Candace ROBB
Crime

Michael CLYNES

Lindsey DAVIS

P.C. DOHERTY

Elizabeth EYRE

D.M. GREENWOOD

Paul HARDING

Domini HIGHSMITH

William KIENZLE

Ellis PETERS

Kate SEDLEY

Derek WILSON

Harold ROBBINS   US   1912-
Glitz & Glamour

Pat BOOTH

Celia BRAYFIELD

Sandra BROWN

Julie BURCHILL

Jackie COLLINS

Joan COLLINS

Shirley CONRAN

Judith KRANTZ

Barbara TRAPIDO

Ann Victoria ROBERTS
Family Stories

Aileen ARMITAGE

Sheelagh KELLY

Beryl KINGSTON

Diane PEARSON

Cynthia S. ROBERTS
Historical
Rosalind LAKER
Agnes SHORT
Barbara WHITNELL
Sarah WOODHOUSE

Keith ROBERTS   1935-
Fantasy
Robert HOLDSTOCK
Christopher PRIEST
John WHITBOURN
Connie WILLIS

Michele ROBERTS   Fr   1949-
General
Angela CARTER
Carol CLEWLOW
Jeanette WINTERSON
Virginia WOOLF

Nora ROBERTS   US   1950-
General
Caroline LLEWELLYN
Anne Rivers SIDDONS
LaVyrle SPENCER
Sally WENTWORTH
Mary WILLIAMS

Denise ROBERTSON
Family Stories
Elizabeth ADLER
Tessa BARCLAY
Louise BRINDLEY
Pamela EVANS
Margaret GRAHAM
Marjorie QUARTON
Susan SALLIS
Eileen STAFFORD
Barbara VICTOR

Wendy ROBERTSON
Family Stories
Josephine COX
Elizabeth ELGIN
Lilian HARRY
Marjorie QUARTON

Patricia ROBINS   1921-
also writes as Claire LORRIMER
Romance
Lucilla ANDREWS
Marion CHESNEY
Elizabeth SEIFERT
Sheila WALSH

Derek ROBINSON   1932-
War
Peter ABRAHAMS
Larry FORRESTER
W.E.B. GRIFFIN

Derek ROBINSON (cont.)

  John HARRIS

  Max HENNESSY

  Robert JACKSON

  Gavin LYALL

  Paul WATKINS

Kim Stanley ROBINSON US

Science Fiction   1952-

  John BARNES

  Greg BEAR

  Ray BRADBURY

  David BRIN

  John BRUNNER

  Orson Scott CARD

  Arthur C. CLARKE

  Philip K. DICK

  William GIBSON

  Larry NIVEN

  Bruce STERLING

  Jack VANCE

  John VARLEY

Peter ROBINSON

Crime

  Colin DEXTER

  Ruth RENDELL

  Dorothy SIMPSON

  R.D. WINGFIELD

C.F. ROE

Crime

  M.C. BEATON

  Christine GREEN

  Janet LAURENCE

  William McILVANNEY

  Sheila RADLEY

Jane ROGERS   1952-

General

  Sally EMERSON

  Jane GARDAM

  Alison LURIE

  Candia McWILLIAM

  Marina WARNER

Michael Scott ROHAN Sco

Fantasy   1951-

  Storm CONSTANTINE

  David GEMMELL

  Colin GREENLAND

  Guy Gavriel KAY

  Sheri S. TEPPER

  J.R.R. TOLKIEN

  Margaret WEIS

  Tad WILLIAMS

  Janny WURTS

  Jonathan WYLIE

Annette ROOME
Crime

Sarah CAUDWELL

Frances FYFIELD

Janet LAURENCE

John SHERWOOD

Kate ROSS   US
Crime

Elizabeth EYRE

Ray HARRISON

Georgette HEYER

M.J. TROW

Nancy Taylor ROSENBERG   US
Crime   1946-

Joy FIELDING

Philip FRIEDMAN

John GRISHAM

Steve MARTINI

Scott TUROW

Malcolm ROSS   1932-
also writes as M.R. O'DONNELL &
                    Malcolm MACDONALD
Family Stories

Donna BAKER

Maeve BINCHY

Sara FRASER

Jonathan GRANT

Evelyn HOOD

Beryl KINGSTON

Mary MINTON

Sue SULLY

Jonathan ROSS   1916-
Crime

W.J. BURLEY

John CREASEY

Eileen DEWHURST

S.T. HAYMON

Reginald HILL

Janet NEEL

Sheila RADLEY

June THOMSON

Michael UNDERWOOD

R.D. WINGFIELD

Stewart ROSS   US
Historical

Dorothy DUNNETT

George Macdonald FRASER

Diana NORMAN

Nigel TRANTER

Judith ROSSNER   US   1935-
General
  Lisa ALTHER
  Marilyn FRENCH
  Toni MORRISON
  Ann OAKLEY
  Anne TYLER

Philip ROTH   US   1933-
General
  Saul BELLOW
  Joseph HELLER
  Jay McINERNEY
  Bernice RUBENS
  Leslie THOMAS

Betty ROWLANDS
Crime
  Catherine AIRD
  Pat BURDEN
  Natasha COOPER
  Ann GRANGER
  Hazel HOLT
  Gwen MOFFAT
  Patricia MOYES
  Sheila RADLEY
  John SHERWOOD
  David WILLIAMS

Kathleen ROWNTREE
General
  Judy ASTLEY
  Marika COBBOLD
  E.M. DELAFIELD
  Maeve HARAN
  Dinah LAMPITT
  Annie LEITH
  Nora NAISH
  Rosamunde PILCHER
  Ann PURSER
  Audrey SLAUGHTER
  Angela THIRKELL

Kenneth ROYCE   1920-
Adventure
  Gavin ESLER
  James MITCHELL
  Paul MYERS
  Lawrence SANDERS
  Glover WRIGHT

Bernice RUBENS   1928-
General
  Patricia ANGADI
  Beryl BAINBRIDGE
  Anita BROOKNER
  Margaret DRABBLE
  Alice Thomas ELLIS
  Iris MURDOCH
  Philip ROTH

Paul THEROUX
A.N. WILSON
Jeanette WINTERSON

David WILTSE
Margaret YORKE

Salman RUSHDIE   1947-
General
  Anthony BURGESS
  Angela CARTER
  Anita DESAI
  Farrukh DHONDY
  John FOWLES
  Gabriel GARCIA MARQUEZ
  Alasdair GRAY
  David GROSSMAN
  Gita MEHTA
  Michael ONDAATJE
  Vikram SETH
  Marianne WIGGINS

Richard RUSSELL
Crime
  Barry CORK
  Mark DANIEL
  Dick FRANCIS
  John FRANCOME
  Paul MYERS
  Richard PITMAN

Mary RYAN   Ire
General
  Maeve BINCHY
  Clare BOYLAN
  Frank DELANEY
  Caro FRASER
  Deirdre PURCELL

Joanna RUSS US   1937-
Science Fiction
  Samuel R. DELANY
  Gwyneth JONES
  Ursula LE GUIN
  Ian WATSON

Fred SABERHAGEN   US 1930-
Science Fiction
  Poul ANDERSON
  Isaac ASIMOV
  Jack L. CHALKER
  Julian MAY
  Robert SILVERBERG

Martin RUSSELL   1934-
Crime
  Dick FRANCIS
  Mary McMULLEN

J.D. SALINGER US   1919-
General

  Russell BANKS

  Truman CAPOTE

  Geoff DYER

  Jane GARDAM

  Cormac McCARTHY

  Carson McCULLERS

  Jay McINERNEY

  Paul MICOU

  Flannery O'CONNOR

Carola SALISBURY   1924-
Historical

  Madeleine BRENT

  Victoria HOLT

  Sara HYLTON

  Phyllis A. WHITNEY

Susan SALLIS   1929-
Family Stories

  Donna BAKER

  Louise BRINDLEY

  Elizabeth ELGIN

  Ruth HAMILTON

  Sybil MARSHALL

  Rosamunde PILCHER

  Deirdre PURCELL

  Elvi RHODES

  Denise ROBERTSON

Sue SULLY

Elizabeth WAITE

R.A. SALVATORE US   1959-
Fantasy

  Raymond E. FEIST

  Mercedes LACKEY

  J.R.R. TOLKIEN

  Margaret WEIS

Lawrence SANDERS US 1920-
Adventure

  Robert LUDLUM

  Ridley PEARSON

  Kenneth ROYCE

  Sidney SHELDON

  Richard STARK

  John TRENHAILE

John SANDFORD US   1944-
Crime

  William BAYER

  James Lee BURKE

  Thomas HARRIS

  David L. LINDSEY

  Philip M. MARGOLIN

  Ridley PEARSON

May SARTON US 1912-
General

Elizabeth BOWEN
Elizabeth PALMER
Rosamunde PILCHER
Barbara PYM
Virginia WOOLF

Walter SATTERTHWAIT US
Crime

Raymond CHANDLER
Tony HILLERMAN
Ross MACDONALD
Gregory McDONALD
Mike RIPLEY

John SAUL
Supernatural

Steve HARRIS
Dean R. KOONTZ
Graham MASTERTON
Christopher PIKE
Dennis WHEATLEY

Kate SAUNDERS
General

Zoe FAIRBAIRNS
Philippa GREGORY
Angela LAMBERT
Mary WESLEY

Alan SAVAGE 1930-
also writes as Christopher NICOLE
Adventure

James CLAVELL
Robert ELEGANT
Eric LUSTBADER
Amin MAALOUF
David MORRELL
Marc OLDEN

Julian Jay SAVARIN
Adventure

Geoffrey ARCHER
Campbell ARMSTRONG
Dale BROWN
Stephen COONTS
Clive CUSSLER
Robert JACKSON
John LE CARRÉ
Wilbur SMITH
Douglas TERMAN
Craig THOMAS

Judith SAXTON 1936-
also writes as Kate FLYNN & Judy TURNER
Family Stories

Harry BOWLING
Teresa CRANE
Janet DAILEY
Judith GLOVER
Mary MACKIE
Erin PIZZEY

Judith SAXTON (cont.)

Claire RAYNER
Danielle STEEL
Janet TANNER
Nicola THORNE

Paul SAYER   1955-
General

Paul BAILEY
David COOK
Janet FRAME
Franz KAFKA
Ken KESEY
Lorrie MOORE

Dorothy L. SAYERS 1893-1957
Crime

Margery ALLINGHAM
John Dickson CARR
Kate CHARLES
Agatha CHRISTIE
Amanda CROSS
Georgette HEYER
Michael INNES
Ngaio MARSH
Rex STOUT
Josephine TEY
Patricia WENTWORTH

Jack SCHAEFER   US   1907-91
Western

John BLAZE
Lee F. GREGSON
Louis L'AMOUR
Bill WADE

Douglas SCOTT   Sco   1926-
Sea

Brian CALLISON
Alan EVANS
Alexander FULLERTON
John HARRIS
Max HENNESSY
Richard HOUGH
A.E. LANGSFORD
Douglas REEMAN
Peter TONKIN
John WINTON

Paul SCOTT   1920-78
General

Nadine GORDIMER
Graham GREENE
Ruth Prawer JHABVALA
Doris LESSING
Olivia MANNING
John MASTERS

Tim SEBASTIAN 1952-
Adventure
  Geoffrey ARCHER
  Lionel DAVIDSON
  Gavin ESLER
  Bryan FORBES
  Gerald SEYMOUR
  Nigel WEST

Kate SEDLEY 1926-
also writes as Brenda CLARKE
Crime
  Kate CHARLES
  Ellis PETERS
  Candace ROBB
  Derek WILSON

Elizabeth SEIFERT US
Romance 1897-1983
  Lucilla ANDREWS
  Anne MATHER
  Patricia ROBINS
  Sheila WALSH

Owen SELA Can
Adventure
  Noel BARBER
  James CLAVELL
  Alan FURST
  Adam HALL

  Robert LITTELL
  Christopher SHERLOCK

Will SELF 1961-
General
  Anne FINE
  Lesley GLAISTER
  Alasdair GRAY
  Patrick McCABE

Vikram SETH Ind 1952-
General
  Amit CHAUDHURI
  Rumer GODDEN
  James A. MICHENER
  V.S. NAIPAUL
  R.K. NARAYAN
  Salman RUSHDIE

Anya SETON 1904-90
Historical
  Pamela BELLE
  Madeleine BRENT
  Elizabeth BYRD
  Daphne DU MAURIER
  Dorothy EDEN
  Elizabeth GOUDGE
  Victoria HOLT
  Jean STUBBS
  Rosemary SUTCLIFF

Gerald SEYMOUR   1941-
Adventure
  Desmond BAGLEY
  Clive CUSSLER
  Gavin ESLER
  Ken FOLLETT
  Robert HARRIS
  Jack HIGGINS
  Gavin LYALL
  Tim SEBASTIAN
  Craig THOMAS
  John TRENHAILE
  Nigel WEST

Dell SHANNON   US   1921-88
also writes as Lesley EGAN
Crime
  Erle Stanley GARDNER
  Susan KELLY
  Ed McBAIN
  Janwillem VAN DE WETERING
  Hillary WAUGH
  Sara WOODS

Tom SHARPE   1928-
Humour
  Guy BELLAMY
  Dan BINCHY
  J.L. CARR
  J.P. DONLEAVY
  George Macdonald FRASER

  Tom HOLT
  Howard JACOBSON
  Leslie THOMAS
  Peter TINNISWOOD
  Keith WATERHOUSE

Bob SHAW   Ire   1931-
Science Fiction
  Douglas ADAMS
  Greg BEAR
  Gregory BENFORD
  C.J. CHERRYH
  Arthur C. CLARKE
  Harry HARRISON
  Stanislaw LEM
  Michael MOORCOCK
  Robert SHECKLEY

Irwin SHAW   US
General
  Arthur HAILEY
  John IRVING
  John STEINBECK
  Herman WOUK

Patricia SHAW   Aus
Historical
  John Gordon DAVIS
  Emma DRUMMOND
  Peter LING

Vivian STUART
E.V. THOMPSON
Eileen TOWNSEND
Dee WILLIAMS

Simon SHAW
Crime
Marian BABSON
Robert BARNARD
Michael BOND
Simon BRETT
Anthea COHEN
Jane DENTINGER
Patricia HIGHSMITH
Neville STEED

Sarah SHEARS
Family Stories
Catrin COLLIER
Jane DUNCAN
Helen FORRESTER
Elizabeth JEFFREY
Brenda McBRYDE
Elisabeth McNEILL
Anne MELVILLE
Mary E. PEARCE
Miss READ
Mary Jane STAPLES
Barbara WHITNELL

Robert SHECKLEY   US   1926-
Science Fiction
Douglas ADAMS
Robert RANKIN
Bob SHAW
Clifford D. SIMAK

Sidney SHELDON   US   1917-
Adventure
Elizabeth ADLER
Jeffrey ARCHER
Pat BOOTH
Richard CONDON
Michael CRICHTON
Nelson DE MILLE
Arthur HAILEY
Robert LUDLUM
Lawrence SANDERS
Wilbur SMITH

Christopher SHERLOCK
Adventure
Robert LITTELL
Owen SELA
Dov SILVERMAN
Wilbur SMITH
Richard STARK

John SHERWOOD 1913-
Crime
  Ann GRANGER
  D.M. GREENWOOD
  Gerald HAMMOND
  Hazel HOLT
  Susan KELLY
  Janet LAURENCE
  Charlotte MACLEOD
  Gladys MITCHELL
  Gwen MOFFAT
  Annette ROOME
  Betty ROWLANDS
  STAYNES & STOREY

Carol SHIELDS Can/US 1935-
General
  Margaret ATWOOD
  Anita BROOKNER
  Susan HILL
  Alice HOFFMAN
  Rona JAFFE
  Alison LURIE
  E. Annie PROULX
  Jane SMILEY
  Anne TYLER
  Marina WARNER
  Marianne WIGGINS

Agnes SHORT Sco
Historical
  Emma BLAIR
  Doris DAVIDSON
  Elisabeth McNEILL
  Cynthia S. ROBERTS
  Emma STIRLING

Anita SHREVE US 1946-
General
  Mary Higgins CLARK
  Carol CLEWLOW
  Alice HOFFMAN
  Judith KELMAN
  Robert James WALLER

Linda Lay SHULER US
Historical
  Jean M. AUEL
  Gary JENNINGS
  Garry D. KILWORTH
  Nicholas LUARD

Nevil SHUTE 1899-1960
Adventure
  Victor CANNING
  Jon CLEARY
  Paul GALLICO
  Hammond INNES

Geoffrey JENKINS

Nicholas MONSARRAT

Elleston TREVOR

Morris WEST

Ursula LE GUIN

Julian MAY

Fred SABERHAGEN

Harry TURTLEDOVE

Jack VANCE

Roger ZELAZNY

Anne Rivers SIDDONS
Family Stories

Gail GODWIN

Olivia GOLDSMITH

Adam KENNEDY

Lewis ORDE

Nora ROBERTS

Rosie THOMAS

Barbara VICTOR

Dov SILVERMAN
Adventure

Eric LUSTBADER

David MORRELL

Christopher SHERLOCK

Richard STARK

Alan SILLITOE   1928-
General

Stan BARSTOW

John BRAINE

D.H. LAWRENCE

David LODGE

Stanley MIDDLETON

David STOREY

Tony WARREN

Clifford D. SIMAK   US   1904-88
Science Fiction

Isaac ASIMOV

Ray BRADBURY

Richard COWPER

Gordon R. DICKSON

Robert SHECKLEY

John WYNDHAM

Georges SIMENON   Fr   1903-89
Crime

John CREASEY

Nicolas FREELING

Mark HEBDEN

H.R.F. KEATING

Robert SILVERBERG US 1935-
Science Fiction

Poul ANDERSON

Jack L. CHALKER

Gordon R. DICKSON

Dan SIMMONS US 1948-
Fantasy
  Nancy COLLINS
  Stephen KING
  Dean R. KOONTZ
  Bentley LITTLE
  Anne RICE

Dorothy SIMPSON 1933-
Crime
  Elizabeth FERRARS
  Caroline GRAHAM
  Hazel HOLT
  P.D. JAMES
  Ngaio MARSH
  Janet NEEL
  Sheila RADLEY
  Ruth RENDELL
  Peter ROBINSON
  STAYNES & STOREY
  Barbara WHITEHEAD

Isaac Bashevis SINGER US
General 1904-
  Saul BELLOW
  Angela CARTER
  David GROSSMAN
  Primo LEVI
  Amos OZ
  Chaim POTOK

June Flaum SINGER
Glitz & Glamour
  Freda BRIGHT
  Jacqueline BRISKIN
  Sandra BROWN
  Jackie COLLINS
  Julie ELLIS
  Elizabeth GAGE
  Judith KRANTZ
  Danielle STEEL
  Alexandra THORNE

Alison Scott SKELTON
General
  Margaret Thomson DAVIS
  Wendy PERRIAM
  Titia SUTHERLAND
  Mary WESLEY

Audrey SLAUGHTER
General
  Charlotte BINGHAM
  Caroline BRIDGWOOD
  Kathleen ROWNTREE
  Titia SUTHERLAND

Jane SMILEY US 1949-
General
  Harry CAULEY
  E.L. DOCTOROW

Louise ERDRICH

Ellen GILCHRIST

Jane HAMILTON

Bobbie Ann MASON

Marge PIERCY

E. Annie PROULX

Carol SHIELDS

Robert James WALLER

John Gordon DAVIS

Peter DRISCOLL

Ken FOLLETT

Arthur HAILEY

Geoffrey JENKINS

Nicholas LUARD

Julian Jay SAVARIN

Sidney SHELDON

Christopher SHERLOCK

Guy N. SMITH
Supernatural

James HERBERT

Shaun HUTSON

Richard LAYMON

Christopher PIKE

C.P. SNOW   1905-80
General

William COOPER

Lawrence DURRELL

L.P. HARTLEY

Pamela Hansford JOHNSON

Anthony POWELL

Joan SMITH   Can   1938-
Crime

Anabel DONALD

Sarah DUNANT

Janet EVANOVICH

Lesley GRANT-ADAMSON

Val McDERMID

Sara PARETSKY

J.B. PRIESTLEY

Frederic RAPHAEL

Evelyn WAUGH

Angus WILSON

Alexander SOLZHENITSYN
General   Rus   1918-

Heinrich BÖLL

Arthur KOESTLER

Primo LEVI

Vladimir NABOKOV

Wilbur SMITH   1933-
Adventure

Jon CLEARY

Bryce COURTENAY

Wole SOYINKA Nigeria
General
  Chinua ACHEBE
  Buchi EMECHETA
  Ben OKRI
  Caryl PHILLIPS

Muriel SPARK 1918-
General
  Lynne Reid BANKS
  Nina BAWDEN
  Brigid BROPHY
  Isabel COLEGATE
  Jane GARDAM
  Pamela Hansford JOHNSON
  Doris LESSING
  Penelope MORTIMER
  Iris MURDOCH
  Elizabeth TAYLOR
  William TREVOR

LaVyrle SPENCER US 1943-
also writes as Elizabeth GAGE
Family Stories
  Charlotte Vale ALLEN
  Virginia COFFMAN
  Janet DAILEY
  Barbara DELINSKY
  Jayne Ann KRENTZ
  Judith McNAUGHT
  Una-Mary PARKER

  Nora ROBERTS
  Danielle STEEL
  Elizabeth VILLARS

Howard SPRING 1889-1965
General
  Thomas ARMSTRONG
  H.E. BATES
  A.J. CRONIN
  R.F. DELDERFIELD
  John GALSWORTHY
  L.P. HARTLEY
  Winifred HOLTBY
  Richard LLEWELLYN
  W. Somerset MAUGHAM
  J.B. PRIESTLEY
  Henry WILLIAMSON

Brian STABLEFORD 1948-
Science Fiction
  Brian W. ALDISS
  Piers ANTHONY
  Richard COWPER
  Colin GREENLAND

Eileen STAFFORD
Family Stories
  Emma BLAIR
  Pamela EVANS
  Connie MONK
  Denise ROBERTSON

Diana STAINFORTH
Family Stories
- Janet DAILEY
- Suzanne GOODWIN
- Margaret GRAHAM
- Maeve HARAN
- Rosie THOMAS

Veronica STALLWOOD
Crime
- Natasha COOPER
- Anabel DONALD
- Susan KELLY
- Neville STEED

Mary Jane STAPLES 1911-
Family Stories
- Lyn ANDREWS
- Philip BOAST
- Harry BOWLING
- Pamela EVANS
- Kate FLYNN
- Sara FRASER
- Ruth HAMILTON
- Peter LING
- Gilda O'NEILL
- Lynda PAGE
- Sarah SHEARS
- Dee WILLIAMS

Richard STARK US 1933-
Adventure
- David MORRELL
- Lawrence SANDERS
- Christopher SHERLOCK
- Dov SILVERMAN
- Douglas TERMAN

Christopher STASHEFF US
Fantasy 1944-
- Robert ASPRIN
- Craig Shaw GARDNER
- Anne McCAFFREY
- Dan McGIRT
- Terry PRATCHETT
- Harry TURTLEDOVE
- John WHITBOURN

STAYNES & STOREY
also write as Elizabeth EYRE
Crime
- Antonia FRASER
- Caroline GRAHAM
- S.T. HAYMON
- Jill McGOWN
- John SHERWOOD
- Dorothy SIMPSON

Christina STEAD Aus 1902-83
General

L.P. HARTLEY

D.H. LAWRENCE

Richard LLEWELLYN

Patrick WHITE

Neville STEED
Crime

Marian BABSON

Jonathan GASH

Gerald HAMMOND

Tim HEALD

Charlotte MACLEOD

John MALCOLM

Gregory McDONALD

Iain PEARS

Simon SHAW

Veronica STALLWOOD

Danielle STEEL US 1947-
Family Stories

Barbara Taylor BRADFORD

Janet DAILEY

Barbara DELINSKY

Cynthia FREEMAN

Una-Mary PARKER

Margaret PEMBERTON

Belva PLAIN

Judith SAXTON

June Flaum SINGER

LaVyrle SPENCER

Elizabeth WARNE

Jessica STEELE 1933-
Romance

Lucilla ANDREWS

Joyce DINGWELL

Jane DONNELLY

Catherine GEORGE

Penny JORDAN

Charlotte LAMB

Audrie MANLEY-TUCKER

Anne MATHER

Carole MORTIMER

Betty NEELS

Kay THORPE

Marguerite STEEN 1894-1975
General

Thomas ARMSTRONG

Taylor CALDWELL

Joyce CARY

Ivy COMPTON-BURNETT

Dorothy EDEN

Norah LOFTS

Colleen McCULLOUGH

John STEINBECK US 1902-68
General

William FAULKNER

F. Scott FITZGERALD

Richard FORD

Ernest HEMINGWAY

William KENNEDY

Harper LEE

Norman MAILER

Irwin SHAW

William STYRON

John UPDIKE

Kay STEPHENS
Family Stories

Aileen ARMITAGE

Brenda CLARKE

Ruth HAMILTON

Brenda JAGGER

Lynda PAGE

Margaret SUNLEY

Elizabeth WALKER

Neal STEPHENSON US
Science Fiction

John BARNES

William GIBSON

Gwyneth JONES

Bruce STERLING

Bruce STERLING US 1954-
Science Fiction

John BARNES

David BRIN

John BRUNNER

William GIBSON

Kim Stanley ROBINSON

Neal STEPHENSON

John VARLEY

Anne STEVENSON US
Romance

Dorothy EDEN

Helen MACINNES

Mary STEWART

Phyllis A. WHITNEY

D.E. STEVENSON Sco
Family Stories 1892-1973

Lucilla ANDREWS

Iris BROMIGE

Elizabeth CADELL

Monica DICKENS

Jane DUNCAN

Mary MELWOOD

Miss READ

Essie SUMMERS

Elswyth THANE

Angela THIRKELL

Mary STEWART 1916-
General
  Madeleine BRENT
  Daphne DU MAURIER
  Dorothy EDEN
  M.M. KAYE
  Caroline LLEWELLYN
  Helen MACINNES
  Barbara MICHAELS
  Sharon PENMAN
  Elizabeth PETERS
  Anne STEVENSON

Caroline STICKLAND
Family Stories
  Harriet HUDSON
  Malcolm MACDONALD
  Patricia WENDORF
  T.R. WILSON

Emma STIRLING Sco
Historical
  Emma BLAIR
  Doris DAVIDSON
  Evelyn HOOD
  Agnes SHORT

Jessica STIRLING
Family Stories
  Emma BLAIR
  Doris DAVIDSON
  Margaret Thomson DAVIS
  Christine Marion FRASER
  Malcolm MACDONALD
  Mary MINTON
  Connie MONK
  Catrin MORGAN
  Maisie MOSCO
  Reay TANNAHILL
  E.V. THOMPSON
  Jan WEBSTER

David STOREY 1933-
General
  Stan BARSTOW
  James KELMAN
  D.H. LAWRENCE
  Stanley MIDDLETON
  Alan SILLITOE

Rex STOUT US 1886-1975
Crime
  John Dickson CARR
  Raymond CHANDLER
  James Hadley CHASE
  Erle Stanley GARDNER
  Dorothy L. SAYERS

Peter STRAUB US 1943-
Supernatural
  Jonathan AYCLIFFE
  John FARRIS
  James HERBERT
  Dean R. KOONTZ
  Richard LAYMON

Whitley STRIEBER
Supernatural
  Ramsey CAMPBELL
  John FARRIS
  Shaun HUTSON
  Dean R. KOONTZ
  Graham MASTERTON

Terence STRONG
War
  Peter ABRAHAMS
  W.E.B. GRIFFIN
  Graham HURLEY
  Gavin LYALL
  L.K. TRUSCOTT

Vivian STUART 1914-86
Historical
  David DONACHIE
  Malcolm MACDONALD
  Colleen McCULLOUGH
  Patricia SHAW

E.V. THOMPSON
Leon URIS

Jean STUBBS 1926-
General
  Donna BAKER
  Elizabeth BYRD
  Winston GRAHAM
  Isabelle HOLLAND
  Susan HOWATCH
  Diane PEARSON
  Jean PLAIDY
  Anya SETON
  Reay TANNAHILL
  E.V. THOMPSON
  Jan WEBSTER

Showell STYLES 1908-
Sea
  C.S. FORESTER
  Patrick O'BRIAN
  Dudley POPE
  Richard WOODMAN

William STYRON US 1925-
General
  Saul BELLOW
  Don DELILLO
  William FAULKNER
  Richard FORD

William STYRON (cont.)

Ernest HEMINGWAY

Norman MAILER

John STEINBECK

Alice WALKER

Sue SULLY
Family Stories

Donna BAKER

Rosemary ENRIGHT

Audrey HOWARD

Mary MACKIE

Rosamunde PILCHER

Malcolm ROSS

Susan SALLIS

Essie SUMMERS   NZ   1912-
Family Stories

Iris BROMIGE

Elizabeth CADELL

Dorothy EDEN

Mary MELWOOD

D.E. STEVENSON

Margaret SUNLEY
Family Stories

Donna BAKER

Janet DAILEY

Mary E. PEARCE

Marjorie QUARTON

Kay STEPHENS

Rosemary SUTCLIFF   1920-92
Historical

Gillian BRADSHAW

Morgan LLYWELYN

Allan MASSIE

Naomi MITCHISON

Diana NORMAN

Edith PARGETER

Mary RENAULT

Anya SETON

Titia SUTHERLAND
General

Patricia ANGADI

Margaret BACON

Anita BROOKNER

Marika COBBOLD

Katie FFORDE

Elizabeth PALMER

Rosamunde PILCHER

Alison Scott SKELTON

Audrey SLAUGHTER

Joanna TROLLOPE

Mary WESLEY

Graham SWIFT 1949-
General

Peter ACKROYD

Paul BAILEY

Julian BARNES

Peter BENSON

John FOWLES

Lesley GLAISTER

Ian McEWAN

Marina WARNER

Gillian WHITE

T.R. WILSON

Julian SYMONS 1912-94
Crime

Agatha CHRISTIE

B.M. GILL

Ray HARRISON

Patricia HIGHSMITH

John Buxton HILTON

Roderic JEFFRIES

Peter LOVESEY

Amy MYERS

Reay TANNAHILL Sco 1929-
Family Stories

Elizabeth BUCHAN

Elizabeth DAISH

Dorothy DUNNETT

Barbara ERSKINE

Margaret ERSKINE

Diana GABALDON

Philippa GREGORY

Susan HOWATCH

Jessica STIRLING

Jean STUBBS

Anne VIVIS

T.R. WILSON

Janet TANNER
Family Stories

Elizabeth ADLER

Aileen ARMITAGE

Noel BARBER

Janice Young BROOKS

Catherine COOKSON

Sara FRASER

Malcolm MACDONALD

Hilda McKENZIE

Deirdre PURCELL

Judith SAXTON

Elizabeth VILLARS

Bernard TAYLOR
Supernatural

Mary Higgins CLARK

James HERBERT

Peter JAMES

Richard LAYMON

Elizabeth TAYLOR   1912-75
General

  Isabel COLEGATE

  Monica DICKENS

  Elizabeth Jane HOWARD

  Rosamond LEHMANN

  Elizabeth PALMER

  Barbara PYM

  Muriel SPARK

Douglas TERMAN US   1933-
Adventure

  Dale BROWN

  Tom CLANCY

  Stephen COONTS

  Richard HERMAN

  David MORRELL

  Julian Jay SAVARIN

  Richard STARK

Emma TENNANT   1937-
General

  Joan AIKEN

  Jane AUSTEN

  A.L. BARKER

  Penelope FITZGERALD

  Iris MURDOCH

  Barbara PYM

  Fay WELDON

Josephine TEY   1897-1952
Crime

  Margery ALLINGHAM

  John Dickson CARR

  Edmund CRISPIN

  Georgette HEYER

  Michael INNES

  Dorothy L. SAYERS

Sheri S. TEPPER US   1929-
Science Fiction

  Marion Zimmer BRADLEY

  Mary GENTLE

  Colin GREENLAND

  Ursula LE GUIN

  Anne McCAFFREY

  Andre NORTON

  Michael Scott ROHAN

  Connie WILLIS

  Janny WURTS

Elswyth THANE US
Romance   1900-deceased

  Iris BROMIGE

  Elizabeth CADELL

  Elizabeth GOUDGE

  D.E. STEVENSON

Paul THEROUX US   1941-
General

  Saul BELLOW

  William BOYD

Anthony BURGESS

Joseph CONRAD

Ernest HEMINGWAY

Brian MOORE

V.S. NAIPAUL

Piers Paul READ

Bernice RUBENS

Colin THUBRON

John UPDIKE

Angela THIRKELL　　1890-1961
General

E.F. BENSON

Vernon COLEMAN

Lettice COOPER

E.M. DELAFIELD

Mary MELWOOD

Miss READ

Kathleen ROWNTREE

D.E. STEVENSON

Craig THOMAS　　1942-
Adventure

Geoffrey ARCHER

Dale BROWN

Harold COYLE

Clive CUSSLER

James FOLLETT

Ken FOLLETT

Jack HIGGINS

Gavin LYALL

Julian RATHBONE

Julian Jay SAVARIN

Gerald SEYMOUR

D.M. THOMAS　　1935-
General

Julian BARNES

John FOWLES

Brian MOORE

Virginia WOOLF

Leslie THOMAS　　1931-
General

John BRAINE

George Macdonald FRASER

Joseph HELLER

David LODGE

David NOBBS

Philip ROTH

Tom SHARPE

Peter TINNISWOOD

Keith WATERHOUSE

Rosie THOMAS　　Wales　　1947-
Family Stories

Sally BRAMPTON

Margaret GRAHAM

Sarah HARRISON

Hilda McKENZIE

Lewis ORDE

Rosie THOMAS (cont.)

Belva PLAIN

Anne Rivers SIDDONS

Diana STAINFORTH

Nicola THORNE

Dee WILLIAMS

Ross THOMAS   US   1926-
Crime

Lawrence BLOCK

James M. CAIN

William DIEHL

Erle Stanley GARDNER

Dashiell HAMMETT

Ross MACDONALD

Leslie WALLER

E.V. THOMPSON   1931-
Historical

Donna BAKER

Pamela BELLE

Alexander CORDELL

R.F. DELDERFIELD

Winston GRAHAM

Cynthia HARROD-EAGLES

Rosalind LAKER

Malcolm MACDONALD

Patricia SHAW

Jessica STIRLING

Vivian STUART

Jean STUBBS

Grace THOMPSON
Family Stories

Catrin COLLIER

Catherine COOKSON

Iris GOWER

Judy TURNER

Jim THOMPSON   US   1906-77
Crime

James M. CAIN

James ELLROY

George V. HIGGINS

Andrew VACHSS

Charles WILLEFORD

June THOMSON   1930-
Crime

Pat BURDEN

W.J. BURLEY

Agatha CHRISTIE

Douglas CLARK

Elizabeth FERRARS

Anthea FRASER

S.T. HAYMON

John Buxton HILTON

Sheila RADLEY

Ruth RENDELL

Jonathan ROSS

Barbara WHITEHEAD

Alexandra THORNE US
Glitz & Glamour
Vanessa FOX
Judith GOULD
Erica JONG
June Flaum SINGER

Kay THORPE
Romance
Charlotte LAMB
Anne MATHER
Judith McNAUGHT
Carole MORTIMER
Jessica STEELE

Nicola THORNE SA
Family Stories
Charlotte Vale ALLEN
Aileen ARMITAGE
Barbara Taylor BRADFORD
Margaret Thomson DAVIS
Cynthia FREEMAN
Evelyn HOOD
Elizabeth MURPHY
Margaret PEMBERTON
Judith SAXTON
Rosie THOMAS
Barbara WHITNELL
T.R. WILSON

Colin THUBRON 1939-
General
Ian McEWAN
Michael ONDAATJE
Paul THEROUX
Jeanette WINTERSON

Patrick TILLEY 1928-
Science Fiction
David A. GEMMELL
Julian MAY
Jack VANCE
David WINGROVE

Margaret THORNTON
Family Stories
Lyn ANDREWS
Ruth HAMILTON
Elizabeth MURPHY
Lynda PAGE
Tony WARREN

Mark TIMLIN
Crime
Simon BRETT
Bill JAMES
Dan KAVANAGH
Michael MOLLOY
Mike RIPLEY

Gillian TINDALL 1938-
General
  Rachel BILLINGTON
  Margaret DRABBLE
  Penelope LIVELY
  Deborah MOGGACH

Peter TINNISWOOD 1936-
Humour
  H.E. BATES
  Guy BELLAMY
  Roy CLARKE
  Ben ELTON
  George Macdonald FRASER
  George GROSSMITH
  Tom HOLT
  David NOBBS
  Tom SHARPE
  Leslie THOMAS
  Keith WATERHOUSE
  P.G. WODEHOUSE

J.R.R. TOLKIEN 1892-1973
Fantasy
  Stephen DONALDSON
  Guy Gavriel KAY
  C.S. LEWIS
  Mervyn PEAKE
  Michael Scott ROHAN
  R.A. SALVATORE

  Margaret WEIS
  Tad WILLIAMS

Peter TONKIN 1950-
Sea
  Alan EVANS
  Duncan HARDING
  A.E. LANGSFORD
  Philip McCUTCHAN
  Douglas SCOTT
  John WINGATE

Eileen TOWNSEND
Family Stories
  Teresa CRANE
  Colleen McCULLOUGH
  Rosamunde PILCHER
  Patricia SHAW
  Judy TURNER

Sue TOWNSEND 1946-
Humour
  Clare BOYLAN
  Roy CLARKE
  Tom HOLT
  Kathy LETTE
  Helen MUIR
  Keith WATERHOUSE
  Nigel WILLIAMS

Nigel TRANTER Sco   1909-
Historical
  D.K. BROSTER
  Philippa CARR
  Bernard CORNWELL
  Dorothy DUNNETT
  Winston GRAHAM
  Neil MUNRO
  Edith PARGETER
  Sharon PENMAN
  Jean PLAIDY
  Stewart ROSS

Barbara TRAPIDO   1941-
General
  Amanda CRAIG
  Alice Thomas ELLIS
  Amanda PRANTERA
  Harold ROBBINS

Peter TREMAYNE
Crime
  Michael CLYNES
  Lindsey DAVIS
  P.C. DOHERTY
  Paul HARDING
  Ellis PETERS

John TRENHAILE   1949-
Adventure
  Jeffrey ARCHER
  Campbell ARMSTRONG
  Nelson DE MILLE
  Daniel EASTERMAN
  Colin FORBES
  Frederick FORSYTH
  Nicholas GUILD
  Stephen LEATHER
  John LE CARRÉ
  Lawrence SANDERS
  Gerald SEYMOUR

Elleston TREVOR   1920-
also writes as Adam HALL
Adventure
  Nicholas GUILD
  Hammond INNES
  J.K. MAYO
  Nevil SHUTE

William TREVOR   1928-
General
  Jane GARDAM
  Graham GREENE
  Roy HATTERSLEY
  Susan HILL
  Jennifer JOHNSTON
  Molly KEANE

William TREVOR (cont.)

  John McGAHERN

  Brian MOORE

  V.S. PRITCHETT

  Muriel SPARK

Antony TREW SA   1906-
Sea

  Brian CALLISON

  Sam LLEWELLYN

  Philip McCUTCHAN

  Douglas REEMAN

  John WINGATE

Joanna TROLLOPE   1943-
General

  Margaret BACON

  Elizabeth BUCHAN

  Marika COBBOLD

  Barbara COMYNS

  E.M. DELAFIELD

  Katie FFORDE

  Angela LAMBERT

  Nora NAISH

  Elizabeth PALMER

  Rosamunde PILCHER

  Titia SUTHERLAND

  Mary WESLEY

  Sarah WOODHOUSE

M.J. TROW
Crime

  W.J. BURLEY

  Ray HARRISON

  Gillian LINSCOTT

  Peter LOVESEY

  Amy MYERS

  Anne PERRY

  Nicholas RHEA

  Kate ROSS

L.K. TRUSCOTT
War

  W.E.B. GRIFFIN

  Graham HURLEY

  Leo KESSLER

  Terence STRONG

Peter TURNBULL   1950-
Crime

  Lesley EGAN

  S.T. HAYMON

  Bill KNOX

  William McILVANNEY

  Frank PALMER

  Sheila RADLEY

  Ian RANKIN

  John WAINWRIGHT

  Janwillem VAN DE WETERING

  R.D. WINGFIELD

Judy TURNER 1936-
also writes as Kate FLYNN & Judith SAXTON
Family Stories

Lewis ORDE

Grace THOMPSON

Eileen TOWNSEND

Barbara VICTOR

Scott TUROW US 1949-
Crime

Alan M. DERSHOWITZ

Dexter DIAS

William DIEHL

Philip FRIEDMAN

John GRISHAM

Phillip M. MARGOLIN

Steve MARTINI

Richard North PATTERSON

Nancy Taylor ROSENBERG

Harry TURTLEDOVE US 1949-
Fantasy

Robert ASPRIN

Tom HOLT

Robert SILVERBERG

Christopher STASHEFF

Roger ZELAZNY

Anne TYLER US 1941-
General

Harry CAULEY

John CHEEVER

Louise ERDRICH

Richard FORD

Jane HAMILTON

Alice HOFFMAN

Alison LURIE

Bobbie Ann MASON

Sue MILLER

Lorrie MOORE

Alice MUNRO

Marge PIERCY

Judith ROSSNER

Carol SHIELDS

Michael UNDERWOOD 1916-
Crime

Gwendoline BUTLER

Gerald HAMMOND

H.R.F. KEATING

Roger ORMEROD

Jonathan ROSS

John WAINWRIGHT

Ted WOOD

Sara WOODS

Barry UNSWORTH 1930-
General
  Peter ACKROYD
  John BANVILLE
  Bruce CHATWIN
  J.M. COETZEE
  John FOWLES
  William GOLDING
  Thomas KENEALLY
  Brian MOORE
  Robert NYE
  Amanda PRANTERA

John UPDIKE US 1932-
General
  Saul BELLOW
  Ethan CANIN
  John CHEEVER
  Don DELILLO
  E.L. DOCTOROW
  Richard FORD
  Joseph HELLER
  John IRVING
  Norman MAILER
  Vladimir NABOKOV
  John STEINBECK
  Paul THEROUX

Leon URIS US 1924-
General
  Howard FAST
  James A. MICHENER

Vivian STUART
Morris WEST

Andrew VACHSS US 1942-
Crime
  James M. CAIN
  Eugene IZZI
  Jim THOMPSON
  Irvine WELSH
  Charles WILLEFORD

Helen VAN SLYKE US 1919-79
Family Stories
  Charlotte Vale ALLEN
  Virginia COFFMAN
  Janet DAILEY
  Cynthia FREEMAN
  Gail GODWIN
  Barbara VICTOR

Jack VANCE US 1916-
Science Fiction
  John BRUNNER
  Frank HERBERT
  Kim Stanley ROBINSON
  Robert SILVERBERG
  Patrick TILLEY
  David WINGROVE

Janwillem VAN DE WETERING
Crime   Neth   1931-

  Lesley EGAN

  Ed McBAIN

  Dell SHANNON

  Peter TURNBULL

  John WAINWRIGHT

John VARLEY US   1947-
Science Fiction

  William GIBSON

  Gwyneth JONES

  Kim Stanley ROBINSON

  Bruce STERLING

Jules VERNE Fr   1828-1905
Science Fiction

  Stephen BAXTER

  Ray BRADBURY

  Robert A. HEINLEIN

  H.G. WELLS

  John WYNDHAM

Barbara VICTOR
Family Stories

  Elizabeth Jane HOWARD

  Ann PURSER

  Denise ROBERTSON

  Anne Rivers SIDDONS

  Judy TURNER

  Helen VAN SLYKE

  Dee WILLIAMS

Gore VIDAL US   1925-
Historical

  Gillian BRADSHAW

  Truman CAPOTE

  John CHEEVER

  Don DELILLO

  Robert GRAVES

  Allan MASSIE

  James A. MICHENER

  Mary RENAULT

  Tom WOLFE

  Herman WOUK

Elizabeth VILLARS
Family Stories

  Elizabeth ADLER

  Barbara Taylor BRADFORD

  Vanessa FOX

  Olivia GOLDSMITH

  Brenda JAGGER

  LaVyrle SPENCER

  Janet TANNER

  Elizabeth WARNE

Penny VINCENZI
Glitz & Glamour

Catherine ALLIOTT

Pat BOOTH

Celia BRAYFIELD

Sandra BROWN

Jackie COLLINS

Shirley CONRAN

Vera COWIE

Shirley ESKAPA

Vanessa FOX

Olivia GOLDSMITH

Judith KRANTZ

Jill MANSELL

Barbara VINE 1930-
also writes as Ruth RENDELL
Crime

Elizabeth GEORGE

Frances HEGARTY

Patricia HIGHSMITH

Susan MOODY

Minette WALTERS

Anne VIVIS Sco
Family Stories

Doris DAVIDSON

Christine Marion FRASER

Reay TANNAHILL

Jan WEBSTER

Dee WILLIAMS

Kurt VONNEGUT US 1922-
Science Fiction

Brian W. ALDISS

J.G. BALLARD

Christopher PRIEST

Roger ZELAZNY

Bill WADE 1928-
Western

Matt CHISHOLM

Louis L'AMOUR

Jack SCHAEFER

John WAINWRIGHT 1921-
Crime

Gerald HAMMOND

Mark HEBDEN

Reginald HILL

Alan HUNTER

Roderic JEFFRIES

H.R.F. KEATING

Bill KNOX

John PENN

Nicholas RHEA

Peter TURNBULL

Michael UNDERWOOD

Janwillem VAN DE WETERING

Eric WRIGHT

Elizabeth WAITE
Family Stories
Harry BOWLING
Barbara Taylor BRADFORD
Janet DAILEY
Pamela EVANS
Helen FORRESTER
Maisie MOSCO
Susan SALLIS
Elizabeth WARNE

Alice WALKER   US   1944-
General
James BALDWIN
Ellen DOUGLAS
Marita GOLDEN
Rosa GUY
Paule MARSHALL
Terry McMILLAN
Toni MORRISON
Gloria NAYLOR
William STYRON

Elizabeth WALKER
Family Stories
Charlotte Vale ALLEN
Aileen ARMITAGE
Barbara Taylor BRADFORD
Maeve HARAN
Sara HYLTON
Penny JORDAN
Kay STEPHENS

Fiona WALKER   1969-
Glitz & Glamour
Jilly COOPER
Lucinda EDMONDS
Rupert LEGGE
Kathy LETTE

Leslie WALLER   US   1923-
Adventure
Richard CONDON
Richard COX
Arthur HAILEY
Ross THOMAS

Robert James WALLER   US
General
Harry CAULEY
Alison LURIE
Anita SHREVE
Jane SMILEY
Larry WATSON

Hugh WALPOLE   1884-1941
General
Melvyn BRAGG
R.F. DELDERFIELD
John GALSWORTHY
J.B. PRIESTLEY

Sheila WALSH 1928-
Romance
- Barbara CARTLAND
- Marion CHESNEY
- Catherine COULTER
- Georgette HEYER
- Patricia ROBINS
- Elizabeth SEIFERT

Minette WALTERS
Crime
- Patricia D. CORNWELL
- Anabel DONALD
- Sarah DUNANT
- Frances FYFIELD
- Patricia HIGHSMITH
- Hazel HOLT
- Ruth RENDELL
- Barbara VINE
- Margaret YORKE

Elizabeth WARNE
Family Stories
- Janet DAILEY
- Pamela EVANS
- Danielle STEEL
- Elizabeth VILLARS
- Elizabeth WAITE

Marina WARNER 1946-
General
- A.S. BYATT
- Angela CARTER
- Lesley GLAISTER
- Candia McWILLIAM
- Amanda PRANTERA
- Jane ROGERS
- Carol SHIELDS
- Graham SWIFT

Tony WARREN
General
- Stan BARSTOW
- Dirk BOGARDE
- John BRAINE
- Michael CARSON
- Stanley MIDDLETON
- Alan SILLITOE
- Margaret THORNTON

Keith WATERHOUSE 1929-
Humour
- Kingsley AMIS
- H.E. BATES
- Malcolm BRADBURY
- Ben ELTON
- George GROSSMITH
- David LODGE
- John MORTIMER
- David NOBBS

Tom SHARPE

Leslie THOMAS

Peter TINNISWOOD

Sue TOWNSEND

Paul WATKINS US 1964-
General

Sebastian FAULKS

Erich Maria REMARQUE

Derek ROBINSON

William WHARTON

Colin WATSON 1920-82
Crime

Michael BOND

Simon BRETT

Edmund CRISPIN

Ruth Dudley EDWARDS

Tim HEALD

Reginald HILL

Joyce PORTER

Ian WATSON 1943-
Science Fiction

J.G. BALLARD

Iain M. BANKS

Philip K. DICK

Gwyneth JONES

Joanna RUSS

Larry WATSON US
General

Pete DEXTER

Louise ERDRICH

David GATES

Jim HARRISON

Harper LEE

Cormac McCARTHY

Robert James WALLER

Evelyn WAUGH 1903-66
General

E.F. BENSON

Ivy COMPTON-BURNETT

Lawrence DURRELL

Aldous HUXLEY

Milan KUNDERA

Paul MICOU

Nancy MITFORD

Anthony POWELL

C.P. SNOW

Hillary WAUGH US 1920-
Crime

K.C. CONSTANTINE

Lesley EGAN

Chester B. HIMES

Dell SHANNON

Anne WEALE
Romance
  Lindsay ARMSTRONG
  Penny JORDAN
  Betty NEELS

Jan WEBSTER   1924-
Family Stories
  Christine Marion FRASER
  Jessica STIRLING
  Jean STUBBS
  Anne VIVIS

Margaret WEIS US   1948-
Fantasy
  Terry BROOKS
  David EDDINGS
  Raymond E. FEIST
  David A. GEMMELL
  Katherine KERR
  Anne McCAFFREY
  Melanie RAWN
  Michael Scott ROHAN
  R.A. SALVATORE
  J.R.R. TOLKIEN

Fay WELDON   1931-
General
  Margaret ATWOOD
  Beryl BAINBRIDGE

  Elizabeth BUCHAN
  Angela CARTER
  Carol CLEWLOW
  Janet FRAME
  Penelope LIVELY
  Edna O'BRIEN
  Wendy PERRIAM
  Emma TENNANT
  Jeanette WINTERSON

H.G. WELLS   1866-1946
Science Fiction
  Stephen BAXTER
  E.M. FORSTER
  Jules VERNE

Irvine WELSH   Sco
General
  Roddy DOYLE
  James KELMAN
  William KENNEDY
  Agnes OWENS
  Andrew VACHSS

Patricia WENDORF
Historical
  Diana GABALDON
  Cynthia HARROD-EAGLES
  Harriet HUDSON
  Claire RAYNER

Caroline STICKLAND

T.R. WILSON

Patricia WENTWORTH
Crime   1878-1961

Catherine AIRD

Margery ALLINGHAM

Agatha CHRISTIE

Georgette HEYER

Michael INNES

Elizabeth LEMARCHAND

Ngaio MARSH

Jennie MELVILLE

Gladys MITCHELL

Gwen MOFFAT

Dorothy L. SAYERS

Sally WENTWORTH
Romance

Penny JORDAN

Charlotte LAMB

Carole MORTIMER

Betty NEELS

Nora ROBERTS

Mary WESLEY   1912-
General

Patricia ANGADI

Judy ASTLEY

Marika COBBOLD

Katie FFORDE

Janice GALLOWAY

Jane GARDAM

Mary HOCKING

Hilary MANTEL

Nora NAISH

Kate SAUNDERS

Alison Scott SKELTON

Titia SUTHERLAND

Joanna TROLLOPE

Morris WEST   Aus   1916-
General

Graham GREENE

Arthur HAILEY

David MALOUF

John MASTERS

W. Somerset MAUGHAM

Nevil SHUTE

Leon URIS

Nigel WEST   1951-
Adventure

Len DEIGHTON

Philip KERR

Tim SEBASTIAN

Gerald SEYMOUR

Rebecca WEST Ire 1892-1983
General

Pat BARKER

Rosamond LEHMANN

Olivia MANNING

Antonia WHITE

Edith WHARTON US 1862-1937
General

Jane AUSTEN

E.M. FORSTER

Henry JAMES

William WHARTON US 1925-
General

Joseph HELLER

Mary McCARTHY

Erich Maria REMARQUE

Paul WATKINS

Dennis WHEATLEY 1897-1977
Supernatural

Jonathan AYCLIFFE

Joe DONNELLY

Graham MASTERTON

Philip RICKMAN

John SAUL

John WHITBOURN
Fantasy

Colin GREENLAND

Keith ROBERTS

Christopher STASHEFF

Connie WILLIS

Antonia WHITE
General

Janet FRAME

Rosamond LEHMANN

Olivia MANNING

Rebecca WEST

Jeanette WINTERSON

Edmund WHITE US 1940-
General

James BALDWIN

Michael CARSON

Patrick GALE

Alan HOLLINGHURST

David LEAVITT

Adam MARS-JONES

Gillian WHITE
General

Patricia ANGADI

Lesley GLAISTER

Deborah MOGGACH

Graham SWIFT

Patrick WHITE   Aus   1912-90
General
  Peter CAREY
  William GOLDING
  Nadine GORDIMER
  Rodney HALL
  Thomas KENEALLY
  V.S. NAIPAUL
  Christina STEAD
  Tim WINTON

Barbara WHITEHEAD
Crime
  Marian BABSON
  Kate CHARLES
  Elizabeth FERRARS
  D.M. GREENWOOD
  Dorothy SIMPSON
  June THOMSON

Charles WHITING   1926-
also writes as Duncan HARDING & Leo KESSLER
War
  Brian CALLISON
  Catherine GAVIN
  John HARRIS
  Robert JACKSON
  Geoffrey JENKINS
  Douglas REEMAN
  John WINTON

Jeanne WHITMEE
Family Stories
  Pamela EVANS
  Suzanne GOODWIN
  Claire LORRIMER
  Gilda O'NEILL
  Pamela OLDFIELD
  Pamela POPE
  Phyllis A. WHITNEY

Barbara WHITNELL
Family Stories
  Elizabeth DAISH
  Dorothy EDEN
  Iris GOWER
  Sarah HARRISON
  Elizabeth Jane HOWARD
  Claire LORRIMER
  Pamela POPE
  Cynthia S. ROBERTS
  Sarah SHEARS
  Nicola THORNE
  Dee WILLIAMS

Phyllis A. WHITNEY   US   1903-
Romance
  Madeleine BRENT
  Virginia COFFMAN
  Ursula CURTISS
  Dorothy EDEN

Phyllis A. WHITNEY (cont.)

Isabelle HOLLAND
Caroline LLEWELLYN
Elizabeth PETERS
Carola SALISBURY
Anne STEVENSON
Jeanne WHITMEE
Daoma WINSTON

Philippa WIAT
Historical

Evelyn ANTHONY
Catherine GAVIN
Pamela HILL
Maureen PETERS
Jean PLAIDY
Judith M. RILEY

Marianne WIGGINS US 1947-
General

Martin AMIS
Margaret ATWOOD
A.S. BYATT
Michael ONDAATJE
Salman RUSHDIE
Carol SHIELDS

Charles WILLEFORD d. 1988
Crime

Lawrence BLOCK
Erle Stanley GARDNER
Carl HIAASEN
George V. HIGGINS
Eugene IZZI
Tom KAKONIS
Elmore LEONARD
John D. MACDONALD
Walter MOSLEY
Jim THOMPSON
Andrew VACHSS

David WILLIAMS 1926-
Crime

Jonathan GASH
Alan HUNTER
Janet LAURENCE
Charlotte MACLEOD
Anne MORICE
Betty ROWLANDS

Dee WILLIAMS
Family Stories

Catherine COOKSON
Peter LING
Brenda McBRYDE
Connie MONK
Gilda O'NEILL

Mary Jane STAPLES

Rosie THOMAS

Barbara VICTOR

Anne VIVIS

Barbara WHITNELL

Anne WORBOYS

Mary WILLIAMS
Romance

Virginia COFFMAN

Barbara MICHAELS

Elizabeth PETERS

Nora ROBERTS

Daoma WINSTON

Nigel WILLIAMS 1948-
Humour

Guy BELLAMY

Mavis CHEEK

Jonathan COE

Colin DOUGLAS

Helen MUIR

David NOBBS

Sue TOWNSEND

Tad WILLIAMS
Fantasy

Marion Zimmer BRADLEY

David EDDINGS

Maggie FUREY

Robert JORDAN

Garry D. KILWORTH

Melanie RAWN

Michael Scott ROHAN

J.R.R. TOLKIEN

Henry WILLIAMSON 1895-1977
General

Richard ADAMS

Heinrich BÖLL

William HORWOOD

A.R. LLOYD

Brian PARVIN

Anthony POWELL

Erich Maria REMARQUE

Howard SPRING

Connie WILLIS US 1945-
Science Fiction

Diana NORMAN

Christopher PRIEST

Keith ROBERTS

Sheri S. TEPPER

John WHITBOURN

Janny WURTS

Tim WILLOCKS
Supernatural

Stephen GALLAGHER

Thomas HARRIS

Dean R. KOONTZ

Richard LAYMON

A.N. WILSON   1950-
General

Kingsley AMIS

Julian BARNES

Malcolm BRADBURY

Roy HATTERSLEY

Bernice RUBENS

Angus WILSON   1913-1991
General

Anthony BURGESS

Robertson DAVIES

Graham GREENE

Iris MURDOCH

J.B. PRIESTLEY

Piers Paul READ

C.P. SNOW

Derek WILSON
Crime

Kate CHARLES

John MALCOLM

Iain PEARS

Ellis PETERS

Candace ROBB

Kate SEDLEY

T.R. WILSON
Family Stories

Tessa BARCLAY

Zoe FAIRBAIRNS

Jonathan GRANT

Malcolm MACDONALD

Caroline STICKLAND

Graham SWIFT

Reay TANNAHILL

Nicola THORNE

Patricia WENDORF

Tim WILSON
Supernatural

Peter JAMES

Stephen LAWS

Mark MORRIS

Philip RICKMAN

David WILTSE
Crime

Mary Higgins CLARK

Thomas H. COOK

Thomas HARRIS

John KATZENBACH

David L. LINDSEY

Ridley PEARSON

Martin RUSSELL

John WINGATE 1920-
Sea
  Brian CALLISON
  Sam LLEWELLYN
  Philip McCUTCHAN
  Dudley POPE
  Douglas REEMAN
  Peter TONKIN
  Antony TREW

R.D. WINGFIELD
Crime
  M.C. BEATON
  Colin DEXTER
  John HARVEY
  Sheila RADLEY
  Ian RANKIN
  Ruth RENDELL
  Peter ROBINSON
  Jonathan ROSS
  Peter TURNBULL

David WINGROVE 1954-
Science Fiction
  Greg BEAR
  Frank HERBERT
  Patrick TILLEY
  Jack VANCE

Daoma WINSTON US 1922-
Romance
  Virginia ANDREWS
  Carol CLEWLOW
  Virginia COFFMAN
  Janet DAILEY
  Barbara MICHAELS
  Phyllis A. WHITNEY
  Mary WILLIAMS

Jeanette WINTERSON 1959-
General
  Angela CARTER
  Carol CLEWLOW
  Michele ROBERTS
  Bernice RUBENS
  Colin THUBRON
  Fay WELDON
  Antonia WHITE
  Virginia WOOLF

John WINTON
Sea
  C.S. FORESTER
  Max HENNESSY
  Philip McCUTCHAN
  Douglas REEMAN
  Douglas SCOTT
  Charles WHITING

Tim WINTON Aus 1960-
General
  Peter CAREY
  Rodney HALL
  L.P. HARTLEY
  Brian MOORE
  Patrick WHITE

P.G. WODEHOUSE 1881-1975
Humour
  E.F. BENSON
  George GROSSMITH
  Tom HOLT
  David NOBBS
  Peter TINNISWOOD

Gene WOLFE US 1931-
Fantasy
  Orson Scott CARD
  Robert HOLDSTOCK
  Ursula LE GUIN
  Julian MAY
  Michael MOORCOCK
  Mervyn PEAKE

Tom WOLFE US 1930-
General
  Dominick DUNNE
  Norman MAILER
  Jay McINERNEY

  Paul MICOU
  Gore VIDAL

Ted WOOD 1931-
Crime
  W.J. BURLEY
  Laurence GOUGH
  Michael UNDERWOOD
  Eric WRIGHT

Sarah WOODHOUSE
General
  Catherine GAVIN
  Pamela OLDFIELD
  Cynthia S. ROBERTS
  Joanna TROLLOPE

Richard WOODMAN
Sea
  Brian CALLISON
  David DONACHIE
  C.S. FORESTER
  Alexander FULLERTON
  Raymond HARDIE
  Alexander KENT
  Philip McCUTCHAN
  Patrick O'BRIAN
  C. Northcote PARKINSON
  Dudley POPE
  Showell STYLES

Sara WOODS 1922-85
Crime
John Dickson CARR
Anthea FRASER
Anne MORICE
Emma PAGE
Dell SHANNON
Michael UNDERWOOD

Virginia WOOLF 1882-1941
General
Elizabeth BOWEN
Rosamund LEHMANN
Iris MURDOCH
Michele ROBERTS
May SARTON
D.M. THOMAS
Jeanette WINTERSON

Anne WORBOYS NZ
Family Stories
Margaret GRAHAM
Mary MINTON
Mary E. PEARCE
Dee WILLIAMS

Herman WOUK US 1915-
General
Howard FAST
James A. MICHENER
Irwin SHAW
Gore VIDAL

Eric WRIGHT Can 1929-
Crime
Jon CLEARY
Laurence GOUGH
James MELVILLE
John WAINWRIGHT
Ted WOOD

Glover WRIGHT
Adventure
James FOLLETT
Jack HIGGINS
Duncan KYLE
Kenneth ROYCE

T.M. WRIGHT US
Supernatural
Ramsey CAMPBELL
Stephen GALLAGHER
Stephen KING
Richard LAYMON

Janny WURTS US 1953-
Science Fiction
Raymond E. FEIST
Guy Gavriel KAY
Anne McCAFFREY
Andre NORTON
Michael Scott ROHAN
Sheri S. TEPPER
Connie WILLIS

Jonathan WYLIE
Fantasy
Terry BROOKS
David EDDINGS
Katherine KERR
Michael Scott ROHAN

John WYNDHAM 1903-69
Science Fiction
Brian W. ALDISS
James BLISH
Harry HARRISON
Robert A. HEINLEIN
Frank HERBERT
Frederik POHL
Clifford D. SIMAK
Jules VERNE
Roger ZELAZNY

Margaret YORKE 1924-
Crime
Catherine AIRD
Ursula CURTISS
Elizabeth FERRARS
Antonia FRASER
Celia FREMLIN
Ann GRANGER
Gerald HAMMOND
Jessica MANN
Mary McMULLEN
Anne MORICE
Martin RUSSELL
Minette WALTERS

Roger ZELAZNY US 1937-
Science Fiction
Poul ANDERSON
Ray BRADBURY
Jack L. CHALKER
Samuel R. DELANY
Gordon R. DICKSON
Robert SILVERBERG
Harry TURTLEDOVE
Kurt VONNEGUT
John WYNDHAM

THE TEENAGE SUPPLEMENT

In this section we present a cross-section of authors who write for teenagers. They range from the established to new voices, and from the challenging to the light-hearted with suggestions for titles to try - there should be something for everyone.

Trish Botten
West Sussex County Council Library Service

Linda Saunders
Birmingham City Libraries

The Teenage Supplement

Lynne Reid BANKS 1929-
With twenty titles for children and adults her most powerful novels for teenagers are based on her first-hand understanding of the Arab/Israeli conflict.

Melusine 1994
One More River 1973
Broken Bridge 1994

Peter BEERE
Fast-moving fantasy thrillers, a number of which have been written for the popular Point Crime and Point Fantasy series.

Underworld trilogy 1992
Riot 1994
Star Warriors 1994

Liz BERRY
Engrossing novels with a heady mix of romance, mystery and everyday problems.

Mel 1988
The China Garden 1994

Judy BLUME US 1938-
Judy Blume was one of the first to write about the dilemmas of being a teenager and 21 years on her novel *Forever*, an explicit account of a teenager's first sexual relationship, is cult reading.

Deenie 1973
Forever 1975
Tiger Eyes 1984

Melvin BURGESS
Difficult and demanding subjects (from life on the streets to the problems of being deaf in a hearing world) are tackled in a challenging and uncompromising style.

Baby and Fly Pie 1993
Angel for May 1994
Loving April 1995

Caroline COONEY US
Accessible stories which get behind the normal facade of everyday life in America.

I'm not your other half 1987
Face on the Milk Carton 1991
The Stranger 1994

Yvonne COPPARD

Hilarious looks at life from a teenage view-point, parents beware!

Everybody else does it, why can't I? 1992
Not dressed like that, you don't! 1995

Robert CORMIER   US   1925-

His views of injustice and violence, both political and personal, challenge and disturb. Boys, in particular, seem to relate to his hard-hitting style.

I am the Cheese 1977
The Chocolate War 1985
We all Fall Down 1992

Gillian CROSS   1945-

Unique novels which defy categorisation whatever their subject matter, be it the ethics of virtual reality games, terrorism or the nature of fear.

The Dark behind the Curtain 1982
Wolf 1990
New World 1994

Annie DALTON   1948-

Fantasy is convincingly linked with everyday life and intertwines the forces of magic, good and evil, with the psychology of adolescence.

Night Maze 1989
The Alpha Box 1991
Naming the Dark 1992

Paula DANZIGER   US   1944-

Younger teenagers love her amusing but sympathetic novels about the problems and pressures of growing up - very American but very funny.

The Pistachio Prescription 1986
The Divorce Express 1987

Peter DICKINSON   1927-

His novels are always thought provoking, often examining difficult ethical and political issues.

Eva 1988
AK 1990
Shadow of a Hero 1994

Berlie DOHERTY   1943-

Social and personal issues which many teenagers face (teenage pregnancy and a boy's quest to find his real mother) are tackled head on.

Dear Nobody 1991
The Snakestone 1995

The Teenage Supplement

Lois DUNCAN   US   1934-
Fast-moving, chilling tales, which often
play with the supernatural, but are
always filled with suspense.

Stranger with my Face 1981
*I know what you did last
   Summer* 1987
Twisted Window 1995

Alan DURANT   1958-
The grittier aspects of teenage life,
football hooliganism and murder, are
explored.

*Hamlet, Bananas and all that
   Jazz* 1991
Blood 1992
The Good Book 1995

Anne FINE   1947-
One of the sharpest and wittiest
observers of family life with a teenager,
but beneath the surface lies compassion
and understanding.

Madame Doubtfire 1989
Book of the Banshee 1991
Flour Babies 1992

Jamila GAVIN   1941-
Her two teenage novels are multi-
layered sagas that look at the powerful
events surrounding the independence of
India.

Wheel of Surya 1992
Eye of the Horse 1994

Adele GERAS   1944-
Atmospheric novels set in a boarding
school, which capture the mood of
dreamy adolescence between girlhood
and maturity.

The Tower Room 1990
Watching the Roses 1991
Pictures of the Night 1992
(Egerton Hall Trilogy)

Rosa GUY   US   1928-
Powerful stories about the lives of
young black people on the streets of
Harlem.

The Friends 1974
And I heard a bird sing 1994
The Disappearance 1996

Nigel HINTON
Best known for his powerful trilogy
about Buddy, named after the legendary
Buddy Holly, and his dreams of
becoming a rock star.

Buddy 1983
Buddy's Song 1989
Buddy's Blues 1995

S.E. HINTON US 1948-

Classic tales of urban American street life with bikers, drug-pushers, rumbles and switchblades, which have converted many reluctant teenage readers.

That was then, this is now 1971
The Outsiders 1972
Rumble Fish 1977

Lesley HOWARTH

Distinctive tales with characters who have extra powers (even extra-terrestrial), which set them apart from normal, everyday life

The Flower King 1993
Maphead 1994
Weather Eye 1995

Brian JACQUES 1939-

Eight riveting and believable epics about a fantasy world of warrior mice and other animals; teenagers and adults love them.

Redwall 1987 (first in series of Redwall Abbey books)
The Outcast of Redwall 1995 (the latest)

Robin JARVIS 1963-

Superbly crafted fantasies about worlds within worlds, and fighting the forces of darkness, his books are tales of endeavour in the tradition of the old sagas ... and hugely popular.

Dark Portal 1989 (Deptford mice)
Alchymist's Cat 1991 (Deptford histories)
Whitby Witches 1991 (Whitby Series)
The Woven Path 1995 (Wyrd Museum)

Pete JOHNSON

Plots of teenage angst and humour spiced with mystery, but the addictive plots include issues concerning the more serious side of life.

Dead Hour 1993
We the Haunted 1993
Ten Hours to Live 1995

Toeckey JONES SA

The focus is on the apartheid years in South Africa and the young people whose lives and loves were exposed to its evils.

Go well, stay well 1979
Skin Deep 1985
Bokkie 1995

The Teenage Supplement

Victor KELLEHER Aus 1939-
Tales of menacing fantasy which are
guaranteed to stay in the mind for some
time.

Brother Night 1990
Del-Del 1991
Parkland 1994

Garry KILWORTH
Three sisters are kept isolated from the
twentieth century in the manner of the
Brontë sisters - the past and the future
feature in his easy-going but intriguing
novels.

The Drowners 1992
The Electric Kid 1994
The Brontë Girls 1995

Louise LAWRENCE 1943-
Fantasy novels which paint a sometimes
grim and realistic picture of the future
forcing the reader to question the world
they know.

Warriors of Tan 1986
Disinherited 1994
Journey through Landor 1995

Joan LINGARD
Her most famous books are set against
the troubles in Northern Ireland but
many more look at some of the core
issues that affect young people in
Britain today.

Twelfth Day of July 1972
The Guilty Party 1989
Lizzie's Leaving 1995

Michelle MAGORIAN 1947-
Convincing and compelling reads about
the fortitude and optimism of young
people in the war-torn Britain of the
1940s.

Goodnight Mister Tom 1981
A Little Love Story 1993
Cuckoo in the Nest 1995

Margaret MAHY NZ 1936-
A storyteller par excellence - the
hallmark of her novels for teenagers are
mystery, fantasy, hauntings and the
unexpected.

The Tricksters 1986
Memory 1987
The Other Side of Silence 1996

Anthony MASTERS
Well-crafted thrillers, some with a hint
of the supernatural, which make for
exciting and compulsive reading

Raven 1993
Whiteout 1994
Roadkill 2 1995

Pat MOON

Satisfying and absorbing mysteries with
original themes, e.g. time-travel for a
GCSE history student!

Double Image 1993
Spying Game 1993
Nathan's Switch 1995

Linda NEWBERY

The two World Wars have proved
fertile ground for these engrossing novels
about the lives of young people at that
time.

Some Other War 1990
Riddle Me This 1993
The Shouting Wind 1995

Bette PAUL

Thought-provoking stories which feature
the lives of young people affected by
things beyond their control - serious
illness or a jail-bird father.

Becca's Race 1992
Variation on a Dream 1996

Gary PAULSEN   US   1939-

His gripping tales of survival in hostile
environments will satisfy younger
teenagers' thirst for good old-fashioned
adventure and escapism.

Hatchet 1991
The Fourteenth Summer 1992
Hatchet: Winter 1996

Terry PRATCHETT   1948-

He has been quoted as being the most
popular author in the universe, his
anarchic and laugh-a-minute fantasy
books enthral teenagers and adults
alike.

Diggers 1990
Johnny and the Dead 1993
Interesting Times 1994

Philip PULLMAN   1946-

His strong, descriptive and detailed
approach conjures up completely
believable societies and worlds
whatever genre he writes in (fantasy,
historical or thriller), many with
courageous heroines.

The White Mercedes 1991
The Ruby in the Smoke 1994
Northern Lights (his Dark
   Materials Bk 1) 1995

Alick ROWE

His two powerful novels for teenagers study the nature of terror, although one is set during the time of the Great War and the other in a secondary school.

Voices of Danger 1992
The Panic Wall 1994

Ian STRACHAN   1938-

Imagine a love story about a boy who has spent his life in a bubble because he has no immune system. These stories *bring alive* the experiences of young people whose lives are out of the ordinary.

Flawed Glass 1990
Boy in the Bubble 1993
Kidnap 1994

Robert SWINDELLS   1939-

Immensely readable stories which all tackle serious, frightening and sometimes controversial themes such as an "after the bomb" society or life in cardboard city.

Brother in the Land 1984
Stone Cold 1993
The Unbelievers 1995

Mildred D. TAYLOR   US

Best known for her trilogy exploring racial tensions in the deep south of 1940's America, her works are a powerful indictment of America's attitudes to its black citizens.

Roll of thunder, hear my Cry 1977
Let the Circle be Unbroken 1995
Road to Memphis 1990

Sue TOWNSEND   1946-

Adrian Mole has become a super-star teenage fictional character in three very funny and irreverent books.

Growing Pains of Adrian Mole 1985
The Secret Diary of Adrian Mole aged thirteen and three quarters 1989
Adrian Mole: The Wilderness Years 1993

Cynthia VOIGHT

Her strong characters linger in the mind in stories which examine tough topics like racism and abandonment, but overall a sense of hope and determination pervades.

Homecoming 1984
Dicey's Song 1985
Solitary Blue 1986 (The Tillerman Saga)
When She Hollers 1995

Sue WELFORD 1942-

Based firmly in the here and now, the adolescents in her novels discover sometimes difficult and unpalatable truths when secrets from the past impact on their lives.

Ghost in the Mirror 1993
In the Shadow of August 1995
Secret Love 1996

Robert WESTALL 1929-1993

A prolific writer of gripping tales, some based on his childhood memories of Tyneside and the Second World War, and many reflecting his interest in the supernatural.

Machine Gunners 1975
The Scarecrows 1984
Falling into Glory 1993

Chris WESTOOD 1959-

Gripping thrillers with sinister undertones which linger in the mind.

Personal Effects 1991
Becoming Julia 1996

Paul ZINDEL US

Quirky tales about American teenage life. Some may seem dated now but they still get a lot of reads.

The Pigman 1992
My Darling, My Hamburger 1992
I never loved your mind 1994

AUTHORS LISTED BY GENRE

It is almost impossible to identify accurately individual authors with one particular section of genre fiction; often there is no 'cut off' point between, for instance, **War** and **Adventure;** between **Fantasy, Science Fiction** and the **Supernatural;** or between **Romance, Historical** and **Family Stories**. So, although in the main sequence this Guide indicates under the names of each author the genre in which they *usually* write and these names are repeated again in the lists that follow, it is suggested that readers also refer to linking genres and in particular to the list of **General** novelists to discover new names that could become firm favourites. In the last edition of the Guide only a broad statement of each genre was used but in this edition some categories - **Adventure, Crime, Fantasy** and **Science Fiction** - have been sub-divided to help readers find novelists they will enjoy.

Do remember that some authors use a different name when they write in another genre and others will produce an occasional book quite different in character to their usual style. Always look at the book jacket and the introduction before you borrow or purchase.

Adventure

Stories with fast moving plots, exotic settings and usually with larger-than-life main characters and the action full of thrilling and daring feats. Many of these authors have specialised in **Spy Stories** often set in the period of the cold war. This sub-genre also can have a political, financial or industrial espionage background. For easier selection the word *spy* **indicates this type of author.**

Ted ALLBEURY *spy*

Eric AMBLER *spy*

Evelyn ANTHONY

Geoffrey ARCHER

Campbell ARMSTRONG *spy*

Desmond BAGLEY

Larry BOND

Martin BOOTH

David BRIERLEY

Dale BROWN

George BROWN

John BUCHAN *spy*

Victor CANNING *spy*

Tom CLANCY *spy*

James CLAVELL

Jon CLEARY

Richard CONDON *spy*

Stephen COONTS

Bernard CORNWELL

Bryce COURTENAY

Richard COX

Harold COYLE

Clive CUSSLER

Lionel DAVIDSON

Nelson DE MILLE

Len DEIGHTON *spy*

Peter DRISCOLL *spy*

Daniel EASTERMAN *spy*

Clive EGLETON *spy*

Gavin ESLER

Alan EVANS

Colin FALCONER

Ian FLEMING *spy*

James FOLLETT *spy*

Ken FOLLETT *spy*

Bryan FORBES

Colin FORBES

Frederick FORSYTH *spy*

Clare FRANCIS

Brian FREEMANTLE *spy*

Alexander FULLERTON

Alan FURST

John GARDNER *spy*

Jack GERSON

Robert GODDARD

Anthony GREY

Nicholas GUILD

William HAGGARD *spy*

Arthur HAILEY

Adam HALL

Palma HARCOURT *spy*

John HARRIS

Robert HARRIS

Michael HARTLAND *spy*

Richard HERMAN

Jack HIGGINS

Geoffrey HOUSEHOLD

Graham HURLEY

Christopher HYDE

Hammond INNES

Geoffrey JENKINS

Gary JENNINGS

John KATZENBACH

Philip KERR

Duncan KYLE *spy*

Derek LAMBERT *spy*

John LE CARRÉ *spy*
James LEASOR *spy*
Stephen LEATHER
Robert LITTELL *spy*
Robert LUDLUM *spy*
Eric LUSTBADER
Gavin LYALL *spy*
Amin MAALOUF
Andrew MACALLAN
David MACE *spy*
Helen MACINNES *spy*
Alistair MACLEAN
David MASON
J.K. MAYO
David MORRELL
Christopher NICOLE *spy*
Marc OLDEN
Anthony PRICE *spy*
Julian RATHBONE
Kenneth ROYCE *spy*

Lawrence SANDERS
Alan SAVAGE
Julian Jay SAVARIN
Tim SEBASTIAN *spy*
Owen SELA
Gerald SEYMOUR *spy*
Sidney SHELDON
Christopher SHERLOCK
Nevil SHUTE
Don SILVERMAN
Wilbur SMITH
Richard STARK
Douglas TERMAN
Craig THOMAS
John TRENHAILE *spy*
Elleston TREVOR *spy*
Leslie WALLER
Nigel WEST
Glover WRIGHT

Crime

This type of novel is usually characterised by the clues which gradually lead the reader to the final solution often within an atmosphere of rising tension or danger. Although there are basically two types of detective, the private investigator and the official policeman, there are an increasing number of sub-genres within these two broad headings. In this edition of the book the style of crime writing has been divided into separate headings and under each is shown the list of authors who **usually but not always** write in that vein. A second index lists writers alphabetically with the sub-genre. A third index is arranged by the name of the principal character or environment.

Golden Age
The masters of the genre whose works are still widely available and read

Margery ALLINGHAM	*Albert Campion*
John Dickson CARR	*Gideon Fell*
Agatha CHRISTIE	*Miss Marple; Hercule Poirot*
Edmund CRISPIN	*Gervaise Fen*
Georgette HEYER	*Supt. Hannasyde & Insp. Hemingway*
Michael INNES	*John Appleby*
Ngaio MARSH	*Insp. Roderick Alleyn*
Gladys MITCHELL	*Dame Beatrice Lestrange Bradley*
Dorothy L. SAYERS	*Lord Peter Wimsey*
Rex STOUT	*Nero Wolfe; Archie Goodwin*
Patricia WENTWORTH	*Miss Silver*

Traditional 'Who Dunnits'

Pat BURDEN	
John Newton CHANCE	
Elizabeth FERRARS	*Toby Dyke & Virginia Freer*
Jill McGOWN	*Ch. Insp. Lloyd & Insp. Judy Hill*
Patricia MOYES	*Henry & Emmy Tibbett*
John PENN	*DCI Dick Tansey*
C.F. ROE	*Jean Montrose*
Julian SYMONS	*Insp. Bland*
Barbara WHITEHEAD	*York Cycle of Mysteries*
Sara WOODS	*Anthony Maitland*

Private Eye (P.I.)

Linda BARNES	*Carlotta Carlyle*
Nicholas BLAKE	*Nigel Strangeways*

Edna BUCHANAN	*Britt Montero*
James Lee BURKE	*Dave Robicheaux: US*
Raymond CHANDLER	*Philip Marlowe: US*
Liza CODY	*Anna Lee*
Natasha COOPER	*Willow King*
Patricia D. CORNWELL	*Dr. Kay Scarpetta: US*
Sarah DUNANT	*Hannah Wolfe*
Martin EDWARDS	*Harry Devlin*
James ELLROY	*Fritz Brown: US*
Loren D. ESTLEMAN	*Amos Walker: US*
Janet EVANOVICH	*Stephanie Plum: US*
Sue GRAFTON	*Kinsey Millhouse*
Christine GREEN	*Nurse Kate Kinsella*
James HALL	*Thorn:US*
Dashiell HAMMETT	*Sam Spade: US*
Hazel HOLT	*Sheila Malory*
P.D. JAMES	*Cordelia Gray*
Dan KAVANAGH	*Nick Duffy*
Karen KIJEWSKI	*Kat Colorado: US*
John D. MACDONALD	*Travis McGee*
Ross MACDONALD	*Lew Archer: US*
Charlotte MACLEOD	*Sarah Kelling*
John MALCOLM	*Tim Simpson*
Jessica MANN	*Tamara Hoyland*
Val McDERMID	*Kate Brannigan; Lindsey Gordon*
Gregory McDONALD	*I.M. Fletcher*
Susan MOODY	*Penny Wanawake*
Walter MOSLEY	*Easy Rawlins:US*
Marcia MULLER	*Sharon McCone: US*
Roger ORMEROD	*Philipa Lowe*
Sara PARETSKY	*V.I. Warshawski: US*
Robert B. PARKER	*Spenser: US*
Walter SATTERTHWAIT	*Joshua Croft: US*
Joan SMITH	*Loretta Lawson*
Veronica STALLWOOD	*Kate Ivory*
Neville STEED	*Peter Marklin*
Ross THOMAS	*Philip St. Ives*
Mark TIMLIN	*Nick Sharman*
Peter TREMAYNE	*Sir Keith Chase*
David WILLIAMS	*Mark Treasure*
R.D. WINGFIELD	*DI Jack Frost*

Police Procedural - British

Catherine AIRD	*Insp. Sloan*
M.C. BEATON	*DI Hamish MacBeth*
W.J. BURLEY	*Insp. Wycliffe*
Gwendoline BUTLER	*Insp. Coffin*
Douglas CLARK	*DCS George Masters*
Ann CLEEVES	*Insp. Ramsay*
Barry CORK	*Angus Straum*
John CREASEY	*Insp. West*
Colin DEXTER	*Insp. Morse*
Elizabeth GEORGE	*Insp. Lynley & Sgt. Havers*
Ann GRANGER	*Ch. Insp. Alan Markey & Meredith Mitchell*
Martha GRIMES	*Ch. Insp. Jury*
John HARVEY	*Charlie Resnick*
S.T. HAYMON	*DI Ben Jurnet*
Reginald HILL	*DI Dalziel & DS Pascoe*
Alan HUNTER	*DI Gently*
Bill JAMES	*Asst. Ch. Const. Desmond Iles & Ch. Supt. Colin Harpur*
P.D. JAMES	*Insp. Dalgleish*
Susan KELLY	*Insp. Nick Trevellyan & Alison Hope*
Bill KNOX	*Ch. Insp. Colin Thane & Insp. Phil Moss*
Elizabeth LEMARCHAND	*Insp. Pollard*
David L. LINDSEY	*Marcus Graver*
William McILVANNEY	*Laidlaw*
Jennie MELVILLE	*DI Charmian Daniels*
Janet NEEL	*Det. Supt. John McLeish & Francesca Wilson*
Emma PAGE	*Insp. Kelsey*
Frank PALMER	*DI Jim Jackson*
Sheila RADLEY	*DCI Quantrill*
Ian RANKIN	*Insp. John Rebus*
Ruth RENDELL	*Insp. Wexford*
Peter ROBINSON	*Insp. Alan Banks*
Jonathan ROSS	*DS Rogers*
John SANDFORD	*Lucas Davenport: US*
Dorothy SIMPSON	*DI Luke Thanet*
STAYNES & STOREY	*Supt. Bone*
June THOMSON	*Insp. Jack Finch*
M.J. TROW	*Insp. Sholto Lestrade*
Peter TURNBULL	*Glasgow Police Force*
John WAINWRIGHT	*Det. Supt. Lewis, Div. Supt. Collins & Supt. Ripley*

Police Procedural - American

Andrew COBURN	*James Morgan - Ch of Police*
K.C. CONSTANTINE	*Mario Balzic*
Lesley EGAN	*Glendale Police Dept*
Chester B. HIMES	*Coffin Ed Johnson & Gravedigger Jones*
Faye KELLERMAN	*Pete Decker & Rina Lazarus*
Jonathan KELLERMAN	*Det. Milo Sturgis*
Ed McBAIN	*Steve Carella*
Dell SHANNON	*Lt. Luis Mendoza*
Hillary WAUGH	*Chief Fred Fellows & Det. Frank Sessions*

Police Procedural - Other Countries

Michael DIBDIN	*Aurelio Zen: Italy*
Nicolas FREELING	*Van der Valk: Netherlands*
Juliet HEBDEN	*Pel: France*
Mark HEBDEN	*Pel: France*
Tony HILLERMAN	*Leaphorn: Navajo*
Roderic JEFFRIES	*Insp. Alvarez: Majorca*
H.R.F. KEATING	*Ganesh Ghote: India*
Donna LEON	*Comm. Guido Brunetti: Venice*
James McCLURE	*Kramer & Zondi: SA*
James MELVILLE	*Comm. Otani: Japan*
Magdalen NABB	*Marshall Guernaccia: Italy*
Georges SIMENON	*Maigret: France*
Janwillem VAN DE WETERING	*Henk Grijpstra: Netherlands*
Ted WOOD	*Reid Bennett & Sam: Canada*
Eric WRIGHT	*Insp. Salter: Canada*

Mysteries with a Specific Occupation or Background

Lawrence BLOCK	*Bernie Rhodenbarr: burglar*
Michael BOND	*Pamplemousse: restaurant critic*
Lilian Jackson BRAUN	*Quilleran: journalist*
Simon BRETT	*Charles Paris: actor*
Kate CHARLES	*David Middleton Brown: ecclesiastical*
Amanda CROSS	*Kate Fansler: academic*
Mark DANIEL	*Horse racing*
Jane DENTINGER	*Jocelyn O'Roarke: theatre*
Dick FRANCIS	*Horse racing*
John FRANCOME	*Horse racing*
Antonia FRASER	*Jemima Shore: TV journalist*
Frances FYFIELD	*Geoffrey Bailey; Helen West: CPS*

Mysteries with a Specific Occupation or Background (cont.)

Erle Stanley GARDNER	*Perry Mason: US lawyer*
Jonathan GASH	*Lovejoy: antique dealer*
Laurence GOUGH	*Canadian police*
Caroline GRAHAM	*English villages: Insp. Tom Barnaby*
Lesley GRANT-ADAMSON	*Rain Morgan: journalist*
D.M. GREENWOOD	*Theodora Braithwaite: ecclesiastical*
Gerald HAMMOND	*Guns and shooting*
Sara LACEY	*Leah Hunter: tax inspector*
Emma LATHEN	*John P. Thatcher: banking*
Janet LAURENCE	*Darina Lisle: cookery*
Charlotte MACLEOD	*Shandy: academic*
Gwen MOFFAT	*Miss Pink: mountaineering*
Anne MORICE	*Tessa Crichton: actress*
Paul MYERS	*Mark Holland: musical world*
Iain PEARS	*Art historical: Jonathan Argyll*
Mike RIPLEY	*Fitzroy Maclean Angel: taxi owner*
Betty ROWLANDS	*Cotswolds: Melissa Craig: writer*
John SHERWOOD	*Celia Grant: gardening*
Derek WILSON	*Art world*

Mysteries with an Historical Slant

Gwendoline BUTLER	*Gothic*
Michael CLYNES	*Sir Roger Shallot: 16th cent.*
Lindsey DAVIS	*Falco: Rome & Roman Britain*
P.C. DOHERTY	*Hugh Corbett: mediaeval*
Elizabeth EYRE	*Sigismondo: renaissance Italy*
Paul HARDING	*Brother Athelstan: mediaeval*
Ray HARRISON	*Victorian police*
John Buxton HILTON	*Insp. Brunt: Derbyshire*
Alanna KNIGHT	*Insp. Faro: Victorian Scotland*
Gillian LINSCOTT	*Nell Bray: Edwardian suffragette*
Peter LOVESEY	*Insp. Dew: Victorian Britain*
Jenny MELVILLE	*Gothic*
Amy MYERS	*Victorian*
Michael PEARCE	*Mamur Zapt: Edwardian Egypt*
Anne PERRY	*Insp. Pitts: Victorian*
Ellis PETERS	*Brother Cadfael: mediaeval*
Candace ROBB	*Owen Archer: mediaeval*
Kate ROSS	*Julian Kestral; gentleman: Victorian*
Kate SEDLEY	*Roger the Chapman: mediaeval*

| Josephine TEY | *Insp. Grant: mediaeval* |
| Peter TREMAYNE | *Sister Fidelma: mediaeval* |

Humorous Mysteries

Marian BABSON	*Evangeline & Trixie*
Sarah CAUDWELL	*Prof. Hilary Tamar*
Ruth Dudley EDWARDS	*Robert Amis*
Tim HEALD	*Simon Bognor*
Frank PARRISH	*Dan Mallett*
Joyce PORTER	*Ch. Insp. Wilfred Dover*
Simon SHAW	*Philip Fletcher: actor*
Colin WATSON	*Insp. Purbright*

Modern Mysteries

Fast moving mystery thrillers reflecting the contemporary scene and language. Often harshly realistic and disturbing.

Robert CAMPBELL	
Thomas H. COOK	
Eileen DEWHURST	
Peter DICKINSON	
Anabel DONALD	
Joy FIELDING	
Anthea FRASER	
Celia FREMLIN	
B.M. GILL	
Thomas HARRIS	
Frances HEGARTY	
George V. HIGGINS	
Patricia HIGHSMITH	
Elmore LEONARD	
Martin RUSSELL	
Andrew VACHSS	
Barbara VINE	
Minette WALTERS	
David WILTSE	*John Becker: US*
Margaret YORKE	

Legal Thrillers (Courtroom dramas)

William J. COUGHLIN	*US*
Alan M. DERSHOWITZ	*US*
Dexter DIAS	

Legal Thrillers *(Courtroom dramas) (cont.)*

Philip FRIEDMAN	*US*
John GRISHAM	*US*
Steve MARTINI	*US*
Richard North PATTERSON	*US*
Nancy Taylor ROSENBERG	*US*
Scott TUROW	*US*
Michael UNDERWOOD	*Rosa Epton*

Unclassified

Robert BARNARD
William BAYER
James M. CAIN
James Hadley CHASE
Anthea COHEN
William DIEHL
Arthur DOUGLAS
Roy HART
Eugene IZZI
Tom KAKONIS
William KIENZLE
Phillip M. MARGOLIN
Mary McMULLEN
T. Jefferson PARKER
James PATTINSON
Ridley PEARSON
Richard PITMAN
Ann QUINTON
Nicholas RHEA
Annette ROOME
Richard RUSSELL
Jim THOMPSON
Charles WILLEFORD

Crime - alphabetical with sub-genre

Catherine AIRD *Police - Br.*
Margery ALLINGHAM *Golden*
Marian BABSON *Humour*
Robert BARNARD *Modern*
Linda BARNES *Pr. Eye*
William BAYER
M.C. BEATON *Police - Br.*
Nicholas BLAKE *Pr. Eye*
Lawrence BLOCK *Specialist*
Michael BOND *Specialist*
Lilian Jackson BRAUN *Specialist*
Simon BRETT *Specialist*
Edna BUCHANAN *Pr. Eye*
Pat BURDEN
James Lee BURKE *Pr. Eye*
W.J. BURLEY *Police - Br.*
Gwendoline BUTLER *Hist.*
James M. CAIN
Robert CAMPBELL *Modern*
John Dickson CARR *Golden*
Sarah CAUDWELL *Humour*
John Newton CHANCE *Trad'l*
Raymond CHANDLER *Pr. Eye*
Kate CHARLES *Specialist*
James Hadley CHASE
Agatha CHRISTIE *Golden*
Douglas CLARK *Police - Br.*
Ann CLEEVES *Police - Br.*
Michael CLYNES *Hist.*
Andrew COBURN *Police - Am.*
Liza CODY *Pr. Eye*
Anthea COHEN
K.C. CONSTANTINE *Police - Am.*
Thomas H. COOK *Modern*
Natasha COOPER *Pr. Eye*
Barry CORK *Police - Br.*
Patricia D. CORNWELL *Pr. Eye*
William J. COUGHLIN *Legal*
John CREASEY *Police - Br.*
Edmund CRISPIN *Golden*

Amanda CROSS *Specialist*
Mark DANIEL *Specialist*
Lindsey DAVIS *Hist.*
Jane DENTINGER *Specialist*
Alan M. DERSHOWITZ *Legal*
Eileen DEWHURST *Modern*
Colin DEXTER *Police - Br.*
Dexter DIAS *Legal*
Michael DIBDIN *Police - world*
Peter DICKINSON *Modern*
William DIEHL
P.C. DOHERTY *Hist.*
Anabel DONALD *Modern*
Arthur DOUGLAS
Sarah DUNANT *Pr. Eye*
Martin EDWARDS *Pr. Eye*
Ruth Dudley EDWARDS
Lesley EGAN *Police - Am.*
James ELLROY *Pr. Eye*
Loren D. ESTLEMAN *Pr. Eye*
Janet EVANOVICH *Pr. Eye*
Elizabeth EYRE *Hist.*
Elizabeth FERRARS *Trad'l*
Joy FIELDING *Modern*
Dick FRANCIS *Specialist*
John FRANCOME *Specialist*
Anthea FRASER *Modern*
Antonia FRASER *Specialist*
Nicolas FREELING *Police - world*
Celia FREMLIN *Modern*
Philip FRIEDMAN *Legal*
Frances FYFIELD *Specialist*
Erle Stanley GARDNER *Specialist*
Jonathan GASH *Specialist*
Elizabeth GEORGE *Police - Br.*
B.M. GILL *Modern*
Laurence GOUGH *Specialist*
Sue GRAFTON *Pr. Eye*
Caroline GRAHAM *Specialist*
Ann GRANGER *Police - Br.*

Crime - alphabetical with sub-genre (cont.)

Lesley GRANT-ADAMSON *Specialist*

Christine GREEN   *Pr. Eye*

D.M. GREENWOOD   *Specialist*

Martha GRIMES   *Police - Br.*

John GRISHAM   *Legal*

James HALL   *Pr. Eye*

Dashiell HAMMETT   *Pr. Eye*

Gerald HAMMOND   *Specialist*

Paul HARDING   *Hist.*

Thomas HARRIS   *Modern*

Ray HARRISON   *Hist.*

Roy HART

John HARVEY   *Police - Br.*

S.T. HAYMON   *Police - Br.*

Tim HEALD   *Humour*

Juliet HEBDEN   *Police - world*

Mark HEBDEN   *Police - world*

Frances HEGARTY   *Modern*

Georgette HEYER   *Golden*

Carl HIAASEN

George V. HIGGINS   *Modern*

Patricia HIGHSMITH   *Modern*

Reginald HILL   *Police - Br.*

Tony HILLERMAN   *Police - world*

John Buxton HILTON   *Hist.*

Chester B. HIMES   *Police - Am.*

Hazel HOLT   *Pr. Eye*

Alan HUNTER   *Police - Br.*

Michael INNES   *Golden*

Eugene IZZI

Bill JAMES   *Police - Br.*

P.D. JAMES   *Pr. Eye; Police - Br.*

Roderic JEFFRIES   *Police - world*

Tom KAKONIS

Dan KAVANAGH   *Pr. Eye*

H.R.F. KEATING   *Police - world*

Faye KELLERMAN   *Police - Br.*

Jonathan KELLERMAN   *Police - Am.*

Susan KELLY   *Police - Br.*

William KIENZLE

Karen KIJEWSKI   *Pr. Eye*

Alanna KNIGHT   *Hist.*

Bill KNOX   *Police - Br.*

Sara LACEY   *Specialist*

Emma LATHEN   *Specialist*

Janet LAURENCE   *Specialist*

Elizabeth LEMARCHAND   *Police - Br.*

Donna LEON   *Police - world*

Elmore LEONARD   *Modern*

David L. LINDSEY   *Police - Br.*

Gillian LINSCOTT   *Hist.*

Peter LOVESEY   *Hist.*

John D. MACDONALD   *Pr. Eye*

Ross MACDONALD   *Pr. Eye*

Charlotte MACLEOD   *Pr. Eye & Specialist*

John MALCOLM   *Pr. Eye*

Jessica MANN   *Pr. Eye*

Phillip M. MARGOLIN

Ngaio MARSH   *Golden*

Steve MARTINI   *Legal*

Ed McBAIN   *Police - Am.*

James McCLURE   *Police - world*

Val McDERMID   *Pr. Eye*

Gregory McDONALD   *Pr. Eye*

Jill McGOWN   *Trad'l*

William McILVANNEY   *Police - Br.*

Mary McMULLEN

James MELVILLE   *Police - world*

Jennie MELVILLE   *Police - Br.*

Gladys MITCHELL   *Golden*

Gwen MOFFAT   *Specialist*

Susan MOODY   *Pr. Eye*

Anne MORICE   *Specialist*

Walter MOSLEY   *Pr. Eye*

Patricia MOYES   *Trad'l*

Marcia MULLER   *Pr. Eye*

Amy MYERS   *Hist.*

Paul MYERS   *Specialist*

Magdalen NABB   *Police - world*

Janet NEEL   *Police - Br.*
Roger ORMEROD   *Pr. Eye*
Emma PAGE   *Police - Br.*
Frank PALMER   *Police - Br.*
Sara PARETSKY   *Pr. Eye*
Robert B. PARKER   *Pr. Eye*
T. Jefferson PARKER
Frank PARRISH   *Humour*
Richard North PATTERSON   *Legal*
James PATTINSON
Michael PEARCE   *Hist.*
Iain PEARS   *Specialist*
Ridley PEARSON
John PENN   *Trad'l*
Anne PERRY   *Hist.*
Ellis PETERS   *Hist.*
Richard PITMAN
Joyce PORTER   *Humour*
Ann QUINTON
Sheila RADLEY   *Police - Br.*
Ian RANKIN   *Police - Br.*
Ruth RENDELL   *Police - Br.*
Nicholas RHEA
Mike RIPLEY   *Specialist*
Candace ROBB   *Hist.*
Peter ROBINSON   *Police - Br.*
C.F. ROE   *Trad'l*
Annette ROOME
Nancy Taylor ROSENBERG   *Legal*
Jonathan ROSS   *Police - Br.*
Kate ROSS   *Hist.*
Betty ROWLANDS   *Specialist*
Martin RUSSELL   *Modern*
Richard RUSSELL
John SANDFORD   *Police - Br.*
Walter SATTERTHWAIT   *Pr. Eye*
Dorothy L. SAYERS   *Golden*
Kate SEDLEY   *Hist.*
Dell SHANNON   *Police - Am.*

Simon SHAW   *Humour*
John SHERWOOD   *Specialist*
Georges SIMENON   *Police - world*
Dorothy SIMPSON   *Police - Br.*
Joan SMITH   *Pr. Eye*
Veronica STALLWOOD   *Pr. Eye*
Neville STEED   *Pr. Eye*
STAYNES & STOREY   *Police - Br.*
Rex STOUT   *Golden*
Julian SYMONS   *Trad'l*
Josephine TEY   *Hist.*
Ross THOMAS   *Pr. Eye*
Jim THOMPSON
June THOMSON   *Police - Br.*
Mark TIMLIN   *Pr. Eye*
Peter TREMAYNE   *Pr. Eye*
M.J. TROW   *Police - Br.*
Peter TURNBULL   *Police - Br.*
Scott TUROW   *Legal*
Michael UNDERWOOD   *Legal*
Andrew VACHSS   *Modern*
Janwillem VAN DE WETERING
                    Police - world
Barbara VINE   *Modern*
John WAINWRIGHT   *Police - Br.*
Minette WALTERS   *Modern*
Colin WATSON   *Humour*
Hillary WAUGH   *Police - Am.*
Patricia WENTWORTH   *Golden*
Barbara WHITEHEAD   *Trad'l*
Charles WILLEFORD
David WILLIAMS   *Pr. Eye*
Derek WILSON   *Specialist*
David WILTSE   *Modern*
R.D. WINGFIELD   *Pr. Eye*
Ted WOOD   *Police - world*
Sara WOODS   *Trad'l*
Eric WRIGHT   *Police - world*
Margaret YORKE   *Modern*

Character or environment of crime author

16th cent.: Sir Roger Shallot	Michael CLYNES
Academic: Shandy	Charlotte MACLEOD
Actor: Philip Fletcher	Simon SHAW
Actor: Charles Paris	Simon BRETT
Actress: Tessa Crichton	Anne MORICE
Insp. Roderick Alleyn	Ngaio MARSH
Insp. Alvarez: Majorca	Roderic JEFFRIES
Robert Amis	Ruth Dudley EDWARDS
Fitzroy Maclean Angel: taxi owner	Mike RIPLEY
Antique dealer: Lovejoy	Jonathan GASH
John Appleby	Michael INNES
Owen Archer: mediaeval	Candace ROBB
Lew Archer: US	Ross MACDONALD
Jonathan Argyll	Iain PEARS
Art historical	Iain PEARS
Art world	Derek WILSON
Brother Athelstan: mediaeval	Paul HARDING
Geoffrey Bailey	Frances FYFIELD
Mario Balzic: US	K.C. CONSTANTINE
Banking: John P. Thatcher	Emma LATHEN
Insp. Alan Banks	Peter ROBINSON
Insp. Tom Barnaby	Caroline GRAHAM
John Becker: US	David WILTSE
Reid Bennett & Sam: Canada	Ted WOOD
Insp. Bland	Julian SYMONS
Simon Bognor	Tim HEALD
Supt. Bone	STAYNES & STOREY
Dame Beatrice Lestrange Bradley	Gladys MITCHELL
Theodora Braithwaite: ecclesiastical	D.M. GREENWOOD
Kate Brannigan	Val McDERMID
Nell Bray: Edwardian suffragette	Gillian LINSCOTT
David Middleton Brown: ecclesiastical	Kate CHARLES
Fritz Brown: US	James ELLROY
Comm. Guido Brunetti: Venice	Donna LEON
Insp. Brunt: Derbyshire	John Buxton HILTON
Burglar: Bernie Rhodenbarr	Lawrence BLOCK
Brother Cadfael: mediaeval	Ellis PETERS
Albert Campion	Margery ALLINGHAM
Canada: Reid Bennett & Sam	Ted WOOD
Canada: Insp. Salter	Eric WRIGHT

Canadian police	Laurence GOUGH
Steve Carella: US	Ed McBAIN
Carlotta Carlyle	Linda BARNES
Sir Keith Chase	Peter TREMAYNE
Insp. Coffin	Gwendoline BUTLER
Div. Supt. Collins, Det. Supt. Lewis & Supt. Ripley	John WAINWRIGHT
Kat Colorado: US	Karen KIJEWSKI
Cookery: Darina Lisle	Janet LAURENCE
Hugh Corbett: mediaeval	P.C. DOHERTY
Cotswolds: Melissa Craig: writer	Betty ROWLANDS
CPS: Helen West	Frances FYFIELD
Melissa Craig: writer: Cotswolds	Betty ROWLANDS
Tessa Crichton: actress	Anne MORICE
Joshua Croft: US	Walter SATTERTHWAIT
Insp. Dalgleish	P.D. JAMES
DI Dalziel & DS Pascoe	Reginald HILL
DI Charmian Daniels	Jennie MELVILLE
Lucas Davenport: US	John SANDFORD
Pete Decker & Rina Lazarus: US	Faye KELLERMAN
Derbyshire: Insp. Brunt	John Buxton HILTON
Harry Devlin	Martin EDWARDS
Insp. Dew: Victorian Britain	Peter LOVESEY
Ch. Insp. Wilfred Dover	Joyce PORTER
Nick Duffy	Dan KAVANAGH
Toby Dyke & Virginia Freer	Elizabeth FERRARS
Ecclesiastical: Theodora Braithwaite	D.M. GREENWOOD
Ecclesiastical: David Middleton Brown	Kate CHARLES
Edwardian Egypt: Mamur Zapt	Michael PEARCE
Edwardian suffragette: Nell Bray	Gillian LINSCOTT
Egypt, Edwardian : Mamur Zapt	Michael PEARCE
English villages	Caroline GRAHAM
Rosa Epton	Michael UNDERWOOD
Evangeline & Trixie	Marion BABSON
Falco: Rome & Roman Britain	Lindsey DAVIS
Kate Fansler: academic	Amanda CROSS
Insp. Faro: Victorian Scotland	Alanna KNIGHT
Gideon Fell	John Dickson CARR
Chief Fred Fellows & Det. Frank Sessions: US	Hillary WAUGH
Gervaise Fen	Edmund CRISPIN
Sister Fidelma: mediaeval	Peter TREMAYNE

Character or environment of crime author *(cont.)*

Insp. Jack Finch	June THOMSON
I.M. Fletcher	Gregory McDONALD
Philip Fletcher: actor	Simon SHAW
France: Maigret	Georges SIMENON
Pel: France	Juliet HEBDEN
Pel: France	Mark HEBDEN
Virginia Freer & Toby Dyke	Elizabeth FERRARS
DI Jack Frost	R.D. WINGFIELD
Gardening: Celia Grant	John SHERWOOD
DI Gently	Alan HUNTER
Ganesh Ghote: India	H.R.F. KEATING
Glasgow Police Force	Peter TURNBULL
Glendale Police Dept: US	Lesley EGAN
Archie Goodwin & Nero Wolfe	Rex STOUT
Lindsey Gordon	Val McDERMID
Celia Grant: gardening	John SHERWOOD
Insp. Grant: mediaeval	Josephine TEY
Marcus Graver	David L. LINDSEY
Cordelia Gray	P.D. JAMES
Henk Grijpstra: Netherlands	Janwillem VAN DE WETERING
Marshall Guernaccia: Italy	Magdalen NABB
Guns and shooting	Gerald HAMMOND
Supt. Hannasyde	Georgette HEYER
Ch. Supt. Colin Harp & Asst. Ch. Const. Desmond Iles	Bill JAMES
Sgt. Havers & Insp. Lynley	Elizabeth GEORGE
Insp. Hemingway	Georgette HEYER
Insp. Judy Hill & Ch. Insp. Lloyd	Jill McGOWN
Mark Holland: musical world	Paul MYERS
Alison Hope & Insp. Nick Trevellyan	Susan KELLY
Horse racing	Mark DANIEL
Horse racing	Dick FRANCIS
Horse racing	John FRANCOME
Tamara Hoyland	Jessica MANN
Leah Hunter: tax inspector	Sara LACEY
Asst. Ch. Const. Desmond Iles & Ch. Supt. Colin Harp	Bill JAMES
India: Ganesh Ghote	H.R.F. KEATING
Italy: Marshall Guernaccia	Magdalen NABB
Italy, Renaissance: Sigismondo	Elizabeth EYRE
Italy: Aurelio Zen	Michael DIBDIN
Kate Ivory	Veronica STALLWOOD

DI Jim Jackson	Frank PALMER
Japan: Comm. Otani	James MELVILLE
Coffin Ed Johnson & Gravedigger Jones: US	Chester B. HIMES
Journalist: Rain Morgan	Lesley GRANT-ADAMSON
Journalist: Quilleran	Lilian Jackson BRAUN
DI Ben Jurnet	S.T. HAYMON
Ch. Insp. Jury	Martha GRIMES
Sarah Kelling: PI	Charlotte MACLEOD
Insp. Kelsey	Emma PAGE
Julian Kestral; gentleman: Victorian	Kate ROSS
Willow King	Natasha COOPER
Nurse Kate Kinsella	Christine GREEN
Kramer & Zondi: SA	James McCLURE
Laidlaw	William McILVANNEY
Loretta Lawson	Joan SMITH
Lawyer: US: Perry Mason	Erle Stanley GARDNER
Rina Lazarus & Pete Decker : US	Faye KELLERMAN
Leaphorn: Navajo	Tony HILLERMAN
Anna Lee	Liza CODY
Det. Supt. Lewis, Div. Supt. Collins & Supt. Ripley	John WAINWRIGHT
Insp. Sholto Lestrade	M.J. TROW
Darina Lisle: cookery	Janet LAURENCE
Ch. Insp. Lloyd & Insp. Judy Hill	Jill McGOWN
Lovejoy: antique dealer	Jonathan GASH
Philipa Lowe	Roger ORMEROD
Insp. Lynley & Sgt. Havers	Elizabeth GEORGE
DI Hamish MacBeth	M.C. BEATON
Maigret: France	Georges SIMENON
Anthony Maitland	Sara WOODS
Majorca: Insp. Alvarez	Roderic JEFFRIES
Dan Mallett	Frank PARRISH
Sheila Malory	Hazel HOLT
Ch. Insp. Alan Markey & Meredith Mitchell	Ann GRANGER
Peter Marklin	Neville STEED
Philip Marlowe: US	Raymond CHANDLER
Miss Marple	Agatha CHRISTIE
Perry Mason: lawyer: US	Erle Stanley GARDNER
DCS George Masters	Douglas CLARK
Sharon McCone: US	Marcia MULLER
Travis McGee	John D. MACDONALD

Character or environment of crime author *(cont.)*

Det. Supt. John McLeish & Francesca Wilson	Janet NEEL
Mediaeval: Owen Archer	Candace ROBB
Mediaeval: Brother Athelstan	Paul HARDING
Mediaeval: Brother Cadfael	Ellis PETERS
Mediaeval: Hugh Corbett	P.C. DOHERTY
Mediaeval: Insp. Grant	Josephine TEY
Mediaeval: Roger the Chapman	Kate SEDLEY
Mediaeval: Sister Fidelma	Peter TREMAYNE
Lt. Luis Mendoza: US	Dell SHANNON
Kinsey Millhouse	Sue GRAFTON
Meredith Mitchell & Ch. Insp. Alan Markey	Ann GRANGER
Britt Montero	Edna BUCHANAN
Jean Montrose	C.F. ROE
James Morgan: Ch of Police: US	Andrew COBURN
Rain Morgan: journalist	Lesley GRANT-ADAMSON
Insp. Morse	Colin DEXTER
Insp. Phil Moss & Ch. Insp. Colin Thane	Bill KNOX
Mountaineering: Miss Pink	Gwen MOFFAT
Musical world: Mark Holland	Paul MYERS
Navajo: Leaphorn	Tony HILLERMAN
Netherlands: Henk Grijpstra	Janwillem VAN DE WETERING
Jocelyn O'Roarke: theatre	Jane DENTINGER
Comm. Otani: Japan	James MELVILLE
Pamplemousse: restaurant critic	Michael BOND
Charles Paris: actor	Simon BRETT
DS Pascoe & DI Dalziel	Reginald HILL
Pel: France	Juliet HEBDEN
Pel: France	Mark HEBDEN
Miss Pink: mountaineering	Gwen MOFFAT
Insp. Pitts: Victorian	Anne PERRY
Stephanie Plum: US	Janet EVANOVICH
Hercule Poirot	Agatha CHRISTIE
Insp. Pollard	Elizabeth LEMARCHAND
Insp. Purbright	Colin WATSON
DCI Quantrill	Sheila RADLEY
Quilleran: journalist	Lilian Jackson BRAUN
Insp. Ramsay	Ann CLEEVES
Easy Rawlins	Walter MOSLEY
Insp. John Rebus	Ian RANKIN
Renaissance Italy: Sigismondo	Elizabeth EYRE

Charlie Resnick	John HARVEY
Restaurant critic: Pamplemousse	Michael BOND
Bernie Rhodenbarr: burglar	Lawrence BLOCK
Supt. Ripley, Div. Supt. Collins & Det. Supt. Lewis	John WAINWRIGHT
Dave Robicheaux	James Lee BURKE
Roger the Chapman: mediaeval	Kate SEDLEY
DS Rogers	Jonathan ROSS
Rome & Roman Britain: Falco	Lindsey DAVIS
Insp. Salter: Canada	Eric WRIGHT
Sam & Reid Bennett: Canada	Ted WOOD
Dr. Kay Scarpetta	Patricia D. CORNWELL
Det. Frank Sessions & Chief Fred Fellows: US	Hillary WAUGH
Sir Roger Shallot: 16th cent.	Michael CLYNES
Shandy: academic	Charlotte MACLEOD
Nick Sharman	Mark TIMLIN
Jemima Shore: TV journalist	Antonia FRASER
Sigismondo: renaissance Italy	Elizabeth EYRE
Miss Silver	Patricia WENTWORTH
Tim Simpson	John MALCOLM
Insp. Sloan	Catherine AIRD
South Africa: Kramer & Zondi	James McCLURE
Sam Spade: US	Dashiell HAMMETT
Spenser: US	Robert B. PARKER
Philip St. Ives	Ross THOMAS
Nigel Strangeways	Nicholas BLAKE
Angus Straum	Barry CORK
Det. Milo Sturgis: US	Jonathan KELLERMAN
Suffragette, Edwardian: Nell Bray	Gillian LINSCOTT
Prof. Hilary Tamar	Sarah CAUDWELL
DCI Dick Tansey	John PENN
Tax inspector: Leah Hunter	Sara LACEY
Taxi owner: Fitzroy Maclean Angel	Mike RIPLEY
Ch. Insp. Colin Thane & Insp. Phil Moss	Bill KNOX
DI Luke Thanet	Dorothy SIMPSON
John P. Thatcher: banking	Emma LATHEN
Theatre: Jocelyn O'Roarke	Jane DENTINGER
Thorn: US	James HALL
Henry & Emmy Tibbett	Patricia MOYES
Mark Treasure	David WILLIAMS
Insp. Nick Trevellyan & Alison Hope	Susan KELLY

Character or environment of crime author (cont.)

Trixie & Evangeline	Marion BABSON
TV journalist: Jemima Shore	Antonia FRASER
Van der Valk: Netherlands	Nicolas FREELING
Venice: Comm. Guido Brunetti	Donna LEON
Victorian	Amy MYERS
Victorian Britain: Insp. Dew	Peter LOVESEY
Victorian: gentleman: Julian Kestral	Kate ROSS
Victorian: Insp. Pitts	Anne PERRY
Victorian police	Ray HARRISON
Amos Walker: US	Loren D. ESTLEMAN
Penny Wanawake	Susan MOODY
V.I. Warshawski: US	Sara PARETSKY
Insp. West	John CREASEY
Helen West: CPS	Frances FYFIELD
Insp. Wexford	Ruth RENDELL
Francesca Wilson & Det. Supt. John McLeish	Janet NEEL
Lord Peter Wimsey	Dorothy L. SAYERS
Hannah Wolfe	Sarah DUNANT
Nero Wolfe & Archie Goodwin	Rex STOUT
Writer: Melissa Craig: Cotswolds	Betty ROWLANDS
Insp. Wycliffe	W.J. BURLEY
York Cycle of Mysteries	Barbara WHITEHEAD
Mamur Zapt: Edwardian Egypt	Michael PEARCE
Aurelio Zen: Italy	Michael DIBDIN
Zondi & Kramer: SA	James McCLURE

Family Stories

A popular genre frequently set against an historical background telling the story of two or more generations of a family with the plot often revolving around the purchase of property or the development of a family business. Included in this genre are **Family Sagas** in which the story is continued in a number of volumes. To help identify this category of author the word *saga* is shown against certain names. This identification also applies in the **Historical** section as many novelists write in both genres.

Elizabeth ADLER	Jane DUNCAN *saga*
Charlotte Vale ALLEN	Elizabeth ELGIN
Lyn ANDREWS	Rosemary ENRIGHT
Aileen ARMITAGE	Margaret ERSKINE
Anne BAKER	Pamela EVANS
Donna BAKER	Zoe FAIRBAIRNS
Tessa BARCLAY *saga*	Kate FLYNN
Maeve BINCHY	Helen FORRESTER *saga*
Emma BLAIR *saga*	Christine Marion FRASER *saga*
Philip BOAST	Sara FRASER *saga*
Rose BOUCHERON	Cynthia FREEMAN
Harry BOWLING *saga*	Gail GODWIN
Clare BOYLAN	Suzanne GOODWIN
Barbara Taylor BRADFORD	Iris GOWER *saga*
Louise BRINDLEY *saga*	Margaret GRAHAM
Patricia BURNS	Ruth HAMILTON
Betty BURTON	Maeve HARAN
Brenda CLARKE	Lilian HARRY
Virginia COFFMAN	Evelyn HOOD
Catrin COLLIER	Audrey HOWARD
Kathleen CONLON	Susan HOWATCH
Catherine COOKSON *saga*	Sara HYLTON
Elaine CROWLEY	Brenda JAGGER *saga*
Janet DAILEY *saga*	Sheila JANSEN
Elizabeth DAISH	Joan JONKER
Elizabeth DARRELL *saga*	Marie JOSEPH *saga*
Doris DAVIDSON	Sheelagh KELLY *saga*
Margaret Thomson DAVIS *saga*	Adam KENNEDY *saga*
Frank DELANEY	Lena KENNEDY *saga*
R.F. DELDERFIELD *saga*	Beryl KINGSTON *saga*
Barbara DELINSKY	Gwen KIRKWOOD
Monica DICKENS	Peter LING

Family Stories *(cont.)*

Claire LORRIMER   *saga*
Malcolm MACDONALD   *saga*
Mary MACKIE
Brenda McBRYDE
Hilda McKENZIE
Elisabeth McNEILL
Anne MELVILLE   *saga*
Mary MELWOOD
Mary MINTON   *saga*
Connie MONK
Catrin MORGAN
Doris MORTMAN
Maisie MOSCO   *saga*
Elizabeth MURPHY
M.R. O'DONNELL
Pamela OLDFIELD   *saga*
Lewis ORDE
Lynda PAGE
Mary E. PEARCE   *saga*
Erin PIZZEY
Belva PLAIN   *saga*
Pamela POPE   *saga*
Deirdre PURCELL
Marjorie QUARTON
Claire RAYNER   *saga*
Miss READ   *saga*
Elvi RHODES
Ann Victoria ROBERTS
Denise ROBERTSON
Wendy ROBERTSON
Malcolm ROSS
Susan SALLIS
Judith SAXTON   *saga*
Sarah SHEARS   *saga*

Anne Rivers SIDDONS
LaVyrle SPENCER
Eileen STAFFORD
Diana STAINFORTH
Mary Jane STAPLES   *saga*
Danielle STEEL
Kay STEPHENS
D.E. STEVENSON   *saga*
Caroline STICKLAND
Jessica STIRLING   *saga*
Sue SULLY
Essie SUMMERS
Margaret SUNLEY
Reay TANNAHILL
Janet TANNER
Rosie THOMAS
Grace THOMPSON
Nicola THORNE   *saga*
Margaret THORNTON
Eileen TOWNSEND
Judy TURNER
Helen VAN SLYKE
Barbara VICTOR
Elizabeth VILLARS
Anne VIVIS
Elizabeth WAITE
Elizabeth WALKER
Elizabeth WARNE   *saga*
Jan WEBSTER
Jeanne WHITMEE
Barbara WHITNELL
Dee WILLIAMS
T.R. WILSON
Anne WORBOYS

Fantasy

Fantasy novels are based on the old folk tales and gothic stories of the eighteenth and nineteenth centuries. Unlike Science Fiction they do not rely on technology but transport the reader to a magical world often linked to the Dark Ages. Some authors specialise in writing in a precise group - **Literary Fantasy** including Myths and Legends; **Epic Fantasy** and **Dark Fantasy** where the author is verging on the supernatural. These authors are identified by the following beside their name:- *lit'y, epic* and *dark.*

Robert ASPRIN	*epic*	Stephen LAWS	
Jean M. AUEL	*epic*	C.S. LEWIS	
Robert BLOCH	*dark*	H.P. LOVECRAFT	*dark*
Ray BRADBURY		Nicholas LUARD	
Marion Zimmer BRADLEY	*epic*	Brian LUMLEY	
Terry BROOKS	*epic*	Julian MAY	
Storm CONSTANTINE		Anne McCAFFREY	*epic*
Louise COOPER		Dan McGIRT	*epic*
August DERLETH	*dark*	Michael MOORCOCK	*epic*
Stephen DONALDSON	*epic*	Andre NORTON	*epic*
Dave DUNCAN		Mervyn PEAKE	*lit'y*
David EDDINGS	*epic*	Terry PRATCHETT	*epic*
Raymond E. FEIST	*epic*	Melanie RAWN	*epic*
Maggie FUREY		Keith ROBERTS	
Craig Shaw GARDNER		Michael Scott ROHAN	
David A. GEMMELL	*epic*	R.A. SALVATORE	
Colin GREENLAND	*lit'y*	Dan SIMMONS	
Robert HOLDSTOCK		Christopher STASHEFF	
Tom HOLT		J.R.R. TOLKIEN	*epic*
Robert JORDAN	*epic*	Harry TURTLEDOVE	
Guy Gavriel KAY	*epic*	Margaret WEIS	*epic*
Patricia KENNEALY		John WHITBOURN	
Katherine KERR	*epic*	Tad WILLIAMS	
Garry D. KILWORTH	*dark*	Gene WOLFE	*lit'y*
Stephen KING		Jonathan WYLIE	
Mercedes LACKEY			

General

Covers a great many authors for whom it is difficult or impossible to establish a genre. Within this **General** category will be found novels exploring personal relationships and the values and meaning of contemporary life. The setting may be in Britain or overseas. This category also includes authors whose plot and/or style change markedly from book to book. It also includes some authors whose writing has the characteristics of several genres.

Chinua ACHEBE
Peter ACKROYD
Richard ADAMS
Joan AIKEN
Isabel ALLENDE
Lisa ALTHER
Stephen AMIDON
Kingsley AMIS
Martin AMIS
Virginia ANDREWS
Patricia ANGADI
Jeffrey ARCHER
Thomas ARMSTRONG
Judy ASTLEY
Margaret ATWOOD
Jane AUSTEN
Margaret BACON
Hilary BAILEY
Paul BAILEY
Beryl BAINBRIDGE
James BALDWIN
Iain BANKS
Lynne Reid BANKS
Russell BANKS
John BANVILLE
Noel BARBER
A.L. BARKER
Pat BARKER
Julian BARNES
Stan BARSTOW
H.E. BATES
Nina BAWDEN

Saul BELLOW
Peter BENCHLEY
Peter BENSON
Phyllis BENTLEY
Rachel BILLINGTON
Charlotte BINGHAM
Dirk BOGARDE
Heinrich BÖLL
Elizabeth BOWEN
William BOYD
Malcolm BRADBURY
Melvyn BRAGG
John BRAINE
Sally BRAMPTON
Caroline BRIDGWOOD
Jane BRINDLE
Andre BRINK
Anita BROOKNER
Janice Young BROOKS
Brigid BROPHY
Fiona BULLEN
Anthony BURGESS
Anita BURGH
Guy BURT
A.S. BYATT
Erskine CALDWELL
Taylor CALDWELL
Albert CAMUS
Ethan CANIN
Truman CAPOTE
Peter CAREY
Michael CARSON

Angela CARTER
Brian CARTER
Raymond CARVER
Joyce CARY
Bruce CHATWIN
Amit CHAUDHURI
John CHEEVER
Mary Higgins CLARK
Aeron CLEMENT
Carol CLEWLOW
Marika COBBOLD
Ian COCHRANE
J.M. COETZEE
Jon COHEN
Martina COLE
Isabel COLEGATE
Vernon COLEMAN
Ivy COMPTON BURNETT
Barbara COMYNS
Joseph CONRAD
David COOK
Lettice COOPER
William COOPER
Alexander CORDELL
Josephine COX
Amanda CRAIG
Michael CRICHTON
A.J. CRONIN
Susan CROSLAND
David DABYDEEN
Robertson DAVIES
John Gordon DAVIS
Louis DE BERNIÈRES
E.M. DELAFIELD
Don DELILLO
Anita DESAI
Pete DEXTER
Farrukh DHONDY
Jenny DISKI
Michael DOBBS

E.L. DOCTOROW
J.P. DONLEAVY
Ellen DOUGLAS
Margaret DRABBLE
Daphne DU MAURIER
Nell DUNN
Dominick DUNNE
Lawrence DURRELL
Geoff DYER
Dorothy EDEN
Robert ELEGANT
Janice ELLIOTT
Alice Thomas ELLIS
Ben ELTON
Buchi EMECHETA
Sally EMERSON
Shusaku ENDO
Louise ERDRICH
Julian FANE
J.G. FARRELL
Howard FAST
William FAULKNER
Sebastian FAULKS
Katie FFORDE
Anne FINE
F. Scott FITZGERALD
Penelope FITZGERALD
Ford Madox FORD
Richard FORD
E.M. FORSTER
Margaret FORSTER
John FOWLES
Janet FRAME
Ronald FRAME
Caro FRASER
Marilyn FRENCH
Patrick GALE
Paul GALLICO
Janice GALLOWAY
John GALSWORTHY

General *(cont.)*

Gabriel GARCIA MARQUEZ

Jane GARDAM

David GATES

Ellen GILCHRIST

Lesley GLAISTER

Rumer GODDEN

Marita GOLDEN

William GOLDING

Nadine GORDIMER

Elizabeth GOUDGE

Winston GRAHAM

Günter GRASS

Robert GRAVES

Alasdair GRAY

Graham GREENE

David GROSSMAN

David GUTERSON

Rosa GUY

Rodney HALL

Jane HAMILTON

James HAMILTON PATERSON

Elizabeth HARRIS

Jim HARRISON

Sarah HARRISON

L.P. HARTLEY

Roy HATTERSLEY

Joseph HELLER

Ernest HEMINGWAY

Domini HIGHSMITH

Susan HILL

Mary HOCKING

Peter HOEG

Alice HOFFMAN

Alan HOLLINGHURST

Winifred HOLTBY

Christopher HOPE

Nick HORNBY

William HORWOOD

Elizabeth Jane HOWARD

Christopher HUDSON

Angela HUTH

Aldous HUXLEY

Elspeth HUXLEY

John IRVING

Susan ISAACS

Kazuo ISHIGURO

Howard JACOBSON

Rona JAFFE

Henry JAMES

Ruth Prawer JHABVALA

Pamela Hansford JOHNSON

Jennifer JOHNSTON

Elizabeth JOLLEY

James JOYCE

Franz KAFKA

Stuart M. KAMINSKY

M.M. KAYE

Molly KEANE

James KELMAN

Judith KELMAN

Thomas KENEALLY

A.L. KENNEDY

William KENNEDY

Jack KEROUAC

Ken KESEY

Francis KING

Arthur KOESTLER

Milan KUNDERA

Hanif KUREISHI

Lynda LA PLANTE

Angela LAMBERT

D.H. LAWRENCE

David LEAVITT

Harper LEE

Rosamond LEHMANN

Annie LEITH

Doris LESSING

Primo LEVI

Sinclair LEWIS

Joan LINGARD

Penelope LIVELY

Caroline LLEWELLYN

Richard LLEWELLYN

A.R. LLOYD

David LODGE

Norah LOFTS

Russell LUCAS

Alison LURIE

Norman MAILER

David MALOUF

Olivia MANNING

Hilary MANTEL

Adam MARS JONES

Paule MARSHALL

Sybil MARSHALL

Bobbie Ann MASON

Allan MASSIE

John MASTERS

W. Somerset MAUGHAM

Armistead MAUPIN

Patrick McCABE

Cormac McCARTHY

Mary McCARTHY

Carson McCULLERS

Colleen McCULLOUGH

Ian McEWAN

John McGAHERN

Thomas McGUANE

Jay McINERNEY

Terry McMILLAN

Larry McMURTRY

Candia McWILLIAM

Gita MEHTA

Barbara MICHAELS

James A. MICHENER

Paul MICOU

Stanley MIDDLETON

Sue MILLER

Yukio MISHIMA

James MITCHELL

Timothy MO

Deborah MOGGACH

Michael MOLLOY

Brian MOORE

Lorrie MOORE

Mary McGarry MORRIS

Toni MORRISON

Penelope MORTIMER

Alice MUNRO

Haruki MURAKAMI

Iris MURDOCH

Vladimir NABOKOV

V.S. NAIPAUL

Nora NAISH

R.K. NARAYAN

Gloria NAYLOR

Robert NYE

Edna O'BRIEN

Flannery O'CONNOR

John O'HARA

Ann OAKLEY

Joyce Carol OATES

Ben OKRI

Michael ONDAATJE

George ORWELL

Agnes OWENS

Amos OZ

Elizabeth PALMER

Brian PARVIN

Alan PATON

Wendy PERRIAM

Elizabeth PETERS

Caryl PHILLIPS

Marge PIERCY

Rosamunde PILCHER

Chaim POTOK

Anthony POWELL

Amanda PRANTERA

General *(cont.)*

J.B. PRIESTLEY

V.S. PRITCHETT

E. Annie PROULX

Ann PURSER

Barbara PYM

Frederic RAPHAEL

Piers Paul READ

Erich Maria REMARQUE

Michele ROBERTS

Nora ROBERTS

Jane ROGERS

Judith ROSSNER

Philip ROTH

Kathleen ROWNTREE

Bernice RUBENS

Salman RUSHDIE

Mary RYAN

J.D. SALINGER

May SARTON

Kate SAUNDERS

Paul SAYER

Paul SCOTT

Will SELF

Vikram SETH

Irwin SHAW

Carol SHIELDS

Anita SHREVE

Alan SILLITOE

Isaac Bashevis SINGER

Alison Scott SKELTON

Audrey SLAUGHTER

Jane SMILEY

C.P. SNOW

Alexander SOLZHENITSYN

Wole SOYINKA

Muriel SPARK

Howard SPRING

Christina STEAD

Marguerite STEEN

John STEINBECK

Mary STEWART

David STOREY

Jean STUBBS

William STYRON

Titia SUTHERLAND

Graham SWIFT

Elizabeth TAYLOR

Emma TENNANT

Paul THEROUX

Angela THIRKELL

D.M. THOMAS

Leslie THOMAS

Colin THUBRON

Gillian TINDALL

Barbara TRAPIDO

William TREVOR

Joanna TROLLOPE

Anne TYLER

Barry UNSWORTH

John UPDIKE

Leon URIS

Alice WALKER

Robert James WALLER

Hugh WALPOLE

Marina WARNER

Tony WARREN

Paul WATKINS

Larry WATSON

Evelyn WAUGH

Fay WELDON

Irvine WELSH

Mary WESLEY

Morris WEST

Rebecca WEST

Edith WHARTON

William WHARTON

Antonia WHITE

Edmund WHITE

Gillian WHITE

Patrick WHITE

Marianne WIGGINS

Henry WILLIAMSON

A.N. WILSON

Angus WILSON

Jeanette WINTERSON

Tim WINTON

Tom WOLFE

Sarah WOODHOUSE

Virginia WOOLF

Herman WOUK

Glitz & Glamour

A fairly recent phenomenon, this genre features the modern world of big business and entertainment with generous proportions of sex, violence and avarice. Identified in libraries and bibliographies by a number of alternative headings including 'Contemporary Glamour', 'Sex and Shopping, 'The Smart Set'.

Catherine ALLIOTT
Sally BEAUMAN
Pat BOOTH
Celia BRAYFIELD
Freda BRIGHT
Jacqueline BRISKIN
Sandra BROWN
Julie BURCHILL
Jackie COLLINS
Joan COLLINS
Shirley CONRAN
Jilly COOPER
Vera COWIE
Laramie DUNAWAY
Lucinda EDMONDS
Julie ELLIS
Shirley ESKAPA

Vanessa FOX
Elizabeth GAGE
Olivia GOLDSMITH
Judith GOULD
Erica JONG
Judith KRANTZ
Jayne Ann KRENTZ
Rupert LEGGE
Kathy LETTE
Susan LEWIS
Jill MANSELL
Una-Mary PARKER
Harold ROBBINS
June Flaum SINGER
Alexandra THORNE
Penny VINCENZI
Fiona WALKER

Historical

Another very popular category where fictional characters are set against an actual historical perspective with close and realistic links between fiction and fact. Some are based on real people and events - others are purely imaginary. Many books in this genre also have a romantic theme and some again, as with family stories, are **Sagas** where the story is continued in a number of volumes. To help identify this category of author the word *saga* is shown against certain names.

Valerie ANAND	Rosalind LAKER
Evelyn ANTHONY	Dinah LAMPITT
Pamela BELLE	Morgan LLYWELYN
Gillian BRADSHAW	Genevieve LYONS
Madeleine BRENT *saga*	Naomi MITCHISON
D.K. BROSTER	Neil MUNRO
Elizabeth BYRD	Dlana NORMAN
Philippa CARR *saga*	Gilda O'NEILL
Elizabeth CHADWICK	Edith PARGETER
Catherine COULTER	Diane PEARSON
Teresa CRANE	Margaret PEMBERTON
Colin DE SILVA	Sharon PENMAN
Emma DRUMMOND	Maureen PETERS
Dorothy DUNNETT *saga*	Jean PLAIDY
Barbara ERSKINE	Mary RENAULT
Diana GABALDON	Judith M. RILEY
Catherine GASKIN *saga*	Cynthia S. ROBERTS
Catherine GAVIN *saga*	Stewart ROSS
Valerie GEORGESON *saga*	Carola SALISBURY
Judith GLOVER *saga*	Anya SETON
Winston GRAHAM *saga*	Patricia SHAW
Jonathan GRANT	Agnes SHORT
Philippa GREGORY	Linda Lay SHULER
Cynthia HARROD-EAGLES *saga*	Emma STIRLING
Georgette HEYER	Vivian STUART *saga*
Pamela HILL	Rosemary SUTCLIFF
Jane Aiken HODGE	E.V. THOMPSON *saga*
Isabelle HOLLAND	Nigel TRANTER
Victoria HOLT	Gore VIDAL
Harriet HUDSON	Patricia WENDORF
Elizabeth JEFFREY	Philippa WIAT

Humour

A select group of authors whose novels are mainly written to amuse.

H.E. BATES
Guy BELLAMY
E.F. BENSON
Dan BINCHY
J.L. CARR
Mavis CHEEK
Roy CLARKE
Jonathan COE
Colin DOUGLAS
Roddy DOYLE
George Macdonald FRASER
Michael FRAYN
George GROSSMITH

Tom HOLT
Garrison KEILLOR
Nancy MITFORD
John MORTIMER
Helen MUIR
David NOBBS
Flann O'BRIEN
Tom SHARPE
Peter TINNISWOOD
Sue TOWNSEND
Keith WATERHOUSE
Nigel WILLIAMS
P.G. WODEHOUSE

Romance

Novels usually written by women for women with a romantic theme.
Some writers specialise in historical settings but for the purposes of this
guide the major theme determines the genre. Many libraries will have a
separate section of shelves for **Romance**.

Lucilla ANDREWS

Lindsay ARMSTRONG

Iris BROMIGE

Elizabeth BUCHAN

Elizabeth CADELL

Barbara CARTLAND

Marion CHESNEY

Caroline COURTNEY

Ursula CURTISS

Clare DARCY

Joyce DINGWELL

Jane DONNELLY

Catherine GEORGE

Penny JORDAN

Charlotte LAMB

Audrie MANLEY-TUCKER

Anne MATHER

Judith McNAUGHT

Carole MORTIMER

Betty NEELS

Patricia ROBINS

Elizabeth SEIFERT

Jessica STEELE

Anne STEVENSON

Elswyth THANE

Kay THORPE

Sheila WALSH

Anne WEALE

Sally WENTWORTH

Phyllis A. WHITNEY

Mary WILLIAMS

Daoma WINSTON

Science Fiction

Books in this genre may be roughly divided into three sub-categories with many authors writing in all three and others changing their style over the years. Most are concerned with **Space and Time** - the exploration of the Universe. Several writers concentrate on the **Technology** of Science Fiction and this forms the second sub-genre. Thirdly we have the world of **Virtual Worlds** where the focus is on information technology. These sub-genres are indicated by the following: *Tech* and *VW*.

Douglas ADAMS	Frank HERBERT
Brian W. ALDISS *Tech*	Gwyneth JONES *VW*
Poul ANDERSON	Ursula LE GUIN
Piers ANTHONY	Stanislaw LEM
Isaac ASIMOV *Tech*	Paul J. McAULEY *Tech*
J.G. BALLARD *Tech/VW*	Grant NAYLOR
Iain M. BANKS	Larry NIVEN
John BARNES *VW*	Frederik POHL *Tech*
Stephen BAXTER	Christopher PRIEST
Greg BEAR *Tech*	Robert RANKIN
Gregory BENFORD *Tech*	Kim Stanley ROBINSON *Tech*
James BLISH *Tech*	Joanna RUSS
David BRIN *Tech/VW*	Fred SABERHAGEN
John BRUNNER *Tech/VW*	Bob SHAW
Orson Scott CARD	Robert SHECKLEY
Jack L. CHALKER	Robert SILVERBERG
C.J. CHERRYH	Clifford D. SIMAK
Arthur C. CLARKE *Tech*	Brian STABLEFORD *Tech*
Richard COWPER	Neal STEPHENSON *VW*
Samuel R. DELANY	Bruce STERLING *VW*
Philip K. DICK *VW*	Sheri S. TEPPER
Gordon R. DICKSON	Patrick TILLEY
Thomas M. DISCH *Tech/VW*	Jack VANCE
Greg EGAN *VW*	John VARLEY
Harlan ELLISON	Jules VERNE
Philip José FARMER	Kurt VONNEGUT
Alan Dean FOSTER	Ian WATSON *Tech*
Mary GENTLE	H.G. WELLS
William GIBSON *VW*	Connie WILLIS
Colin GREENLAND	David WINGROVE
Joe HALDEMAN	Janny WURTS
Harry HARRISON	John WYNDHAM
Robert A. HEINLEIN *Tech*	Roger ZELAZNY

Sea

A popular category where many authors have made a well-deserved reputation for writing about the sea either in an historical or contemporary setting. Many novelists in this genre will also be found under **Adventure** and also under **War Stories**.

Brian CALLISON
David DONACHIE
C.S. FORESTER
Raymond HARDIE
Duncan HARDING
Alexander KENT
A.E. LANGSFORD
Sam LLEWELLYN
Philip McCUTCHAN
Nicholas MONSARRAT
Patrick O'BRIAN

C. Northcote PARKINSON
Dudley POPE
Douglas REEMAN
Douglas SCOTT
Showell STYLES
Peter TONKIN
Antony TREW
John WINGATE
John WINTON
Richard WOODMAN

Supernatural

This section includes authors who frequently write suspense and horror where the story line involves pursuit and eventual escape often from the supernatural, demonic or the occult.

Jonathan AYCLIFFE
Chaz BRENCHLEY
Ramsey CAMPBELL
Nancy COLLINS
Joe DONNELLY
John FARRIS
Christopher FOWLER
Stephen GALLAGHER
Steve HARRIS
James HERBERT
Shaun HUTSON
Peter JAMES
Stephen KING
Dean R. KOONTZ
Richard LAYMON
Bentley LITTLE
George R. MARTIN

Graham MASTERTON
Robert McCAMMON
Mark MORRIS
Kim NEWMAN
Christopher PIKE
Anne RICE
Philip RICKMAN
John SAUL
Guy N. SMITH
Peter STRAUB
Whitley STRIEBER
Bernard TAYLOR
Dennis WHEATLEY
Tim WILLOCKS
Tim WILSON
T.M. WRIGHT

War

Authors who have written widely but not exclusively about war generally within the 19th and 20th centuries. Many books about war will also be found under **Adventure** and **Sea Stories**. Some novelists listed in the **General** category have also written individual books about war.

Peter ABRAHAMS	Richard HOUGH
Doug ARMSTRONG	Robert JACKSON
Peter CAVE	Robin JAMES
Shaun CLARKE	Leo KESSLER
Larry FORRESTER	David MONNERY
W.E.B. GRIFFIN	Derek ROBINSON
John HARRIS	Terence STRONG
Sven HASSEL	L.K. TRUSCOTT
Max HENNESSY	Charles WHITING

Western

Books set in the old American West with a range of plots from romance to adventure. Only a selection of the many authors who write in this genre are included in the Guide and, as with **Romance** many libraries will have a separate section for **Western Stories**.

John BLAZE	Chuck MARTIN
Max BRAND	Nelson NYE
Matt CHISHOLM	Clint OGDEN
Al CODY	T.C. OLSEN
Jess CODY	Lauran PAINE
J.T. EDSON	Gary PAULSEN
Lee F. GREGSON	Jack SCHAEFER
Zane GREY	Bill WADE
Louis L'AMOUR	

LITERARY PRIZES AND AWARDS

There are well over 200 prizes and awards currently on offer to writers and publishers. The following list, covers the period from 1970 to date and contains most of those for which works of fiction are eligible. Further information on the awards themselves, may be found in the **Guide to Literary Prizes** (Book Trust, 1995).

AUTHORS' CLUB FIRST NOVEL AWARD

This is given to the most promising First Novel published by a writer in Great Britain. Introduced by Laurence Meynell in 1954.

1970	Rachel INGALLS	Theft
1971	Rosemary Hawley JARMAN	We speak no Treason
1973	Jennifer JOHNSTON	The Captains and the Kings
1975	Sasha MOORSOM	A Lavender Trip
1977	Barbara BENSON	The Underlings
1978	Katherine GORDON	The Emerald Peacock
1979	Martin PAGE	The Pilate Plot
1980	Dawn LOWE-WATSON	The Good Morrow
1981	Dr Anne SMITH	The Magic Glass
1982	Frances VERNON	The Privileged Children
1983	Katharine MOORE	Summer at the Haven
1984	Frederick HYDE-CHAMBERS	Lama, a Novel of Tibet
1985	Magda SWEETLAND	Eightsome Reel
1986	Helen HARRIS	Playing Fields in Winter
1987	Peter BENSON	The Levels
1988	Gilbert ADAIR	The Holy Innocents
1989	Lindsey DAVIS	The Silver Pigs
1990	Alan BROWNJOHN	The Way You Tell Them
1991	Zina ROHAN	The Book of Wishes and Complaints
1992	David PARK	The Healing
1993	Nadeem ASLAM	Season of the Rainbirds
1994	Andrew COWAN	Pig
1995	T.J. ARMSTRONG	Walter and the Resurrection of G

JAMES TAIT BLACK MEMORIAL PRIZES

The James Tait Black Memorial Prizes, founded in memory of a partner in the publishing house A & C Black Ltd, were instituted in 1918. Two prizes are awarded annually: one for the best biography or work of that type and the other for the best work of fiction published during the calendar year.

joint winners	1981	Salman RUSHDIE	Midnight's Children
	1981	Paul THEROUX	The Mosquito Coast
	1982	Bruce CHATWIN	On the Black Hill
	1983	Jonathan KEATES	Allegro Postillions
joint winners	1984	J.G. BALLARD	Empire of the Sun
	1984	Angela CARTER	Nights at the Circus
	1985	Robert EDRIC	Winter Garden
	1986	Jenny JOSEPH	Persephone
	1987	George Mackay BROWN	The Golden Bird: Two Orkney Stories
	1988	Piers Paul READ	A Season in the West
	1989	James KELMAN	A Disaffection
	1990	William BOYD	Brazzaville Beach
	1991	Iain SINCLAIR	Downriver
	1992	Rose TREMAIN	Sacred Country
	1993	Caryl PHILLIPS	Crossing the River
	1994	Alan HOLLINGHURST	The Folding Star
	1995	Christopher PRIEST	The Prestige

BOARDMAN TASKER AWARD FOR MOUNTAIN LITERATURE

This award commemorates the lives of Peter Boardman and Joe Tasker and is given to the author of an original work, either fiction or non-fiction, which has made an outstanding contribution to mountain literature. Since its inception in 1983 two novels have won the award:-

1989	M. John HARRISON	Climbers
1991	Alison FELL	Mer de Glace
1993	Jeff LONG	The Ascent

BOOKER PRIZE FOR FICTION

Established in 1968 by Booker McConnell Ltd., eligible novels must be written in English by a citizen of Britain, the Commonwealth and the Republic of Ireland.

The announcement of the winner has been televised live since 1981.

1969	P.H. NEWBY	Something to Answer For
1970	Bernice RUBENS	The Elected Member
1971	V.S. NAIPAUL	In a Free State
1972	John BERGER	G
1973	J.G. FARRELL	The Siege of Krishnapur
1974	Nadine GORDIMER	The Conservationist
1974	Stanley MIDDLETON	Holiday
1975	Ruth Prawer JHABVALA	Heat and Dust
1976	David STOREY	Saville
1977	Paul SCOTT	Staying On
1978	Iris MURDOCH	The Sea, The Sea
1979	Penelope FITZGERALD	Offshore
1980	William GOLDING	Rites of Passage
1981	Salman RUSHDIE	Midnight's Children
1982	Thomas KENEALLY	Schindler's Ark
1983	J.M. COETZEE	Life & Times of Michael K
1984	Anita BROOKNER	Hotel du Lac
1985	Keri HULME	The Bone People
1986	Kingsley AMIS	The Old Devils
1987	Penelope LIVELY	Moon Tiger
1988	Peter CAREY	Oscar and Lucinda
1989	Kazuo ISHIGURO	The Remains of the Day
1990	A.S. BYATT	Possession
1991	Ben OKRI	The Famished Road
1992	Michael ONDAATJE	The English Patient
1992	Barry UNSWORTH	Sacred Hunger
1993	Roddy DOYLE	Paddy Clarke Ha Ha Ha
1994	James KELMAN	How Late it Was, How Late
1995	Pat BARKER	The Ghost Road

joint winners { 1974 / 1974

joint winners { 1992 / 1992

BRITISH FANTASY AWARDS

Originally termed the August Derleth Fantasy Award, the British Fantasy Society announced its first award in 1972 for the best novel of the previous year.

1971	Michael MOORCOCK	The Knight of the Swords
1972	Michael MOORCOCK	The King of the Swords
1973	Poul ANDERSON	Hrolf Kraki's Saga
1974	Michael MOORCOCK	The Sword and the Stallion
1975	Michael MOORCOCK	The Hollow Lands
1976	Gordon DICKSON	The Dragon and the George
1977	Piers ANTHONY	A Spell for Chameleon
1978	Stephen DONALDSON	The Chronicles of Thomas Covenant
1979	Tanith LEE	Death's Master
1980	Ramsey CAMPBELL	To Wake the Dead
1981	Stephen KING	Cujo
1982	Gene WOLFE	Sword of the Lictor
1983	Peter STRAUB	Floating Dragon
1984	Ramsey CAMPBELL	Incarnate
1985	T.E.D. KLEIN	The Ceremonies
1986	Stephen KING	It
1987	Ramsey CAMPBELL	The Hungry Moon
1988	Ramsey CAMPBELL	The Influence
1989	Dan SIMMONS	Carrion Comfort
1990	Ramsey CAMPBELL	Midnight Sun
1991	Jonathan CARROLL	Outside the Dog Museum
1992	Graham JOYCE	Dark Sister
1993	Ramsey CAMPBELL	The Long Lost
1994	Michael Marshall SMITH	Only Forward

BRITISH SCIENCE FICTION ASSOCIATION AWARD

Awarded annually, after a ballot of members, by the British Science Fiction Association. Given in four categories: Best Novel; Best Short Fiction; Best Media Presentation; and Best Artwork. Novel winners since 1982 are:-

1982	Gene WOLFE	The Shadow of the Torturer
1983	Brian ALDISS	Helliconia Spring
1984	John SLADEK	Tik-Tok
1985	Robert HOLDSTOCK	Mythago Wood
1986	Brian ALDISS	Helliconia Winter
1987	Bob SHAW	The Ragged Astronauts
1988	Keith ROBERTS	Grainne
1989	Robert HOLDSTOCK	Lavondyss
1990	Terry PRATCHETT	Pyramids
1991	Colin GREENLAND	Take Back Plenty
1992	Dan SIMMONS	The Fall of Hyperion
1993	Christopher EVANS	Aztec Century
1994	Iain M. BANKS	Feerum Endjinn

ARTHUR C. CLARKE AWARD

This award, established in 1986, is for a Science Fiction novel and there are no limits on country of origin.

Horror and Fantasy are excluded unless there is a strong SF element in the book.

1987	Margaret ATWOOD	The Handmaid's Tale
1988	George TURNER	The Sea and Summer
1989	Rachel POLLACK	Unquenchable Fire
1990	Geoff RYMAN	The Child Garden
1991	Colin GREENLAND	Take Back Plenty
1992	Pat CADIGAN	Synners
1993	Marge PIERCY	Body of Glass
1994	Jeff NOON	Vurt
1995	Pat CADIGAN	Fools
1996	Paul J. McAULEY	Fairyland

DAVID COHEN BRITISH LITERATURE PRIZE

This latest award is supported and administered by the Arts Council of Great Britain. The prize money is put up by the David Cohen Family Charitable Trust. It is awarded every two years for a lifetime of achievement to a distinguished writer of British citizenship who works in the English, Gaelic, or Welsh languages.

1993	Sir Vidia NAIPAUL
1995	Harold PINTER

COMMONWEALTH WRITERS PRIZE

Established in 1987 by the Commonwealth Foundation in association with the Book Trust and the Royal Overseas League, the award is administered annually within one of four regions of the Commonwealth. Entries submitted by publishers must be novels or short stories.

1987	Olive SENIOR	Summer Lightning
1988	Festus IYAYI	Heroes
1989	Janet FRAME	The Carpathians
1990	Mordecai RICHLER	Solomon Gursky
1991	David MALOUF	The Great World
1992	Rohinton MISTRY	Such a Long Journey
1993	Alex MILLER	The Ancestor Game
1994	Vikram SETH	A Suitable Boy
1995	Louis DE BERNIÈRES	Captain Corelli's Mandolin

CATHERINE COOKSON FICTION PRIZE

A new award founded in 1992 by Transworld Publishers to celebrate the achievement of Catherine Cookson.

Awarded to a novel of at least 70,000 words in length that possesses features of strong characterisation, authentic background and story telling ability.

1992	Valerie WOOD	The Sea is my Companion
1993	Susanna KEARSLEY	Mariana
1994	Anna GILBERT	The Treachery of Time
1995	*No Award*	

CRIME WRITERS' ASSOCIATION

The first meeting of the Association was convened by John Creasey in November 1953 and awards have been presented since 1955 for the best crime novel of the year. Originally called the Crossed Red Herrings Award it is now the Gold Dagger. The Silver Dagger goes to the runner up. The John Creasey Memorial Award (JCMA), instituted to commemorate his death in 1973, is for the best crime novel by an author who has not previously published a full length work of fiction. From 1985 to 1987, the Police Review sponsored an award for the crime novel which best portrayed police work and procedure. In 1988 for one year only, Punch magazine sponsored a prize for the funniest crime book of the year. It has now been superseded by The Last Laugh Award. In 1990, Hazel Wynn Jones instituted the CWA '92 Award to run for three years for a crime novel partly or wholly set in Europe. Also in 1990 the New Law Journal sponsored the biennial Rumpole Award for a crime novel with a British legal setting. All these awards are set out below under each year.

1970	Joan FLEMING	*Gold Dagger*	Young Man I Think You're Dying
	Anthony PRICE	*Silver Dagger*	The Labyrinth Makers
1971	James McCLURE	*Gold Dagger*	The Steam Pig
	P.D. JAMES	*Silver Dagger*	Shroud for a Nightingale
1972	Eric AMBLER	*Gold Dagger*	The Levanter
	Victor CANNING	*Silver Dagger*	The Rainbird Pattern
1973	Robert LITTELL	*Gold Dagger*	The Defection of A.J. Lewinter
	Gwendoline BUTLER	*Silver Dagger*	A Coffin for Pandora
	Kyril BONFIGLIOLI	*J.C.M.A.*	Don't Point That Thing at Me
1974	Anthony Price	*Gold Dagger*	Other Paths to Glory
	Francis CLIFFORD	*Silver Dagger*	The Grosvenor Square Goodbye
	Roger L. SIMON	*J.C.M.A.*	The Big Fix

CRIME WRITERS' ASSOCIATION (cont.)

1975	Nicholas MEYER	*Gold Dagger*	The Seven Per Cent Solution
	P.D. JAMES	*Silver Dagger*	The Black Tower
	Sara GEORGE	*J.C.M.A.*	Acid Drop

1976	Ruth RENDELL	*Gold Dagger*	A Demon in my View
	James McCLURE	*Silver Dagger*	Rogue Eagle
	Patrick ALEXANDER	*J.C.M.A.*	Death of a Thin Skinned Animal

1977	John LE CARRÉ	*Gold Dagger*	The Honourable Schoolboy
	William McILVANNEY	*Silver Dagger*	Laidlaw
	Jonathan GASH	*J.C.M.A.*	The Judas Pair

1978	Lionel DAVIDSON	*Gold Dagger*	The Chelsea Murders
	Peter LOVESEY	*Silver Dagger*	Waxwork
	Paula GOSLING	*J.C.M.A.*	A Running Duck

1979	Dick FRANCIS	*Gold Dagger*	Whip Hand
	Colin DEXTER	*Silver Dagger*	Service of all the Dead
	David SERAFIN	*J.C.M.A.*	Saturday of Glory

1980	H.R.F. KEATING	*Gold Dagger*	The Murder of the Maharajah
	Ellis PETERS	*Silver Dagger*	Monk's Hood
	Liza CODY	*J.C.M.A.*	Dupe

1981	Martin Cruz SMITH	*Gold Dagger*	Gorky Park
	Colin DEXTER	*Silver Dagger*	The Dead of Jericho
	James LEIGH	*J.C.M.A.*	The Ludi Victor

1982	Peter LOVESEY	*Gold Dagger*	The False Inspector Dew
	S.T. HAYMON	*Silver Dagger*	Ritual Murder
	Andrew TAYLOR	*J.C.M.A.*	Caroline Minuscule

1983	John HUTTON	*Gold Dagger*	Accidental Crimes
	William McILVANNEY	*Silver Dagger*	The Papers of Tony Veitch
Tied {	Carol CLEMEAU	*J.C.M.A.*	The Ariadne Clue
	Eric WRIGHT	*J.C.M.A.*	The Night the Gods Smiled

1984	B.M. GILL	*Gold Dagger*	The Twelfth Juror
	Ruth RENDELL	*Silver Dagger*	The Tree of Hands
	Elizabeth IRONSIDE	*J.C.M.A.*	A Very Private Enterprise

1985	Paula GOSLING	*Gold Dagger*	Monkey Puzzle
	Dorothy SIMPSON	*Silver Dagger*	Last Seen Alive
	Robert RICHARDSON	*J.C.M.A.*	The Latimer Mercy
	Andrew ARNCLIFFE	*Police Review Award*	After the holiday

1986	Ruth RENDELL	*Gold Dagger*	Live Flesh
	P.D. JAMES	*Silver Dagger*	A Taste for Death
	Neville STEED	*J.C.M.A.*	Tinplate
	Bill KNOX	*Police Review Award*	The Crossfire Killings

1987	Barbara VINE	*Gold Dagger*	A Fatal Inversion
	Scott TUROW	*Silver Dagger*	Presumed Innocent
	Denis KILCOMMONS	*J.C.M.A.*	Dark Apostle
	Roger BUSBY	*Police Review Award*	Snowman

1988	Michael DIBDIN	*Gold Dagger*	Ratking
	Sara PARETSKY	*Silver Dagger*	Toxic Shock
	Janet NEEL	*J.C.M.A.*	Death's Bright Angel
	Nancy LIVINGSTON	*Punch Prize*	Death in a Distant Land

CRIME WRITERS' ASSOCIATION (cont.)

1989	Colin DEXTER	*Gold Dagger*	The Wench is Dead
	Desmond LOWDEN	*Silver Dagger*	The Shadow Run
	Annette ROOME	*J.C.M.A.*	A Real Shot in the Arm
	Mike RIPLEY	*Last Laugh Award*	Angel Touch
1990	Reginald HILL	*Gold Dagger*	Bones and Silence
	Mike PHILLIPS	*Silver Dagger*	The Late Candidate
	Patricia D. CORNWELL	*J.C.M.A.*	Postmortem
	Simon SHAW	*Last Laugh Award*	Killer Cinderella
	Michael DIBDIN	*CWA '92 Award*	Vendetta
	Frances FYFIELD	*Rumpole Award*	Trial by Fire
1991	Barbara VINE	*Gold Dagger*	King Solomon's Carpet
	Frances FYFIELD	*Silver Dagger*	Deep Sleep
	Walter MOSLEY	*J.C.M.A.*	Devil in a Blue Dress
	Mike RIPLEY	*Last Laugh Award*	Angels in Arms
	Barbara WILSON	*CWA '92 Award*	Gaudi Afternoon
1992	Colin DEXTER	*Gold Dagger*	The Way Through the Woods
	Liza CODY	*Silver Dagger*	Bucket Nut
	Minette WALTERS	*J.C.M.A.*	The Ice House
	Carl HIAASEN	*Last Laugh Award*	Native Tongue
	Timothy WILLIAMS	*CWA '92 Award*	Black August
	Peter RAWLINSON	*Rumpole Award*	Hatred and Contempt
1993	Patricia D. CORNWELL	*Gold Dagger*	Cruel and Unusual
	Sarah DUNANT	*Silver Dagger*	Fatlands
	No Award	*J.C.M.A.*	
	Michael PEARCE	*Last Laugh Award*	The Marmur Zapt and the Spoils of Egypt

1994	Minette WALTERS	*Gold Dagger*	The Scold's Bridle
	Peter HOEG	*Silver Dagger*	Miss Smilla's Feeling for Snow
	Doug J. SWANSON	*J.C.M.A.*	Big Town
	Simon SHAW	*Last Laugh Award*	The Villain of the Earth
1995	Val McDERMID	*Gold Dagger*	The Mermaid's Singing
	Peter LOVESEY	*Silver Dagger*	The Summons
	Jane EVANOVICH	*J.C.M.A.*	One for the Money
	Laurence SHAMES	*Last Laugh Award*	Sunburn

ENCORE AWARD

Awarded to the best second novel of the year published in that calendar year. The winner is chosen by a panel of judges from entries submitted by publishers.

joint winners	1990	Peter BENSON	A Lesser Dependency
	1990	Paul WATKINS	Calm at Sunset, Calm at Dawn
	1991	Carey HARRISON	Richard's Feet
	1992	Iain SINCLAIR	Downriver
	1993	Colm TOIBIN	The Heather Blazing
	1994	Amit CHAUDHURI	Afternoon Raag
	1995	Dermot HEALY	A Goat's Song

GEOFFREY FABER MEMORIAL PRIZE

As a memorial to the founder and first Chairman of the firm, Faber and Faber Limited established the prize in 1963. Awarded annually it is given in alternate years for a volume of verse and for a volume of prose fiction published originally in this country by writers who are under 40 years of age. The following is the list of fiction prize winners:-

1971	J.G. FARRELL	Troubles
1973	David STOREY	Pasmore
1975	Richard WRIGHT	The Middle of a Life
1977	Carolyn SLAUGHTER	The Story of the Weasel
1979	Timothy MO	The Monkey King
1981	J.M. COETZEE	Waiting for the Barbarians
1983	Graham SWIFT	Shuttlecock
1985	Julian BARNES	Flaubert's Parrot
1987	Guy VANDERHAEGHE	Man Descending
1989	David PROFUMO	Sea Music
1991	Carol BIRCH	The Fog Line
1993	Will SELF	The Quantity Theory of Insanity
1995	Livi MICHAEL	Their Angel Reach

FAWCETT SOCIETY BOOK PRIZE

An annual award, made until 1993 alternately to a work of fiction and non-fiction, which has made a substantial contribution to the understanding of women's concerns, attitudes and place in society. From 1993 the prize will always be awarded to a work of non-fiction.

1983	Pat BARKER	Union Street
1985	Zoe FAIRBAIRNS	Here Today
1987	Shena MACKAY	Redhill Rococo
1989	Stevie SMITH	Boy Blue
1991	Jennifer DAWSON	Judasland

GUARDIAN FICTION PRIZE

Awarded annually since 1965 to a work of fiction by a British or Commonwealth writer and published in the United Kingdom. The winner is chosen by a panel of five judges.

1965	Clive BARRY	Crumb Borne
1966	Archie HIND	The Dear Green Place
1967	Eva FIGES	Winter Journey
1968	P.J. KAVANAGH	A Song and Dance
1969	Maurice LEITCH	Poor Lazarus
1970	Margaret BLOUNT	When Did You Last See Your Father?
1971	Thomas KILROY	The Big Chapel
1972	John BERGER	G
1973	Peter REDGROVE	In the Country of the Skin
1974	Beryl BAINBRIDGE	The Bottle Factory Outing
1975	Sylvia CLAYTON	Friends and Romans
1976	Robert NYE	Falstaff
1977	Michael MOORCOCK	The Condition of Muzak
1978	Roy A.K. HEATH	The Murderer
1979	Neil JORDAN	Night in Tunisia
1980	J.L. CARR	A Month in the Country
1981	John BANVILLE	Kepler
1982	Glyn HUGHES	Where I Used to Play on the Green
1983	Graham SWIFT	Waterland
1984	J.G. BALLARD	Empire of the Sun
1985	Peter ACKROYD	Hawksmoor
1986	Jim CRACE	Continent
1987	Peter BENSON	The Levels
1988	Lucy ELLMAN	Sweet Desserts
1989	Carol LAKE	Rosehill: Portraits from a Midlands City
1990	Pauline MELVILLE	Shape-Shifter
1991	Alan JUDD	The Devil's Own Work
1992	Alasdair GRAY	Poor Things

GUARDIAN FICTION PRIZE (cont.)

1993	Pat BARKER	The Eye in the Door
1994	Candia McWILLIAM	Debatable Land
1995	James BUCHAN	Heart's Journey into Winter

RUTH HADDEN MEMORIAL AWARD

Created in memory of Ruth Hadden, who died in the Marchioness Riverboat tragedy. This is awarded annually to the publishers of a first book by a previously unpublished author born in the British Isles, non-fiction and poetry are all eligible.

1991	Elean THOMAS	The Last Room
1992	Catherine MERRIMAN	Leaving the Light On
1993	Tim PEARS	In the Place of Fallen Leaves
1994	Andrew COWAN	Pig
1995	Alan WARNER	Morvern Callar

HAWTHORNDEN PRIZE

Founded in 1919 by Miss Alice Warrender, it is the oldest of the famous British literary prizes. Awarded annually to an English writer for the best work of imaginative literature, it is especially designed to encourage young authors and the word 'imaginative' is given a broad interpretation.

The following dates are the years for which the award was given to a work of fiction:-

1970	Piers Paul READ	Monk Dawson
1975	David LODGE	Changing Places
1976	Robert NYE	Falstaff
1978	David COOK	Walter
1979	P.S. RUSHFORTH	Kindergarten
1982	Timothy MO	Sour Sweet
1983	Jonathan KEATES	Allegro Postillions
1992	Ferdinand MOUNT	Of Love and Asthma
1993	Andrew BARROW	The Tap Dancer
1994	Tim PEARS	In the Place of Fallen Leaves
1995	*No Award to Fiction*	
1996	Hilary MANTEL	An Experiment in Love

DAVID HIGHAM PRIZE FOR FICTION

An annual award for a first novel or book of short stories published in the UK in the year of the award, by an author who is a citizen of Britain, the Commonwealth or the Republic of Ireland.

joint winners { 1975	Jane GARDAM	Black Faces/White Faces
1975	Matthew VAUGHAN	Chalky
1976	Caroline BLACKWOOD	The Stepdaughter
1977	Patricia FINNEY	A Shadow of Gulls
1978	Leslie NORRIS	Sliding
1979	John HARVEY	The Plate Shop
1980	Ted HARRIOT	Keep on Running
1981	Christopher HOPE	A Separate Development
1982	Glyn HUGHES	Where I Used to Play on the Green
1983	R.M. LAMMING	The Notebook of Gismondo Cavalletti
1984	James BUCHAN	A Parish of Rich Women
1985	Patricia FERGUSON	Family Myths and Legends
1986	Jim CRACE	Continent
1987	Adam ZAMEENZAD	The 13th House
1988	Carol BIRCH	Life in the Palace
1989	Timothy O'GRADY	Motherland
1990	Russell Celyn JONES	Soldiers and Innocents
1991	Elspeth BARKER	O Caledonia
1992	John LOVEDAY	Halo
1993	Nicola BARKER	Love your Enemies
1994	Fred D. AGUIAR	The Longest Memory
1995	Vikram CHANDRA	Red Earth and Pouring Rain

WINIFRED HOLTBY MEMORIAL PRIZE

In 1966 Vera Brittain gave to the Royal Society of Literature a sum of money to provide an annual prize in honour of Winifred Holtby. It is for the best regional novel of the year written in the English Language. Winners since 1981 are:-

1980	Elsa JOUBERT	Poppie
1981	Alan JUDD	A Breed of Heroes
1982	Kazuo ISHIGURO	A Pale View of Hills
1983	Graham SWIFT	Waterland
1984	Balraj KHANNA	Nation of Fools
1985	*No Award*	
1986	Maggie HEMINGWAY	The Bridge
1987	*No Award*	
1989	Shusha GUPPY	The Blindfold Horse
1990	Hilary MANTEL	Fludd
1991	Nino RICCI	The Lives of the Saints
1992	Elspeth BARKER	O Caledonia
1993	Adam THORPE	Ulverton
1994	Jim CRACE	Signals of Distress
1995	Paul WATKINS	Archangel

McKITTERICK PRIZE

Endowed by the late Tom McKitterick the Award is made to a first novel (published or unpublished) by an author over the age of 40.

1990	Simon MAWER	Chimera
1991	John LOVEDAY	A Summer to Halo
1992	Alberto MANGUEL	News from a Foreign Country Came
1993	Andrew BARROW	The Tap Dancer
1994	Helen DUNMORE	Zennor in Darkness
1995	Christopher BIGSBY	Hester
1996	Stephen BLANCHARD	Gagarin and I

MAIL ON SUNDAY / JOHN LLEWELLYN RHYS PRIZE

Founded in 1942 by Jane Oliver, the widow of John Llewellyn Rhys a young writer killed in action in World War II. Open to writers aged under 35 the work may be any form of literature:- fiction, short stories, poetry, drama, biography or literary non-fiction written by a British or Commonwealth writer.

1970	*No Award to Fiction*	
1971	Shiva NAIPAUL	Fireflies
1972	Susan HILL	The Albatross
1973	Peter SMALLEY	A Warm Gun
1974	Hugh FLEETWOOD	The Girl who Passed for Normal
1975	Tim JEAL	Cushing's Crusade
1976	*No Award*	
1977	*No Award to Fiction*	
1978	A.N. WILSON	The Sweets of Pimlico
1979	*No Award to Fiction*	
1980	Desmond HOGAN	The Diamonds at the Bottom of the Sea
1981	*No Award to Fiction*	
1982	William BOYD	An Ice-Cream War
1983	Lisa ST AUBIN DE TERAN	The Slow Train to Milan
1984	*No Award to Fiction*	
1985	John MILNE	Out of the Blue
1986	Tim PARKS	Loving Roger
1987	Jeanette WINTERSON	The Passion
1988	Matthew YORKE	The March Fence
1989	*No Award to Fiction*	
1990	*No Award to Fiction*	
1991	*No Award to Fiction*	
1992	Matthew KNEALE	Sweet Thames
1993	*No Award to Fiction*	
1994	Jonathan COE	What a Carve Up!
1995	Melanie McGRATH	Motel Nirvana

THE ORANGE PRIZE

Founded in 1996 this new award is open to women authors of any nationality provided that all entries have been published in the United Kingdom.

1996   Helen DUNMORE   A Spell of Winter

PULITZER PRIZE FOR FICTION

Joseph Pulitzer, reporter, editor, publisher and a founder of the Graduate School of Journalism at Columbia University established in 1903 a system of prizes to encourage 'public service, public morals, American literature and the advancement of education'. The Fiction Prize was first awarded in 1948.

1970	Jean STAFFORD	Collected Stories
1971	*No Award*	
1972	Wallace STEGNER	Angle of Repose
1973	Eudora WELTY	The Optimist's Daughter
1974	*No Award*	
1975	Michael SHAARA	The Killer Angels
1976	Saul BELLOW	Humboldt's Gift
1977	*No Award*	
1978	James Alan McPHERSON	Elbow Room
1979	John CHEEVER	The Stories of John Cheever
1980	Norman MAILER	The Executioner's Song
1981	John Kennedy TOOLE	A Confederacy of Dunces
1982	John UPDIKE	Rabbit is Rich
1983	Alice WALKER	The Color Purple
1984	William KENNEDY	Ironweed
1985	Alison LURIE	Foreign Affairs
1986	Larry McMURTRY	Lonesome Dove
1987	Peter TAYLOR	A Summons to Memphis
1988	Toni MORRISON	Beloved
1989	Anne TYLER	Breathing Lessons
1990	Oscar HIJUELOS	The Mambo Kings Play Songs of Love
1991	John UPDIKE	Rabbit at Rest
1992	Jane SMILEY	A Thousand Acres
1993	Robert OLEN	Butler A Good Scent from a Strange Mountain
1994	E. Annie PROULX	The Shipping News
1995	Carol SHIELDS	The Stone Diaries
1996	Richard FORD	Independence Day

ROMANTIC NOVELISTS' ASSOCIATION
MAJOR AWARD

Established in 1960 the award, now sponsored by Boots the Chemists is for the best romantic novel of the year.

joint winners	1970	Margaret MADDOCKS	Thea
	1970	Joanne MARSHALL	Cat on a Broomstick
	1970	Rona RANDALL	Broken Tapestry
	1971	Joanne MARSHALL	Flower of Silence
	1972	Maynah LEWIS	The Pride of Innocence
	1973	Constance HEAVEN	The House of Kuragin
	1974	Frances MURRAY	The Burning Lamp
	1975	Jay ALLERTON	Vote for a Silk Gown
	1976	Anna GILBERT	The Look of Innocence
	1977	Anne WORBOYS	Every Man a King
	1978	Madeleine BRENT	Merlin's Keep
	1979	Josephine EDGAR	Countess
	1980	Joanna TROLLOPE	Parson Harding's Daughter
	1981	Gwendoline BUTLER	The Red Staircase
	1982	Valerie FITZGERALD	Zemindar
	1983	Eva IBBOTSON	Magic Flutes
	1984	Sheila WALSH	A Highly Respectable Marriage
	1985	Rosie THOMAS	Sunrise
	1986	Brenda JAGGER	A Song Twice Over
	1987	Marie JOSEPH	A Better World Than This
	1988	Audrey HOWARD	The Juniper Bush
	1989	Sarah WOODHOUSE	The Peacock's Feather
	1990	Reay TANNAHILL	Passing Glory
	1991	Susan KAY	Phantom
	1992	June KNOX-MAWER	Sandstorm
	1993	Cynthia HARROD-EAGLES	Emily
	1994	Elizabeth BUCHAN	Consider the Lily
	1995	Charlotte BINGHAM	Change of Heart
	1996	Rosamunde PILCHER	Coming Home

SAGA PRIZE

First awarded in 1995 this prize will be made for a manuscript by an unpublished writer of Black African descent. Entrants must have been born and consider their main residence to be in the United Kingdom or the Republic of Ireland.

| 1995 | Diran ADEBAYO | Some Kind of Black |

THE STEINBECK AWARD

Awarded to a young writer for a new work of fiction written in the spirit of John Steinbeck, that is involving the issues of poverty, race, political injustice etc.

| 1995 | Pinckney BENEDICT | The Dogs of God |
| 1996 | John Gregory BROWNE | Decorations in a Ruined Cemetery |

SUNDAY TIMES YOUNG WRITER OF THE YEAR AWARD

Awarded to a writer who is under the age of 35 on the strength of the promise shown by a full-length published work of fiction, non-fiction or poetry.

1991	Helen SIMPSON	Four Bare Legs in a Bed
1992	Caryl PHILLIPS	Cambridge
1993	*No Award to Fiction*	
1994	*No Award to Fiction*	
1995	Andrew COWEN	Pig

THUMPING GOOD READ BOOK AWARD

Awarded to a novel that is judged by a panel of W.H. Smith's customers to be an "accessible and page turning good read".

1992	Robert GODDARD	Into the Blue
1993	Robert HARRIS	Fatherland
1994	Dominick DUNNE	A Season in Purgatory
1995	Thomas EIDSON	St Agnes' Stand
1996	Andrew KLAVAN	True Crime

TOM-GALLON TRUST

Founded by the late Miss Nellie Tom-Gallon the Award is made biennially to fiction writers of limited means who have had a least one short story accepted for publication. The Award is made for a short story.

	1943	Elizabeth MYERS	A Well Full of Leaves
	1945	Jack AISTROP	Death in the Midst of What
	1947	Dorothy K. HAYNES	The Head
	1949	Olivia MANNING	The Children
	1951	Fred URQUHART	The Ploughing Match
	1953	Maurice CRANSTON	A Visit to the Author
	1955	Robert ROBERTS	Conducted Tour
	1957	E.W.HILDICK	A Casual Visit
	1959	Harold ELVIN	God's Right Hand Upon My Shoulder
	1961	*No Award*	
	1963	*No Award*	
joint winners	1964	Peter GREAVE	The Wonderful Day
	1964	Jean STUBBS	A Child's Four Seasons
	1966	Gillian EDWARDS	An Evening in September
	1968	*No Award*	
joint winners	1970	A. Craig BELL	The Nest
	1970	Aileen PENNINGTON	The Princess and the Pussycat
	1972	Kathleen JULIAN	Catch Two
	1974	Neilson GRAHAM	Anscombe
	1976	Jackson WEBB	Vassili
	1978	Michael MORRISSEY	An Evening with Ionesco
	1980	A. McCONNELL-DUFF	The Comrades Marathon
	1982	Dermot HEALY	The Tenant
	1984	Janni HOWKER	The Egg Man
	1986	Lawrence SCOTT	The House of Funerals
	1988	Alan BEARD	Taking Doreen Out of the Sky
	1990	Richard AUSTIN	Sister Monica's Last Journey
	1992	David CALLARD	Reading the Signals
	1994	Janice FOX	A Good Place to Die

BETTY TRASK AWARDS

Started in 1984 and administered by the Society of Authors, the awards are for the benefit of young authors (under 35) and are given on the strength of the manuscript of a first novel of a romantic or traditional rather than experimental nature. The winners are required to use the money for foreign travel. The principal winners are:-

joint winners {	1984	Ronald FRAME	Winter Journey
	1984	Clare NONHEBEL	Cold Showers
	1985	Susan KAY	Legacy
	1986	Tim PARKS	Tongues of Flame
	1987	James MAW	Hard Luck
	1988	Alex MARTIN	The General Interruptor
	1989	Nigel WATTS	The Life Game
	1990	Robert McLiam WILSON	Ripley Bogle
	1991	Amit CHAUDHURI	A Strange and Sublime Address
	1992	Liane JONES	The Dream Stone
	1993	Mark BLACKABY	You'll Never be Here Again *(unpublished)*
	1994	Colin BATEMAN	Divorcing Jack
	1995	Robert NEWMAN	Dependence Day
	1996	John LANCHESTER	The Debt to Pleasure

WHITBREAD BOOK OF THE YEAR AND LITERARY AWARDS

Established in 1971, five categories of book are now rewarded by Whitbread & Co. These are Novel; First Novel; Children's Novel; Poetry and Biography. Writers must have been resident in Great Britain or the Republic of Ireland for three years or more. Nominations are selected by the panel of judges from each category and one of the category winners is then voted Whitbread Book of The Year. The awards are administered by the Booksellers Association.

	1971	Gerda CHARLES	The Destiny Waltz
	1972	Susan HILL	The Bird of Night
	1973	Shiva NAIPAUL	The Chip Chip Gatherers
	1974	Iris MURDOCH	The Sacred and Profane Love Machine
	1975	William McILVANNEY	Docherty
	1976	William TREVOR	The Children of Dynmouth
	1977	Beryl BAINBRIDGE	Injury Time
	1978	Paul THEROUX	Picture Palace
	1979	Jennifer JOHNSTON	The Old Jest
'Book of The Year'	1980	David LODGE	How Far Can You Go?
	1981	Maurice LEITCH	Silver's City
First Novel	1981	William BOYD	A Good Man in Africa
	1982	John WAIN	Young Shoulders
First Novel	1982	Bruce CHATWIN	On the Black Hill
	1983	William TREVOR	Fools of Fortune
First Novel	1983	John FULLER	Flying to Nowhere
	1984	Christopher HOPE	Kruger's Alp
First Novel	1984	James BUCHAN	A Parish of Rich Women
	1985	Peter ACKROYD	Hawksmoor
First Novel	1985	Jeanette WINTERSON	Oranges are not the Only Fruit
'Book of The Year'	1986	Kazuo ISHIGURO	An Artist of the Floating World
First Novel	1986	Jim CRACE	Continent
	1987	Ian McEWAN	The Child in Time

WHITBREAD BOOK OF THE YEAR
AND LITERARY AWARDS (cont.)

First novel	1987	Francis WYNDHAM	The Other Garden
	1988	Salman RUSHDIE	The Satanic Verses
First Novel & 'Book of The Year'	1988	Paul SAYER	The Comforts of Madness
	1989	Lindsay CLARKE	The Chymical Wedding
First Novel	1989	James Hamilton PATERSON	Gerontius
'Book of The Year'	1990	Nicholas MOSLEY	Hopeful Monsters
First Novel	1990	Hanif KUREISHI	The Buddha of Suburbia
	1991	Jane GARDAM	The Queen of the Tambourine
First Novel	1991	Gordon BURN	Alma Cogan
	1992	Alasdair GRAY	Poor Things
First Novel & 'Book of The Year'	1992	Jeff TORRINGTON	Swing Hammer Swing!
'Book of The Year'	1993	Joan BRADY	Theory of War
First Novel	1993	Rachel CUSK	Saving Agnes
'Book of The Year'	1994	William TREVOR	Felicia's Journey
First Novel	1994	Fred D'AGUIAR	The Longest Memory
	1995	Salman RUSHDIE	The Moor's Last Sigh
First Novel	1995	Kate ATKINSON	Behind the Scenes at the Museum

WRITERS' GUILD AWARDS

Three sponsored awards are made each year to fiction, non-fiction and childrens' books selected by a jury of writers and critics. Entries must be written by British citizens or by a writer resident in Britain. Fiction winners are:

1991	Alice Thomas ELLIS	The Inn at the Edge of the World
1992	Lee LANGLEY	Persistent Rumours
1993	Edna O'BRIEN	Time and Tide
1994	James KELMAN	How Late it Was, How Late
1995	Nick HORNBY	High Fidelity

YORKSHIRE POST BOOK OF THE YEAR AWARD

An annual award for the book, either fiction or non-fiction, which, in the opinion of the judges, is the best work published in the preceding year.

1970	Edna O'BRIEN	A Pagan Place
1971	Paul SCOTT	Towers of Silence
1972	Margaret DRABBLE	The Needle's Eye
1973	Evelyn ANTHONY	The Occupying Power
1974	Kingsley AMIS	Ending Up
1975	David LODGE	Changing Places
1976	Nina BAWDEN	Afternoon of a Good Woman
1977	Olivia MANNING	The Danger Tree
1978	Sian JAMES	Yesterday
1979	Jennifer JOHNSTON	The Old Jest
1980	Anthony BURGESS	Earthly Powers
1981	Paul THEROUX	Mosquito Coast
1982	Elizabeth Jane HOWARD	Getting it Right
1983	Francis KING	Act of Darkness
1984	Kingsley AMIS	Stanley and the Women
1985	Alice Thomas ELLIS	Unexplained Laughter
1986	*No Award to Fiction*	
1987	*No Award to Fiction*	
1988	William TREVOR	The Silence in the Garden
1989	*No Award to Fiction*	
1990	*No Award to Fiction*	
1991	*No Award to Fiction*	
1992	*No Award to Fiction*	
1993	*No Award to Fiction*	
1994	*No Award to Fiction*	

BIBLIOGRAPHY

Many of the books in this short list should be readily available in the larger public libraries. Together they form an invaluable complement to **Who Else Writes Like ... ?** and will help the user find specific authors or titles, pursue the reading of a series, enjoy exploring a particular genre or discover novels set in a particular place or period of history.

In addition to these published titles many libraries now issue excellent local guides to fiction. Always remember to ask the library staff who will be pleased to help.

BLOOMSBURY GOOD READING GUIDE; by Kenneth McLeish.
 Bloomsbury Publishing Ltd, 3rd revised ed., 1994.

Contains articles on some 350 authors describing the type of books they write - listing over 3,500 books and suggesting alternative and 'follow-up' authors and titles.

BLOOMSBURY GOOD READING GUIDE TO MURDER, CRIME
 FICTION AND THRILLERS; by Kenneth and Valerie McLeish.
 Bloomsbury Publishing Ltd, 1990.

Describes the work of 250 crime and thriller writers and suggests follow-up reading by the same author and others.

BLOOMSBURY GOOD READING GUIDE TO SCIENCE FICTION AND
 FANTASY; by M.H. Zool.
 Bloomsbury Publishing Ltd, 1989.

An invaluable complement to the other guides in the series.

BOOK TRUST GUIDE TO LITERARY PRIZES; edited by Huw Molseed.
 8th ed., 1995.

Lists nearly 200 Literary Prizes in the United Kingdom of which 50 are awarded to adult fiction.

CHAMBERS FICTION FILE; compiled and edited by Roger Prebble. Chambers, 1992.

Divided into three fully cross-referenced sections - authors, titles and characters. Covers over 1,000 authors, over 10,000 novels and over 2,000 characters.

CONTEMPORARY NOVELISTS; edited by Lesley Henderson. Gale/St James Press, 6th ed., 1995.

An alphabetical list of over 600 novelists. Each entry contains a bibliography, a complete list of separately published books and a signed essay. In addition authors were invited to comment on their work.

CRIME AND MYSTERY - THE 100 BEST BOOKS; by H.R.F. Keating. Xanadu, 1987.

Arranged chronologically from Edgar Allen Poe (1845) to P.D. James (1986): these short essays are one person's authoritative and entertaining choice.

CUMULATED FICTION INDEX; Association of Assistant Librarians.
1945-1960	by G.B. Cotton and Alan Glencross
1960-1969	by Raymond Smith
1970-1974	by Raymond Smith and Anthony J. Gordon
1975-1979	by Marilyn E. Hicken
1980-1989	by Marilyn E. Hicken

Taken together this series indexes the majority of novels published in the United Kingdom since the end of the Second World War. The choice of headings continues to be based on the scheme devised by Cotton and Glencross. It would be particularly helpful to readers looking for crime fiction as the index divides this genre into fifteen groups. This series of cumulations is supplemented by Annual Volumes.

DICTIONARY OF LITERARY PSEUDONYMS IN THE ENGLISH LANGUAGE; compiled by Terence Carty. Mansell, 1995.

Lists 12,000 English language literary pseudonyms to give the real names of around 7,500 authors from the early seventeenth century to the present day.

ENCYCLOPAEDIA OF SCIENCE FICTION; edited by John Clute and
Peter Nichols. 2nd ed., Orbit, 1993.

The essential reference work on Science Fiction for its coverage and scholarship.

AN ENGLISH LIBRARY; edited by Nigel Farrow, Brian Last and
Vernon Pratt. Gower Publishing Co. Ltd with The Book Trust,
6th ed., 1990.

*First published in 1943, the first five editions were edited by F. Seymour
Smith. Its objective is to identify the books from the classical and modern
heritage that will extend the enjoyment of reading. Nearly 250 writers of
adult fiction are included with lists of their most significant works.*

MURDER IN PRINT: A GUIDE TO TWO CENTURIES OF CRIME
FICTION; edited by Melvyn Barnes.
Barn Owl Books, 1986.

*Illustrates the development of the genre by a selection of almost 500 titles
chosen to represent the best examples of the work of 260 writers. A personal
selection by an acknowledged expert in the field.*

THE NOVELS OF WORLD WAR TWO: AN ANNOTATED
BIBLIOGRAPHY OF WORLD WAR TWO FICTION; edited by
Michael Paris. The Library Association, 1990.

*Lists over 2,000 novels published in English and in translation from
September 1939 to 1988. Arranged in four parts:- (1) Chronological list with
annotations; (2) Subject index; (3) Author index; (4) Title index.*

NOW READ ON: A GUIDE TO CONTEMPORARY POPULAR FICTION;
by Mandy Hicken and Ray Prytherch.
Gower Publishing Co. Ltd, 1990.

*This is a similar publication to the Bloomsbury Guide but is arranged in
nineteen different genres of fiction. It gives short biographies of the principal
authors included and lists their books' titles.*

READERS' COMPANION TO THE TWENTIETH CENTURY NOVEL;
edited by Peter Parker. Fourth Estate & Helicon, 1994.

*Detailed accounts of some 750 novels from Britain, the USA and many
Commonwealth countries, supplying a summary of the plot, placing the book
in its context and providing a critical assessment.*

ST. JAMES GUIDE TO FANTASY WRITERS; edited by David Pringle.
Gale/St. James Press, 1st ed., 1995.

*This new work is the first of a two volume set, the second of which will cover
Horror, Ghost and Gothic writers. Lists over 400 Fantasy novelists each entry
comprising a brief biography, a complete list of separately published books and
a signed essay.*

SCIENCE FICTION: THE ILLUSTRATED ENCYCLOPAEDIA; edited by
John Clute. Dorling Kindersley, 1995.

*Contains over 100 biographies of Science Fiction writers and lists their work
from Mary Shelley to the mid 1990's. Traces the history of Science Fiction in
print, in graphics, in the cinema and in television.*

SEQUELS. VOL. 1: ADULT BOOKS; compiled by Marilyn E. Hicken.
The Association of Assistant Librarians, 10th revised ed., 1992.

*Lists novels in which the same characters appear; sequences of novels connected
by theme; sequences of novels with a geographical or historical connection; and
non-fiction, mainly autobiographical, which is intended to be read in sequence.
The arrangement is primarily under the author with an index of series and
characters.*

TWENTIETH-CENTURY CRIME AND MYSTERY WRITERS; edited by
Lesley Henderson. Gale/St. James Press, 3rd ed., 1991.

*Provides detailed information on more than 700 English language writers of
mystery fiction including biographical and bibliographical information
together with a signed critical essay.*

TWENTIETH-CENTURY ROMANCE AND HISTORICAL WRITERS;
edited by Lesley Henderson.
Gale/St. James Press, 3rd ed., 1994.

This new edition has been broadened to include historical fiction writers as well as writers of romance. A good, concise reference tool to the genre.

TWENTIETH-CENTURY SCIENCE FICTION WRITERS; edited by
Noelle Watson and Paul E. Schellinger.
Gale/St. James Press, 4th ed., 1995.

Over 600 writers are represented - ranging from the traditional favourites to the most recent novelists who have altered the style and parameters of this constantly evolving genre.

TWENTIETH-CENTURY WESTERN WRITERS; edited by Geoff Sadler.
Gale/St. James Press, 2nd ed., 1991.

More than 450 entries are included in this edition, chosen to reflect the current state of this complex and diverse genre.

ULTIMATE GUIDE TO SCIENCE FICTION; edited by David Pringle.
Scolar Press, 2nd ed., 1995.

Valuable for its listing by title of the popular and important work of Science Fiction.

WHAT DO I READ NEXT? A READER'S GUIDE TO CURRENT GENRE
FICTION; edited by Neil Barron and others.
Gale Research Inc., published annually, 1995 ed.

A large and elaborate publication. Contains over 1300 entries for titles published during the previous year. Divided into six genre sections. Extremely detailed entries with alternative titles. Only US editions quoted. Demonstrates how much American popular fiction is unknown across the Atlantic, and vice versa.

STRATEGIC AIMS

1. LISU's primary aim is to act as the UK national centre for the collation, analysis and dissemination of statistical data relating to library and information activities.

2. In pursuit of this aim, LISU will, wherever appropriate, work in co-operation with other individuals and organisations in the library, information and book trade communities.

3. If there are significant gaps in the statistical information available, LISU will examine these with a view to initiating or assisting in the collection of data required to fill such gaps.

4. LISU also aims to fill gaps in the supply of trade and general statistics to librarians and other information workers to meet their needs.

5. LISU will provide information and advice to librarians on statistical sources.

6. LISU aims to develop and encourage good practice in librarians' knowledge and use of statistics.

7. LISU aims to act as a source of statistical information on the features of libraries and other information work for people outside the profession (particularly those in the book trade, specialist journalists, and politicians).

8. LISU will, where appropriate, undertake or initiate research projects in connection with any of these aims.

9. LISU will, where appropriate, examine and analyse statistics of library and book trade operations abroad to compare with the British position.